Scars to Prove It

SCARS TO PROVE IT

The Civil War Soldier and American Fiction

CRAIG A. WARREN

The Kent State University Press
Kent, Ohio

© 2009 by The Kent State University Press, Kent, Ohio 44242
ALL RIGHTS RESERVED
Library of Congress Catalog Card Number 2009001492

ISBN 978-1-60635-015-7

Manufactured in the United States of America

Library of Congress Cataloging-in-Publication Data

Warren, Craig A.
    Scars to prove it : the Civil War soldier and American fiction / Craig A. Warren.
        p. cm.
    Includes bibliographical references and index.
    ISBN 978-1-60635-015-7 (pbk. : alk. paper) ∞
1. American fiction—History and criticism.
2. United States—History—Civil War, 1861–1865—Literature and the war.
3. Soldiers—United States—Biography—History and criticism.
4. Soldiers' writings, American—History and criticism.
5. War and literature—United States—History.
6. Soldiers in literature.
7. War in literature. I. Title.
    PS374.C53W37 2009
    813.009358737—dc22

                                              2009001492

British Library Cataloging-in-Publication data are available.

To my parents, Linda and Gary Warren

Contents

Acknowledgments ix

Introduction 1

1 Various Veterans Had Told Him Tales:
   The Red Badge of Courage and an Inclusive Civil War
   Literature 9

2 For Was I Not a Soldier, Enlisted for the War?
   Female Veterans in *Gone with the Wind* and *None Shall
   Look Back* 39

3 The Eggshell Shibboleth of Caste and Color Too:
   Civilian Narrators in *Absalom, Absalom!* and
   The Unvanquished 83

4 Each Man Has His Own Reason to Die:
   The Triumph of the Individual in *The Killer Angels* 118

   Conclusion: Grief Crowded the Secret Rooms of Their Hearts:
   Haunted Veterans in *The Judas Field* 160

   Notes 170

   Bibliography 200

   Index 215

Acknowledgments

I wish to thank the many friends, colleagues, and mentors who encouraged me during the writing of this book. Because it would be impossible to name every person to whom I am indebted, I will use this space to thank my teachers and family especially.

My professors at the University of Virginia taught me the joys of research and the responsibilities of teaching. Stephen Cushman led the graduate seminar on Civil War literature that inspired this project (and that introduced me to my wife!). As a dissertation director, Steve was an enthusiastic sponsor and an insightful critic. As a teacher, he is the model against whom I compare all others. I owe him a great deal. Gary Gallagher may be the busiest person I have ever met, and yet he always finds time for his students—even those working in disciplines other than his own. I thank him for his excellent advice regarding this project and for his ongoing support of my research and writing. I am also deeply grateful to the following individuals, each of whom shaped me as a scholar, writer, and teacher: Stephen Arata, Paul Cantor, Greg Colomb, Jon D'Errico, the late Robert Kellogg, Jerome McGann, Franny Nudelman, and Stephen Railton. I could not have asked for a more generous or gifted group of mentors.

My mother and father, Linda and Gary Warren, have never failed to encourage me at whatever I have attempted. I admire no people more than my parents; this book is dedicated to them. Thanks, too, to my grandmothers, Valda Warren and Margaret Wharton, and to my brother Eric and his family: Karen, Lexi, and Emily. Each has done more for me than they can possibly know. My wonderful in-laws, Jim and Mary Whitney, share my passion for the study of history and literature. Our conversations about the

Civil War, and day trips to historical sites in and around Richmond, stand among my favorite memories of the last several years.

The greatest thanks go to my best friend and wife, Sarah Whitney. Sarah has been a true comrade throughout the writing process, from the early drafts in Charlottesville through the final revisions in Erie. Her wisdom and advice have enhanced my work immeasurably. Moreover, Sarah has inspired me to grow as a reader, scholar, housemate, and human being. Any virtues of this book, and of its author, are hers to claim.

Introduction

When the first cannon sounded over Charleston Harbor in 1861, it announced the beginning of an American literary phenomenon. Readers North and South hungered for imaginative writing about the escalating war, and canny publishers were swift to deliver. Short fiction about the conflict appeared with growing regularity, followed by the first Civil War novels in 1862. These early works commenced a literary genre that continues to grow to this day. Not since the fall of Fort Sumter have Americans ceased to read and write fictions about the American Civil War. By the late 1930s, the Library of Congress listed three hundred Civil War novels in its catalogs.[1] The next twenty years produced at least two hundred more, a spike reflecting the approaching Civil War centennial. Today even the most conservative estimate would place the total number of Civil War novels at well over one thousand, and this figure does not account for the thousands of war-related stories published in journals, newspapers, and magazines since 1861. New fictions about the war continue to appear in libraries and bookstores. The David Madden Collection of Civil War Fiction, housed at Louisiana State University, contains almost five hundred titles published between 1950 and 2005 alone. Of those, nearly 150 are works of the twenty-first century.

Within this enormous body of literature, no figure stands taller than the Civil War soldier. Thousands of pages of fiction have confirmed that Union and Confederate soldiers occupy an essential, even iconic, place in the American imagination. Surely other familiar types populate the landscape of Civil War fiction as well—among them, slaves, Southern belles, politicians, journalists, abolitionists, and children. But soldiers dominate the genre, and not only for the obvious reason that millions of men performed military service between 1861 and 1865. In *Memoranda during the War* (1875), Walt Whitman reflected on the centrality of soldiers to his own understanding of the struggle: "[These] two or three millions of American young and middle-aged men, North and South, embodied in the armies . . . were of more significance even than the Political interests involved." Whitman had served as a nurse during those dark years, however, and he expected that those less familiar with the troops would not view them as "the main interest of the War."[2]

Yet the public has indeed shared Whitman's fascination with the men clothed in blue and gray. The Civil War soldier, by virtue of his flesh-and-blood humanity, has appealed to generations of Americans as the most compelling and accessible aspect of the crisis. Even when fiction writers have examined the principles at stake in the war, both sacred and mundane, they have usually done so in terms of the words and actions of men in uniform. Admittedly, some novels do push fighting men offstage, focusing instead on civilians and families on the home front. But almost always the presence of soldiers can be felt in the background, the men who fought the battles that determined the future of America and its people.

In the chapters that follow, I examine seven novels published between 1895 and 2006, with an eye to how each portrays and responds to the figure of the Civil War soldier. The specific themes of each chapter differ, but throughout I have maintained an interest in how the featured novels interact with the recorded words of veterans themselves. Perhaps no voice did more to shape popular understanding of the war than that of the Civil War veteran. Far from ceding the war to novelists and historians, veterans came to command memory of the conflict during the late nineteenth and early twentieth centuries. In many respects, soldiers ensured their importance to Civil War fiction by themselves taking up the pen. Some chose to author their own stories, novels, and poems of the war, but most embraced different forms of writing: the memoir, the reminiscence, the regimental history.

Why did veterans become writers? In the weeks and months following Appomattox and the close of the American Civil War, soldiers North and South removed the faded uniform and returned to their farms, cities, and ports of home. Freed from the boredom of camp and the trauma of combat, most veterans embraced civilian life with enthusiasm. Yet for many former combatants, the war remained a prominent part of everyday thought and conversation. Even as they raised families, rebuilt devastated cities, and secured the future of a reunited nation, these men actively sought to interpret their wartime experiences. Many wished to develop answers to their own questions about the war and to cope with horrific memories of battle or prison. Others desired to educate younger generations, to create a record of their accomplishments, or to heap glory upon themselves. Over time, writing became a means to accomplish each of these goals and also fulfilled an array of financial, personal, and familial needs. During a span of nearly six decades, Civil War participants published a vast body of literature consisting of memoirs, diaries, debates, regimental and unit histories, poems, speeches, sermons, and annotated maps. By the 1880s the outpouring of veterans' writing outpaced the publication of Civil War fictions. Although stories and novels of the war had predated the memoirs of combatants, new fictions came to reflect the common emphases found in veterans' narratives: primarily the soldier in camp and combat.

It is surprising that literary critics have largely ignored the important influence of veterans' narratives over the shape and character of Civil War fiction. In his landmark study of the war's literature, *Patriotic Gore* (1962), Edmund Wilson devoted ample space to the postwar writing of such famous officers as Ulysses S. Grant, Robert E. Lee, John S. Mosby, and William T. Sherman. But largely because the scope of his project involved only the first generation of Civil War narratives, Wilson did not explore in detail how soldiers' works informed such celebrated novels as *The Red Badge of Courage* (1895), *The Long Roll* (1911), and *Gone with the Wind* (1936).[3]

The only other major study of Civil War literature, Daniel Aaron's *The Unwritten War*, appeared in 1973. A respected scholar with a strong command of American letters, Aaron addressed the prose and poetry penned by those who lived through the war, as well as "The War at Second Hand"—his term for the conflict's battles, causes, and consequences as they appeared in literature from 1865 through the Agrarian movement and the novels of William Faulkner. Ultimately, however, *The Unwritten War* glosses over the writing of Civil War veterans. In those pages where soldiers' memoirs received Aaron's undivided attention (three pages out of nearly four hundred), he more or less dismissed these works as sentimental, tedious, or both. The critic showed himself to be particularly unimpressed with the idea that such narratives influenced directly the work of true literary talents. For example, at one point Aaron explained that "[even had] Crane read none of the books whose impress has been detected in *The Red Badge,* he could have pieced together his novel from the spoken and pictorial accounts of the War." More generally, he described the soldier-turned-author as a kind of literary pest infesting late nineteenth-century America ("[the] land swarmed with veterans more than ready to reminisce about the most exciting years of their lives") and chalked up veterans' writing to nostalgia more than to political or cultural purpose.[4]

Aaron's assessment is typical of the way academics have, at least since the mid-twentieth century, distanced veterans' narratives from any serious consideration of American literary history. Today, few scholars writing about Civil War literature take time to investigate what memoirs Ellen Glasgow read, or to learn how regimental histories contributed to the diverse historical visions of Shelby Foote, Mary Lee Settle, Charles Frazier, and Allen B. Ballard. Why has this been the case? Certainly veterans' narratives are often not to the taste of readers accustomed to highbrow literature. While military historians and Civil War enthusiasts may devour memoirs that obsess over battlefield tactics and the personalities of obscure officers, literary critics tend to find such writing slow and even infuriating. They exhibit an equally low tolerance for memoirs written in a lofty, overblown style—a category into which scores of memoirs admittedly fall, and which can be easily (if unfairly) dismissed as silly. Last, critics have shown little patience for soldiers' narratives that take a romantic view of an undeniably brutal war that was inspired, to a great extent, by racism and human bondage.

The problem presented by the critical disdain for veterans' memoirs is that the authors of Civil War literature have not always viewed these texts as romantic, silly, or racist. Scholars have sometimes projected their own disregard for soldiers' writing onto the novelists they discuss, not believing that Stephen Crane or William Faulkner might take seriously the contents of a Yankee or Confederate remembrance. My contention here is that the relationship between veterans' narratives and Civil War fiction deserves careful study by anyone interested in the war and its literature. As writers of later generations have sought to understand their own moment in time, they have often looked back on the Civil War as the central crisis in the nation's past, the forge responsible for the shaping of modern American identity. How did the war define relationships between combatants and noncombatants, men and women, rich and poor, native and immigrant, black and white? Veterans understood that they had participated in the nation's greatest and most awful struggle, and they left their countrymen thousands of reflections about the war and its meaning for America. Some novelists have entered into direct conversation with one or two memoirs, while others have responded more generally to the collective power of veterans' accounts. How authors of fiction have embraced, celebrated, resisted, and rejected those published reflections, while in pursuit of their own artistic and cultural objectives, is the subject of this book.

It is fitting to begin with Stephen Crane's *The Red Badge of Courage* (1895), the novel often revered as the greatest—and perhaps *only* great—fiction about the war. In this chapter I consider the impressive and intimidating stature of the Civil War veteran within the literary marketplace of the late nineteenth century. Living veterans enjoyed great authority over memory of the war, especially the arena exclusive to soldiers: the battlefield. By writing an account of Civil War combat from the vantage point of a participant, Crane breached the cultural barriers dividing veterans from noncombatants. Although he outraged some former soldiers with this act of literary trespassing, Crane relied primarily on veterans' own published accounts to imagine and experience the traumas of the war. I argue that *The Red Badge of Courage* inaugurated an inclusive Civil War literature, one that invited all Americans to participate in the nation's most transformative event.

The next chapter examines how Margaret Mitchell's *Gone with the Wind* (1936) and Caroline Gordon's *None Shall Look Back* (1937) responded to the prevailing martial vision of the war.[5] By at once embracing and revising the Confederate military narratives they used as material for their fiction, Mitchell and Gordon asserted that many women deserved recognition as true Civil War veterans. I believe the pairing of these novels strengthens my discussion of each and reveals how women—especially those writing for a competitive literary market—could respond to veterans' memoirs in diverse and complex ways. My study of these fictions occurs against the backdrop of 1930s America, a period after World War I and the ratification of the Nineteenth Amendment had seemingly created new cultural and professional roles for women. Writers such as Mitchell and Gordon used female participation in the Civil War to comment on women's larger contributions to American nationhood.

The focus of the third chapter shifts to the crises of racism and race relations within American culture, both in the 1860s and in the decades leading up to the civil rights movement of the twentieth century. I argue that in *Absalom, Absalom!* (1936) and *The Unvanquished* (1938), William Faulkner grappled with these issues only by first demythologizing and demilitarizing the South's Civil War.[6] By transferring the responsibility of narrating the war from veterans to civilians, Faulkner suggested that slavery functioned as the moral center of the Civil War and that Lost Cause narratives must be silenced if we are to understand the common humanity of both the slave and the soldier. Like the novels of Mitchell and Gordon, Faulkner's works demonstrate that the Civil War involved both men and women, in the field and at home. But by staking a claim for black participation in the conflict, and by de-centering the figure of the uniformed soldier, Faulkner more fully contested the war as described in veterans' memoirs.

A discussion of Michael Shaara's *The Killer Angels* occupies the fourth chapter.[7] Although the novel is admired by both general and academic readers, few scholars have written at length about its structure, interpretation of the war, and source materials. More than any other novel, *The Killer Angels* illustrates the legacy of soldiers' narratives within contemporary Civil War fiction. Published in 1974, the book combines elements from different veterans' traditions in order to package the war in a way attractive to readers of the late twentieth and early twenty-first centuries. Looking beyond an emancipationist vision of the conflict, Shaara collapsed race into a larger narrative about the enduring power of the individual within American culture.

The conclusion considers Civil War fictions first published after *The Killer Angels* and the close of the Vietnam War—a period during which the nation grew increasingly aware of the horrors of modern warfare and of the psychological burdens carried by veterans. Taking Howard Bahr's 2006 work *The Judas Field* as an exemplary text, I discuss how recent Civil War novels have responded to memoirs published by veterans of America's twentieth-century military conflicts.[8] This section both begins and ends by reflecting on the participatory nature of Civil War fiction and on its enduring place in American letters.

Some readers will wonder how I chose to examine these seven novels out of the many hundreds published since 1861. I do not mean to suggest that these works are representative of Civil War fiction in any systematic sense, nor that each represents a pivotal moment in the evolution of the genre. But all have been judged, by the public and scholars alike, to have contributed something meaningful to American literature and culture. Two of my selections, *Gone with the Wind* and *The Killer Angels,* won the Pulitzer Prize for fiction and enjoy considerable attention within any discussion of popular Civil War literature. Both have spawned feature films, inspired numerous sequels and imitations, and continue to attract and excite the reading public. Critical consensus holds that *The Red Badge of*

Courage and *Absalom, Absalom!* stand among the most important works in American literary history. As for the last three works, I initially chose to include the well-respected *None Shall Look Back* and *The Unvanquished* in order to comment on *Gone with the Wind* and *Absalom, Absalom!* respectively. But I soon came to appreciate how these novels' own interest in Civil War veterans and cultural memory made them just as valuable to my study as the other texts. The inclusion of the award-winning *The Judas Field*, which I first read long after the completion of the rest of this study, owes to its success at crystallizing some of the major trends in recent Civil War literature.

I do regret that my choice of works may seem to suggest that white novelists alone write Civil War fiction. As students of American literature know, several African American writers—from Charles W. Chesnutt to Toni Morrison—have made the causes and consequences of 1861–65 a subject of their work, and to powerful effect. Nonetheless, the overwhelming majority of Civil War narratives have been the work of white authors, a fact reflected in my selection of novels. And while I certainly recognize the importance of short fiction to the body of Civil War literature, I have focused on the novel for two reasons. First, those Civil War fictions that have most influenced public memory of the war, and best captured the popular imagination, have almost always been novels. Second, the novelistic form, due to its length and depth, has allowed for a more sustained analysis of the subject at hand. Many short stories about the war do exhibit the same qualities I discuss in this book, however; I therefore hope that my observations will be read as pertaining not to one literary form alone but to a wide range of fictions about the conflict.

Undoubtedly there exist many other imaginative works, including poems and film scripts, that stand in conversation with the memoirs of veterans— perhaps even more obviously than those I have selected. I believe this fact ultimately strengthens my observations, insofar as it shows that the authors and novels featured here represent larger trends and developments in literature about the war.

Last, I will add just a word about the poor reputation that has hounded Civil War fiction nearly since its origins. Scores of commentators have lampooned the genre as silly, sensational, romantic, lowbrow, boring, and just plain bad. These criticisms have been deserved in many cases but at other times have been exaggerated and misplaced. Many novels and short stories have been unjustly dismissed, not because of their own faults, but because they do not live up to some set of ill-defined but nonetheless lofty expectations. Literary critics are especially guilty in this regard, irritated that American writers have failed to produce an epic masterpiece about a historical event that would seem to be rich with dramatic possibilities. Stephen Cushman has offered the best rejoinder to such critics: "I often hear someone say that we have yet to see the great Civil War novel, adding something like, 'Where is the *War and Peace* of the American Civil War?' This question makes as much sense to me as asking, Where is the *Moby-Dick* of the Russian whaling industry? But even if I could take the question seriously, I wonder... how many good Russian novels about the Napoleonic wars never got written because other novelists felt intimidated by *War and Peace*? If the price of an American counterpart to Tolstoy's tome were the loss of most of the books we now have, would we be willing to pay it?"[9]

For the record, I believe that all seven novels discussed here are artistic successes and that each reflects well upon its author. But I also believe that the success and value of these works owe a great deal to the literary efforts of an earlier group of American writers—the soldiers who fought the Civil War and who later recorded in print their experiences and interpretations. No less than the authors of Civil War fiction, these men helped to produce a branch of imaginative literature fascinating for what it can teach us about the evolution of American culture and identity.

Chapter One

Various Veterans Had Told Him Tales
The Red Badge of Courage and an Inclusive Civil War Literature

For many readers, *The Red Badge of Courage* (1895) occupies a curious place in the history of Civil War literature. Although routinely celebrated as our greatest novel of the war, the book has surprisingly little to say about the conflict beyond the heat and crash of battle. No matter that Stephen Crane chose *An Episode of the American Civil War* as his subtitle. As scholars are fond of pointing out, the novel appears uninterested in secession, emancipation, and the other cultural and political phenomena that inspired the war. The book likewise ignores the military specifics available in countless other Civil War fictions. While almost certainly set at the battle of Chancellorsville, *The Red Badge of Courage* forgoes most place names, as well as the names of military leaders, famous engagements, and most units other than the fictional 304th New York, a regiment whose "preposterously high number" seems intended to slight those who would read for historical accuracy.[1]

Crane's decision to empty his novel of historical details has not bothered those who interpret the work as an experiment in literary impressionism or naturalism, nor those who read it as a universal portrait of "every man who goes to war, no matter the cause."[2] But for readers interested in the evolution of Civil War literature, *The Red Badge of Courage* represents a challenge. Exactly why have so many Americans agreed with Ernest Hemingway's famous remark that there was virtually "no real literature of our Civil War" until Crane published his "episode"?[3] Moreover, why was Crane—himself not born until six years after the war—the first major writer to pen a Civil War novel? I believe the answers to these questions depend on the relationship of *The Red Badge of Courage* to the vast body of veterans' memoirs that preceded it into print. Critics have widely acknowledged the role that soldiers' narratives played in inspiring and informing Crane's novel.[4] Wilbur F. Hinman's fictionalized reminiscence, *Corporal Si Klegg and His "Pard"* (1887), has been suggested as one source from which Crane drew, as have a number of more traditional soldiers' memoirs. Such works include *Our Boys* by Alonzo F. Hill (1864), *Hardtack and Coffee* by John D. Billings (1888), *Recollections of a Private Soldier in the Army of the Potomac* by Frank Wilkeson (1887), and *Recollections of a Private* by Warren Lee Goss (1890).[5]

Few scholars, however, have appreciated the degree to which those memoirs, and the middle-aged veterans themselves, represented a formidable obstacle to any nonveteran wishing to write about the war during the 1880s and 1890s. By examining this cultural and literary context, we can better understand the striking achievement of Crane. Far from rejecting the world of old soldiers, the young author seized upon and exploited the very ideal that veterans had guarded jealously and hence made sacred: individual participation in America's greatest conflict. As I argue, this strategy explains how *The Red Badge of Courage*, more than any other work of fiction, helped transform Civil War literature from an exclusive genre into an inclusive one.

I.

Today it is difficult for us to imagine the stature of the Civil War veteran during the last two decades of the nineteenth century. Veterans of America's later wars have at times enjoyed the thanks and adoration of their countrymen, but no soldiers in living memory experienced the kind of long-standing and heartfelt celebration that came to envelop veterans blue and gray. Even the recent efforts to honor veterans of World War II, although at times robust, cannot begin to compare with the veritable culture of commemoration that Americans built around the figure of the Civil War soldier. By 1890, the holidays of Decoration Day and Memorial Day had become grand affairs, during which Americans adorned the graves of soldiers, participated in parades, and turned out by the thousands to listen to patriotic orations. The celebration was pervasive. Writing in 1898, a contributor to the *New York Times* reported that there was "scarcely a hamlet in the United States" that did not display "a tiny flag or bit of bunting on Decoration Day." She recounted having once come across a "wretched hut" among the "wild mountain country" of West Virginia. Upon asking the hut's impoverished inhabitants why they displayed a red rag at the door, she was surprised when the occupants cried out: "Decoration Day!" Even these "untamed, untamable people respected the day." Accounts such as this one lend credence to David W. Blight's observation that, during the late nineteenth century, "one could not live in or near an American city or village, North or South, and remain unaware of the ritual of decorating the graves of the Civil War dead."[6]

With the veneration of the dead came the championing of the living veteran. Granted, historians have shown that the lionization of veterans often had less to do with the events of 1861–65 than with the political, economic, and cultural landscape of the 1880s and 1890s. Dissatisfaction with the excesses and corruption of the Gilded Age, for example, led many thousands of Americans to embrace a nostalgic vision of the nation's recent past—one represented by aging veterans whose patriotism and self-sacrifice stood as a reminder of what had been lost, after the war, to the decadent and self-interested world of commerce. But most Americans who came to revere former Yankees and Confederates did not explore their motivations for doing so, nor did the veterans themselves question the parades, speeches, and holidays that honored them. On the contrary, many thousands of veterans threw themselves wholeheartedly into the culture of remembrance, sometimes with more passion than they had ever displayed as youths in uniform.[7]

Whether by presiding over commemorative events or simply marching in Decoration Day parades with ribbons pinned to their chests, veterans North and South stood "very much in public view" throughout the late nineteenth century. In this respect they were flesh-and-blood counterparts to the marble and bronze figures then appearing atop new monuments to common soldiers of the war. Monuments to the rank and file were virtually nonexistent in Europe at the time, but they came to dominate America's public squares and cemeteries by the early twentieth century. As art historian Kirk Savage has explained, these monuments honored "not only the dead but the living veteran," and "it was the veterans themselves, or their loved ones, who mobilized to erect this new form of war memorial." So popular were these monuments to America's citizen-soldiers that a "monument industry developed to meet the demand, packaging the services of granite companies, marble quarries, and metal foundries directly to the monument consumers." Just as former soldiers lived in virtually every American community, such statuary came to occupy not only large cities but also "tiny hamlets that had never before seen a single public statue." Americans of Crane's generation therefore found themselves surrounded, on a daily basis, by reminders of the unsurpassed valor and sacrifices of Civil War veterans.[8]

Keeping apace with their high profile in American public spaces, veterans also made deep inroads into the literary marketplace. Some publications featured reflective speeches delivered by veterans at battlefield reunions. Others, in the form of articles or sketches by old soldiers, looked back on particular episodes or personalities of the war. Veterans sought to write history as well as to reminisce; they consulted old comrades and enemies alike when preparing manuscripts. They produced scores of regimental and unit histories. Most notably, thousands of veterans embarked on the often-daunting task of penning their wartime memoirs, recording for posterity the experiences that defined their personal lives as well as the life of the nation. In these works, veterans asked and sought to answer important questions about the conflict. What did the war mean for America and for its different regions, races, and ethnic groups? For what purpose did more than six hundred thousand Americans die of wounds and disease? How should future generations remember America's great sectional struggle? "They created one of the most remarkable bodies of literature in American history," one recent historian observed: "Whatever they lacked in terms of accepted style these books, articles, and essays made up for in candor and sincerity." Several hundred of these works enjoyed a wide circulation, and the reading public devoured them voraciously.[9]

Literary critics have long marveled at the astounding popularity of soldiers' memoirs, but most have too quickly dismissed these works as the byproduct of a national love for nostalgia and adventure. More careful scholars have considered what the popularity of these narratives said about American democracy, and American literature, at the dawn of the twentieth century. This approach seems necessary when we consider that Civil War memoirs reflected far more than a brief literary fad. Stephen Cushman has noted that "the flash flood of personal reminiscences washed the country for a good sixty years," from 1866 to the late 1920s: "[During] the convulsive stretch that literary histories describe as running from the emergence of realism to the flourishing of high modernism, a stretch that included the Spanish-American War and World War I, Americans steadily wrote and read personal narratives of the Civil War." As suggested by the durability of the genre, the spoken and published accounts of veterans were more than simple entertainment for the public at large.[10]

For example, few genres of American literature more clearly celebrated the democratic voice than the soldier's narrative, a quality that undoubtedly attracted many readers. "No other historical experience in America has given rise to such a massive collection of personal narrative 'literature' written by ordinary people," Blight explained. "They published themselves, and provided each other with audiences. If any former private, captain, or brevet-general was willing to write an account, it was generally published." Admittedly, the memoirs of Civil War generals and their high-ranking subordinates drew the most widespread audiences. The *Century* magazine's *Century* War Series—a three-year run of articles written mostly by officers North and South—fed the public's fascination with those leaders who directed the legendary battles of the war. The magazine's monthly circulation soared from 127,000 to 225,000 in the year following the 1884 release of the series. In turn, the *Century* War Series begot the popular *Battles and Leaders of the Civil War* (1887–88), a four-volume bound collection of illustrated articles culled from the magazine. But for all the attention given to the words of leaders, the published narratives of common soldiers also found their way into the hands of thousands of readers. To be sure, the literary phenomenon cut across lines of class and rank. For instance, in the same year that *Battles and Leaders* first appeared in print, Union private John D. Billings published his now classic *Hardtack and Coffee: Or, the Unwritten Story of Army Life*. Designed by Billings to complement "the more majestic" histories penned by generals, the book set out to record the experiences of the common Civil War soldier, in camp and on the march. Surrounded by the words and writings of generals, privates, and soldiers everywhere in between, Americans of Crane's era knew the Civil War veteran in all his manifestations.[11]

Yet if the memoirs of veterans represented a democratic voice, they also stood for an exclusionary one. No matter how plain the prose nor how lowly the author's rank, these narratives all flowed from the pens of Civil War participants—men whose military service set them apart from their fellow Americans. Having survived the physical and psychological horrors of the battlefield, and having dedicated body and soul to the flag, veterans often came to prize their service above all else. In an article appearing in the *Southern Historical Society Papers* in 1895, the same year that Crane published *The Red Badge of Courage*, one Virginian declared: "There is not enough money in the coffers of all the banks to buy the proud claim that I was a loyal soldier." The old Confederate urged his fellow veterans to recognize their elite status among men: "It is not often the privilege of a man to serve his country for years without pay and on half rations. This has been your privilege, my dear comrades. Wear this badge of royalty upon your hearts, while they beat proudly your grand and solemn march to eternity." Similarly, another Southern veteran ended his memoir with the avowal that his wartime experiences, no matter how inconsequential, were priceless: "That I view my participation in the stirring events herein narrated with some pride is freely admitted, and, in conclusion, I confidently assert I would not part with my own inconsiderable share of the glories of the Army of Northern Virginia for a fortune of wealth."[12]

Such sentiments were shared by old soldiers both North and South and repeated for years in commemorative speeches, articles, and memoirs. A Union veteran sounded the familiar note in 1888: "The veteran soldiers are the aristocracy of the land. I do not refer to the distinctions which society may try to make supreme, or the glitter with which misers of gold may seek to dazzle the people. I mean by aristocracy, the heroes who have proven the best men in the land." The Civil War veteran, he argued, "has proved the possession of immortal and self-sacrificing courage. He has recorded himself by his deeds as immensely superior to the devotees of fashion, or the worshippers of gold."[13]

In their published memoirs, veterans found ample opportunities to remind readers of the distance between the soldier and the civilian, and between the Civil War veteran and the soldier of later generations. A veteran of the 4th Rhode Island hoped that the Star-Spangled Banner would always "be supported with arms and hearts as brave and loyal as those which have once and forever redeemed it from the curse of slavery." But sensing that readers might doubt the fortitude of America's young men, he assured them that the flag would remain safe so long as its old defenders remained alive: "Thus supported, it can never fall; and while our hearts beat, and our arms can be raised in its defense, it shall have our sympathy and aid 'against all its enemies or opposers whatsoever.'" Some veterans never again saw themselves as civilians, even decades after taking off the uniform. This mentality created problems for more than a few memoirists, because they found it difficult to write for civilian readers. When "writing for the information of the citizen," one former soldier suggested, the veteran "should forget his own familiarity with the every-day scenes of soldier life and strive to record even those things which seem to him too common to mention." Still other veterans thought it best not to convey too much about battle in their narratives, as naïve youngsters might romanticize their combat experiences.

So horrific and costly was the Civil War, one Union veteran argued, that the nations of the earth should abolish war and erect an "international arbitration court." This measure would in turn force America's young men to abandon dreams of soldiering and instead lead them to serve "Uncle Sam" as ministers, schoolteachers, and mailmen. The old soldier wanted none of his young readers to ever know a battlefield firsthand.[14]

Many thousands of Americans who had not fought in the war, or who were not yet born before Appomattox, came to respect and awe this fraternity of men whose exceptional status could not be bought, matched, or shared. Gerald Linderman has examined the process by which the reputation of veterans grew in the American consciousness, noting that as the Civil War "was incorporated in public ritual and the reputation of soldiering rose, participation in war became an important mark of merit. Honor attached itself less to courageous or cowardly conduct, battles won or lost, causes preserved or destroyed than to one's simple presence in the war." While the nation never ceased to celebrate those soldiers who had given their lives in the struggle, there emerged—both in veterans' writings and in the public imagination—a conviction that survivors of the war deserved special distinction. "Survival, too, by whatever circumstances actually achieved, became a source of pride," Linderman argued. Veterans "told themselves that it could not have been mere chance, that they must have possessed certain worthy attributes or acted in certain meritorious ways that accounted for their survival. As community ritual magnified the war, the war began to magnify all those who had fought and lived."[15]

The premium placed on survival reflected the public's fascination with the exhilarating and terrifying world of the Civil War battlefield. Indeed, the combat experience underscored and united all those attributes that Americans most admired about veterans: patriotism, courage, gallantry, sacrifice, fortitude, and grit. In popular memory, the war's skirmishes, cavalry charges, and full-scale engagements functioned as the stage on which soldiers had refined and perfected American heroism. Linderman quoted the pioneering Civil War historian Bruce Catton, who as a child had idolized the Union veterans in his hometown, recognizing them as living links to the past. "The Civil War veterans were men set apart," Catton recalled. "They were pillars . . . of the community; the keepers of its patriotic traditions, the living embodiment, so to speak, of what it most deeply believed about the nation's greatness and high destiny." The historian left no doubt that the mystique of the aging soldiers derived from their past experiences in battle: "Years ago they had marched thousands of miles to legendary battlefields.... And we were in awe of them. Those terrible names out of the history books—Gettysburg, Shiloh, Stone's River, Cold Harbor—came alive through these men. They had *been* there."[16]

As Catton's memoirs confirm, by the early twentieth century veterans and their admirers had succeeded in defining the war—and the virtues it inspired—in terms of the battlefield. Considering the dramatic courage and bloodshed witnessed during the war's many campaigns, it is not surprising that the battlefield became synonymous with the Civil War experience. Yet social and political matters also played a role in pushing the field to the forefront of soldiers' narratives. Many historians have suggested that veterans-turned-writers focused on combat, rather than on the ideological issues of the war, in an attempt to heal the wounds of the nation. By ignoring the subject of slavery, and denying the centrality of emancipation to the war, white Americans North and South could forget old animosities and confirm the honor and manhood of each section. Reflections on battlefield heroics, rather than on the war's moral and political contests, would prove the easier route toward peace and prosperity.[17]

But it is, of course, also true that former soldiers had their own interests in mind when choosing how to remember the conflict. It is indeed little wonder that veterans, when writing and speaking about the war, chose to focus on the battlefield: an arena virtually exclusive to men in uniform. By doing so, they played down the wartime roles of civilians, noncombatants, journalists, and politicians. And they hence reserved for themselves nearly all the honor and glory reaped from the nation's most devastating, yet also most captivating and defining, experience. As Stuart McConnell has explained, veterans "tried to institutionalize the memory of the war as a radically unique event, a one-time-only drama of national salvation" in which they had served as the principal players.[18]

Old Yankee and Rebel soldiers established their elite fraternity not only via public addresses and memoirs but also in the more structured form of veterans' organizations such as the Grand Army of the Republic (GAR) and the United Confederate Veterans (UCV). Membership in these organizations climbed steadily during the 1880s and into the 1890s, in part for reasons related to politics and pensions. However, as McConnell has shown in his book on the GAR, these associations also functioned as exclusive fraternal orders. While that exclusivity could at times bend (noncombatants could visit GAR posts and take part in some "campfire" activities), it would not break. For example, although many GAR events involved the families of veterans, its members refused to merge with the Sons of Veterans, a society of men whose fathers had fought for the Union. Like the Sons of Confederate Veterans and United Daughters of the Confederacy, the Sons of Veterans sought to bask in the reflected glow of the Civil War soldier. But many veterans frowned on the imitative and parasitic nature of hereditary organizations and urged Americans to remember that their experiences could not be shared. As one high-ranking GAR official declared, "No one, not even our sons, can appreciate the memories of camp and march, of bivouac and battle, as those who were participants therein; the scenes of the great struggle can never be to them what they are to us."[19]

By closely monitoring the literary marketplace, veterans found an effective way to safeguard their authority over the war and its meanings. Old soldiers routinely scrutinized the printed accounts and memoirs of one another, sometimes crossing pens in earnest over the smallest details in the historical record. Such scrutiny also applied to histories, articles, and accounts of the war written by authors who had not participated in the contest. Not only could veterans cast doubt on the historical accuracy of such works, but they at times also responded with indignation when a civilian dared to evaluate or critique the war's causes, battles, or leaders. Generally speaking, few Americans found fault with former soldiers for at times frustrating the literary and historicizing ambitions of others. Indeed, most recognized the right of veterans to dominate and police the literary legacy of the war. As a result, book reviewers sometimes found it necessary to explain *why* a civilian's account of the conflict might have real value for readers. When reviewing *A Short History of the War of Secession* (1888) by Rossiter Johnson, the New York *Critic* explained that Johnson, as a civilian, "is free from the ambitions and jealousies that almost inevitably mar the value of the reports of even the highest military participants in such a struggle." Taking a more deferential approach, the *Buffalo Express* played down Johnson's lack of military experience by noting that he "writes of military events like a soldier." The newspaper further pointed out that Gen. William T. Sherman himself admired the historian's earlier book about the War of 1812. Employing a similar strategy, the *Chicago-Tribune* used military language to describe Johnson's narrative enterprise, noting that "his commission" was to present an honest portrait of the Civil War, a duty he had fulfilled with soldierly "courage, taste, and skill." As these reviews illustrate, any noncombatant wishing to write about the war during the late nineteenth century risked facing a skeptical and unreceptive audience. It could take finesse and wordplay, especially on the part of booksellers and reviewers, to attract a readership for such works.[20]

Scholars have not usually considered the imposing presence of veterans when questioning why the war produced hundreds of memoirs but few great works of literature. Elizabeth Young has observed that "there is, in fact, no male canon of great American Civil War novels as such but, rather, a hole precisely where one ought to be. None of the most canonical authors of the immediate postwar period—Twain, Howells, James—fought at any length in the war; neither they nor the next generation of American naturalists wrote Civil War novels; and the most 'authentic' of Civil War novels, *The Red Badge of Courage*, was a retroactive version of the war invented by a man born after it had ended." Young's portrait of this "curiously impotent male canon" lines up with the observations of editors David Madden and Peggy Bach, who in the introduction to *Classics of Civil War Fiction* (1991) outlined critical complaints about the absence of "the great Civil War novel." While praising the bold literary contributions of veterans John W. De Forest and Ambrose Bierce, the editors seem perplexed and troubled by the fact that the most famous literary talents of the age produced no Civil War novels. Overcompensating for the lack of war fiction by Henry James or Mark Twain, they suggested with enthusiasm that the *Adventures of Huckleberry Finn* (1885) "should be considered one of the great Civil War novels," even if some will consider that designation "perverse."[21]

Rather than reinvent a work like *Huckleberry Finn* as a war novel, I believe students of Civil War literature should instead consider how the postwar culture imposed restrictions on those who would write about the conflict. The climate of nostalgia and martial exaltation helps explain why men of letters, if they had not fought for North or South, were reluctant to write directly about the war. Many felt it was not their place to do so, and, in light of the wholesale celebration of veterans during the 1880s and 1890s, few wished to draw attention to the fact that they had not served in uniform. In his classic study of Civil War literature, *The Unwritten War* (1973), Daniel Aaron considered the postwar careers of Henry Adams, William Dean Howells, Henry James, and Mark Twain. Naming these men "the Malingerers," Aaron noted that the "four most talented writers in post-War America did indeed shun the battlefields." I cannot agree with Aaron's claim that each may have "suffered psychic abrasions no less grievous to him than real wounds incurred by real soldiers on real battlefields." But I believe he correctly concluded that although Adams, Howells, James, and Twain never "condemned the American War openly or disparaged the contestants, [each] covertly resented the demands of the War on his mind and body and felt guilt of some sort about his failure to meet them." For these and other American men who had not enlisted, feelings of guilt and shame compelled silence, as did deference to contemporaries who had shouldered arms. For example, Aaron noted that while Henry James surely admired his two youngest brothers for volunteering, their participation in the war "filled him with remorse and humiliation." Such complex feelings stilled James's pen every time he thought to write about the war; as a spectator who "knew nothing of bivouacs and skirmishes," he could do no more than "nourish himself on the crumbs of [his brothers'] experiential feast."[22]

Mark Twain perhaps best exhibited the mixed emotions with which the nation's most gifted authors approached the war. His career as a soldier was as undistinguished as it was brief: the future celebrity left Missouri for Nevada in 1861 after just two weeks' service as a Confederate volunteer. Although the details of his short-lived stint as a soldier remain elusive, he did write up a comic account of his "service" for *Century*, under the title "The Private History of a Campaign That Failed" (1885). Published as part of the War Series (but not included in the bound *Battles and Leaders* collection), the piece shows Twain by turn to be both sardonic and deferential toward the veterans with whom he shared the pages of the magazine. As he told it, in the summer of 1861 Twain joined the Marion Rangers, an irregular Missouri unit whose members eschewed orders, ignored rank, and avoided most other military protocol. Humorously deficient in any sense of duty or patriotism, the band regularly retreated and hid in order to avoid contact with the enemy. This "idly delicious" life ended abruptly when the Rangers shot and killed a man who may or may not have been a Union scout. For the first time facing the reality of war, "the killing of strangers against whom you feel no personal animosity," Twain and several comrades decided to give up military service altogether.[23]

Because of its comic delivery and antiwar message, Twain's article differed dramatically from virtually every other piece published in the series. While some critics have concluded that Twain used "the jester's license to undercut the reverential and celebratory *Century* series," that judgment seems only half correct. As the first and last paragraphs of "The Private History" indicate, Twain oscillated between mocking and admiring those men who contributed more to the war effort than he had. "You have heard from a great many people who did something in the war," he began boldly. "[Is] it not fair and right that you listen a little moment to one who started out to do something in it, but didn't?" The confident tone faded noticeably, however, as he proceeded: "Thousands entered the war, got just a taste of it, and then stepped out again, permanently. These, by their very numbers, are respectable, and are therefore entitled to a sort of voice—not a loud one, but a modest one; not a boastful one, but an apologetic one. They ought not to be allowed much space among better people—people who did something—I grant that; but they ought at least to be allowed to state why they didn't do anything. . . . Surely this kind of light must have some sort of value." Undoubtedly, irony shined through Twain's statement that veterans were "better people" than nonparticipants. But he appeared less ironic when describing the civilian's voice as "modest" and "apologetic," and less bold when asserting that his own experiences have a "sort of value."[24]

Although the majority of his article cast doubt on the valor of the Civil War soldier, Twain seemed unable or unwilling to sustain the critique without backpedaling. For example, when characterizing his comrades-in-arms as lacking the necessary obedience and gallantry for war, he paused to make an exception: "[There] were those among us who afterward learned the grim trade; learned to obey like machines; became valuable soldiers; fought all through the war, and came out at the end with excellent records." Similarly, the final paragraph reflected Twain's knowledge that most readers of *Century* would have little patience with criticism of the men in blue and gray. There he tried to explain the real contribution that his article made to the history of the war. "The thoughtful will not throw this war-paper of mine lightly aside as being valueless," Twain declared. "It has this value: it is a not unfair picture of what went on in many and many a militia camp in the first months of the rebellion . . . before the invaluable experience of actual collision in the field had turned them from rabbits into soldiers. If this side of the picture of that early day has not before been put into history, then history has been to that degree incomplete, for it had and has its rightful place there." Today few would doubt that Twain's account had a rightful place in the story of the war, and few would fault the satirist for wishing to deflate the swelling ego of the Civil War veteran. Yet what remains most intriguing about "The Private History" is the degree to which Twain reigned in his own satirical powers. He did so not merely because he stood as a humorist reliant on the goodwill of his audience, but because—as his account betrayed—he felt unjustified in using a voice as loud and as sharp as did those who "did something in the war."[25]

Evidence of Twain's conflicting views on the heroes of the Civil War can be found beyond the pages of *Century* magazine. On the one hand, he seemed determined to show that great soldiers achieved their fame as a result of happenstance rather than destiny. In his *Autobiography* (1924), for example, Twain paused to discuss his work "Captain Stormfield's Visit to Heaven" (1909), in which the protagonist arrived in heaven "eager to get a sight of those unrivaled and incomparable military geniuses, Caesar, Alexander and Napoleon." But the newcomer "was told by an old resident of heaven that they didn't amount to much there as military geniuses, that they ranked as obscure corporals only, by comparison with a certain colossal military genius, a shoemaker by trade, who had lived and died unknown in a New England village and had never seen a battle in all his earthly life." In Twain's imagination, the "most prodigious military genius the planet had ever produced" had not been discovered on Earth simply because war never arrived at his doorstep. Beneath the humor and wit, this and other satirical passages reflected the writer's resentment and envy for those soldiers whose military prowess and bearing cast a shadow over those who had not served.[26]

Yet on the other hand, no matter how much he loathed war itself, or how much he worried over his decision in 1861 to abandon a soldier's life, Twain maintained a true respect for the martial heroes of his day. He at times sought the company of renowned officers and cultivated a friendship with one of the war's most towering figures, Ulysses S. Grant. In fact, Twain eventually marketed and published Grant's memoirs. The friendship certainly benefited the public image of Twain; as Aaron has observed, he "acquired a kind of derived honor" from the connection to Grant, "the man of peace linked in the public's eye with the man of war and gaining credit by this affiliation." But the relationship meant more to Twain than publicity or publishing revenue. It likely benefited his self-image as well, helping to reduce his anxieties about not participating in the Civil War. Perhaps most important, the friendship allowed Twain, whose civilian status inhibited him from writing fully of the war, to make an enduring mark on the literary heritage of the conflict. By encouraging, publishing, and popularizing Grant's *Personal Memoirs* (1885), he affixed himself to one of the most admired and well-read narratives by any Civil War soldier, one that Edmund Wilson has called "a unique expression of the national character."[27]

II.

With *The Red Badge of Courage*, Stephen Crane broke with literary tradition and changed the very nature of Civil War literature. In hindsight, Crane was better equipped than most writers to attempt a battlefield narrative, a mode of writing that had for more than twenty years been dominated by Civil War veterans. Born too late to bear the stigma of having declined or fled from service, he also enjoyed the benefits of his own obscurity and precocity. A virtual unknown during the early 1890s, Crane had no real reputation to lose by raising the ire of veterans or by upsetting a public sensitive to soldiers' authority over the battlefield. And yet because he wrote with skill, wisdom, and artistry beyond his years (he was just twenty-four when the novel appeared in hard covers), he was able to produce the kind of powerful narrative that readers expected from the pens of older talents, those established men of letters who felt unable to write of the conflict.

The iconoclastic young author did not take propriety into account when he set out to compose his novel. Whereas Twain carefully began and concluded his "Private History" with a half-ironic, half-heartfelt apology for entering the conversation, Crane felt no obligation to do so. He made no effort to justify his writing a Civil War novel, nor did he prepare a preface meant to pay homage to the soldiers he wrote about (a convention practiced by some Civil War novelists right up to the present day). In fact, many scholars have seen in his fiction and comments a tendency to scorn veterans and the narratives they created or inspired. Eric Solomon argued in 1966 that, from start to finish, "Crane's war novel is shot through with mockery of the common views of war." In recent decades, scholars have continued to argue that *The Red Badge of Courage* parodies veterans' written narratives. "Crane's parody questions the pedagogical value of those memoirs that made up such popular works as *Battles and Leaders*," Amy Kaplan observed. Other critics have concluded that veterans' accounts "disappointed" Crane, a writer who wanted to read less about tactics and romance than about the blood, dirt, and fear of combat.[28]

Crane's written and reported remarks indeed reflect frustration over his own distance from the experiences described by veterans. According to his friend Corwin K. Linson, the young novelist became annoyed when surveying the War Series in *Century* magazine. "I wonder that *some* of these fellows don't tell how they *felt* in those scraps!" Crane groused. "They spout eternally of what they *did*, but they are as emotionless as rocks!"

While these words may at first seem unequivocally dismissive, we should be careful not to exaggerate Crane's misgivings about the *Century* and *Battles and Leaders* contents he read before drafting *The Red Badge of Courage*. Contrary to the conclusions of some scholars, I do not believe that Crane found personal histories of the war so flat and irritating that he sought to rewrite them or that he set out to travesty veterans' "lifeless and dry" narratives. Crane surely realized that his powers as a writer far exceeded those of most former soldiers. His object was not to outdo and embarrass these men, but to delve deeper into the war than the standard accounts allowed. In short, Crane wanted to discover what Walt Whitman termed the "real war." And that meant not "just getting the surface appearance right," but also "imparting to it some kind of meaning or feeling."[29]

In order to find the real war, Crane relied on the imaginative possibilities of fiction. Writing a few weeks after Crane's death in 1900, William L. Alden reflected on how fiction enabled the young author to portray "the vivid truthfulness" of the war: "To many people, it may seem strange that an author's imagination can be more truthful than his facts; but that this is often the case has been demonstrated times without number. Why should it not be so? Is not the creator superior to the mere reporter? We see the same thing in painting. A portrait is never as true to life in its lines as is a photograph, but it is infinitely truer in its effect." Alden argued that first-person remembrances depended primarily on facts and that facts were the enemy of the imagination: "Facts are in the way of a man of real genius when he undertakes descriptive writing. They hamper and restrain him. In a real battle there are many things which the reporter who is present cannot see, but in the imaginary battle the writer plans and fights it through in the way that suits him best."[30]

I agree with Alden that the "truth" of a battle is more than the sum of its facts. But not all soldiers wrote memoirs in order to be "mere reporters." As Cushman has observed, former Yankees and Confederates wrote for numerous reasons: among them the desire to record history, to praise and discredit others, to conceal and deny past blunders, to bolster one's own reputation, and to make money. Moreover, some memoirists felt free to describe happenings that they did not themselves witness, relying on the reports of others and, importantly, on their own imaginations. For example, Union veteran Theodore Gerrish did not witness the events described in the most famous passage of his memoir, *Army Life: A Private's Reminiscences of the Civil War* (1882). Although Gerrish served in the 20th Maine, he was absent from Gettysburg during July 1863 when his unit helped turn back Confederate assaults on Little Round Top. Therefore what Gerrish knew of the fighting was drawn from the stories of comrades who had survived the battle. The suspense and sweep of his narrative, especially as it involves the regiment preparing for combat, reflected his own imaginative powers. "How can I describe the scenes that followed?" Gerrish wondered, as if uncertain how to best relate an episode he had not witnessed. He answered with two breathless and dramatic sentences: "Imagine, if you can, nine small companies of infantry; numbering perhaps three hundred men, in the form of a right angle, on the extreme flank of an army of eighty thousand men, put there to hold the key of the entire position against a force at least ten times their number, and who are desperately determined to succeed in the mission upon which they came. Stand firm, ye boys from Maine, for not once in a century are men permitted to bear such responsibilities for freedom and justice, for God and humanity, as are now placed upon you." Tellingly, despite the fact that these lines lionized the 20th Maine, some of Gerrish's old companions complained. By writing as though he had been present at Little Round Top, the memoirist had covered himself with borrowed glory.[31]

How might we distinguish between the writing of Crane and Gerrish? Both works sought to collapse the boundaries between past and present, and both depended on the ability of the author to imagine what he did not witness firsthand. It would therefore be wrongheaded to conclude that veterans' narratives always treasured the past over the present, and facts over the imagination. But I want to suggest that two factors do separate these works. The first is the fact that Gerrish himself had served during the Civil War. Veterans of the 20th Maine may have disapproved of him for letting readers believe he had fought at Gettysburg, but as a veteran of the war, it was surely his right to discuss the shock, blaze, and roar of combat. The civilian Crane, by contrast, did not enjoy the same privilege. And this factor leads to the second difference between the novel and the memoir: Crane's use of the imagination. Memoirists began with the remembered experience of war (even a second-hand memory), and then used their imagination and literary talents to transform those memories into a written account. *The Red Badge of Courage* moved in the opposite direction. Crane began with published accounts of the war and used his imagination and literary skill to work backward to the experience itself. Like no writer before him, he sought to close the temporal and experiential gap between himself and the veterans whose narratives he read.

Early in *The Red Badge of Courage*, Crane revealed the process by which soldiers' words informed his novel. In writing that his young protagonist, Henry Fleming, had "read of marches, sieges, conflicts, and he had longed to see it all," Crane spoke in part for himself, another youth fascinated by veterans' accounts of "Greeklike struggles": "Various veterans had told him tales. Some talked of gray, bewhiskered hordes who were advancing with relentless curses and chewing tobacco with unspeakable valor; tremendous bodies of fierce soldiery who were sweeping along like the Huns. Others spoke of tattered and eternally hungry men who fired despondent powders. 'They'll charge through hell's fire an' brimstone t' git a holt on a haversack, an' sech stomachs ain't a-lastin' long,' he was told. From the stories, the youth imagined the red, live bones sticking out through slits in the faded uniforms." Just as old soldiers bombarded Crane's generation with countless stories of the war, so do veterans' dramatic tales assail Henry. Full of "fierce soldiery" and "eternally hungry" men, these stories offer alternately dramatic or silly phrases that hold little meaning for the novice. But Henry suspects that grim truths must lie beneath that language, and his imagination transforms romance into reality. "From the stories," the paragraph concludes, "the youth imagined the red, live bones sticking out through slits in the faded uniforms." Here Crane reunited the threadbare uniform, so often sanitized in postwar writing, to the blood and sinew of the war as it happened. To a degree, this sentence characterizes the entirety of *The Red Badge of Courage*; it shows how Crane, like Henry, used his imagination to breathe life, color, and horror into the words of former soldiers, producing a vivid narrative.[32]

To be sure, *The Red Badge of Courage* almost always takes a more complex approach to veterans' narratives than it may at first appear. No doubt Crane did mean to poke fun at some of the more quixotic memoirs, such as when writing of Confederate troops "chewing tobacco with unspeakable valor" and when voicing Henry's belief that veterans "were in no wise to be trusted" (87). However, at other points his novel suggested that veterans had much to teach. For example, on the brink of the 304th New York's first taste of battle, Henry and his untried comrades are uncertain of how to behave. Some began to build small entrenchments in front of their line with shoveled earth, sticks, and rocks: "This procedure caused a discussion among the men. Some wished to fight like duelists, believing it to be correct to stand erect and be, from their feet to their foreheads, a mark. They said they scorned the devices of the cautious. But the others scoffed in reply, and pointed to the veterans on the flanks who were digging at the ground like terriers. In a short time there was quite a barricade along the regimental fronts" (103–4). Running counter to the idea that Crane merely parodied the writing of old soldiers, he here showed that veterans might dispel romantic notions of war as well as perpetuate them. In his study of the *Century* War Series and other narratives, Crane would have read many accounts of Civil War veterans hunkering down behind entrenchments and makeshift cover. Similarly "reading" the actions of veterans, the soldiers of the 304th come to discard their romantic ideas and build a barricade along their front. This scene makes literal one of Crane's primary projects—digging into veterans' narratives and using the realities found there as a barricade against the world of romance. The accounts of veterans therefore became more than sources to plunder for plot and detail, and more than targets for parody; they became Crane's primary vehicle for exploring the Civil War.

Probably more than anything else, Crane's deft use of irony explains why scholars have usually concluded that the novel rejects outright the memoirs of veterans. Many have seen Henry's ironic "red badge," a welt on the head masquerading as a bullet wound, as the quintessential example of the novel's critique of standard war narratives. But readers familiar with soldiers' accounts know that irony played a crucial role in how veterans themselves recalled the conflict. In turn, Crane's brand of irony reflected the wry commentary of those veterans who had grown uncomfortable with how the nation had come to remember the war. Confederate veteran Sam Watkins ended his narrative, *Co. Aytch: A Side Show of the Big Show* (1882), by winking at the idea of national unity. He stated that "impartial" historians will conclude, in the postwar era, "'The United States has no North, no South, no East, no West.' '*We are one and undivided.*'" Many readers, filmmaker Ken Burns among them, have missed the irony in these lines, despite the fact that Watkins began his memoir mocking the very idea of Union: "We can laugh now at the absurd notion of there being a north and south. . . . Well, reader, let me whisper in your ear. I was in the row, and the following pages will tell what part I took in the little unpleasant misconception of there being such a thing as a north and south." Crane found himself drawn to such moments in veterans' narratives, precisely because they dipped beneath the standard, mythic surface of the war.[33]

In engaging the ironies exhibited in *Battles and Leaders*, *The Red Badge of Courage* probably depended most on the account of Capt. Andrew B.

Wells, a member of the 8th Pennsylvania, who dismissed his unit's supposed heroics at Chancellorsville. Harold R. Hungerford has noted that when the Confederate flank attack crushed the Eleventh Corps and menaced the entire Federal army, the 8th purportedly "held Jackson's corps off long enough to enable artillery to be dragged into place and charged with canister.... Theirs was the only cavalry charge at Chancellorsville, and it became famous not only because it had saved the Union army—perhaps even the Union—but also because no two observers could agree on its details." In a section titled "The Charge of the Eighth Pennsylvania Calvary," Captain Wells undercut what has gone down as "one of history's more extraordinary military maneuvers."

> The whole affair was accidental. We were on our way to report to General Howard, some three miles from where we were encamped, and the country that General Howard's staff-officer had just passed over in quest of the cavalry had in the meantime been crossed by Stonewall Jackson's troops, and in following the same track we naturally ran into them.... We could not turn around and get out in the face of the enemy, and the only thing left for us was to go through them, "sink or swim."
>
> Can any man who was a soldier for one moment imagine an officer deliberately planning a charge by a regiment of cavalry, strung out by twos in a column half a mile long in a thick wood?

In Wells's view, the 8th's famous charge "was accidental," not the brave and self-sacrificing effort so often described. And by appealing to "any man who was a soldier" to verify his words, his account offered a backhanded critique of the postwar mythmaking that thrived on accounts of troops making hopeless assaults against impossible odds.[34]

Crane linked Henry's ironic "wounding" to the account by Wells of the 8th Pennsylvania's inadvertent charge. Clubbed by one of the Eleventh's stampeding soldiers, Henry stumbles groggily around the scene described by the cavalryman. The novel there makes the youth a witness to the famed episode: "Into the unspeakable jumble in the roadway rode a squadron of cavalry. The faded yellow of their facings shone bravely. There was a mighty altercation" (150). The squadron here adds to the "unspeakable jumble" instead of performing a heroic stand before the reader's eyes. And as Henry reels away from the scene, he shares something of the 8th's postbattle experience. Like so many of Wells's companions, he first allows others—such as the Cheery Man—to assume he fought heroically on the Union right while others fled (152). And by the time he returns to his regiment, he has decided to make that claim himself. "Over on th' right, I got shot," he told a companion. "In th' head. I never see sech fightin'. Awful time. . . . I got shot, too" (154).

Here Crane showed how quickly memory of one's own actions might dim the harsh light of reality. As early as the next morning, "when [Henry] remembered his fortunes of yesterday, and looked at them from a distance he began to see something fine there. He had license to be pompous and veteranlike" (165). Conflating the words *pompous* and *veteranlike*, the novel acknowledged that many veterans sang their own praises while shying away from accidents and mistakes performed "in the dark" (165). Crane's investigation of that process, made possible by his familiarity with accounts like Wells's, lent credibility to his representation of the battle. Realizing the ironies of the field, and seeing them working in the words of his sources, Crane granted Henry an ironic wound that furthers the novel's "authenticity."

In some respects, however, Crane's novel did challenge the narratives of Civil War combatants, even those that eschewed romantic myth. Most important, *The Red Badge of Courage* seized upon the very terrain that veterans had made sacred in their remembrances: the battlefield. The novel engaged unwaveringly this one arena of the war exclusive to soldiers and sent its protagonist marching, charging, retreating, and fleeing wildly over it. Whether or not Crane had trespassed on privileged territory, there can be no doubt that his version of the Civil War battlefield appeared quite unlike the hallowed ground described by most veterans. Specifically, he upset the sentimental and sterile portrait of combat common to remembrances of the struggle. One extreme example of that sanitized war can be found in the regimental history of the 116th Pennsylvania, written by Union veteran St. Clair A. Mulholland. When describing the battle of Fredericksburg, Mulholland reported: "Here there was no disorder. The men were calm, silent, cheerful. The commands of the officers, given in a quiet, subdued voice, were distinctly heard and calmly obeyed, and the regiments manoeuvred without a flaw." The soldier altogether denied the chaos of battle: "The destruction of human beings [was] done with order and system. . . . As for the screams and shrieks, no one heard anything of that kind, either on the field or in the hospitals. . . . The men of the War of 1861 took their punishment without a complaint or murmur."[35]

Like Mulholland, many who saw battle did not wish to remember, or record for posterity, the horrific and sickening details of combat. Others believed, as Aaron has suggested, that such details were not appropriate for a general reading audience: "Polite literature before and after the War excluded certain kinds of experience, and it is not surprising that the territory of the common soldier should have been placed 'off bounds' by America's cultural guardians." The very details Crane included in his novel—"powder-blackened, lousy combatants daily exposed to bullets and shells, resenting their superiors"—were by most standards "hardly presentable subjects." Yet the young author refused to temper his portrait of combat. Henry Fleming and his comrades inhabit a field marked by trash, obscenities, cowardice, and inglorious death. The lieutenant curses relentlessly, the ground is littered with debris, and men are heard grunting, crying out, babbling, and "laughing hysterically" (130).[36]

Among those few veterans whose writing granted the public a glimpse of the war's dark and tawdry side, Ambrose Bierce stood foremost. The cantankerous Bierce did not himself admire Crane's writing style, reportedly saying, "I had thought there could be only two worse writers than Stephen Crane, namely, two Stephen Cranes." Yet he conceded that the young author had indeed envisioned qualities of battle known almost exclusively to combatants: "This young man . . . has the power to feel. He knows nothing of war, yet he is drenched in blood. Most beginners who deal with this subject spatter themselves merely with ink." Bierce's statement goes a long way toward explaining how *The Red Badge of Courage* altered the course of Civil War literature. Crane sought to overcome his inexperience by exercising his powers to "feel," and by pushing those powers to the extreme. In turn, his published episode made that exploration available to generations of readers who likewise knew nothing of the battlefield. Via the senses, body, and mind of Henry Fleming, Crane's literary reenactment offers readers the chance to experience the nation's greatest crisis from the front lines. The novel in fact anticipated the large- and small-scale battlefield reenactments popular today, events at which spectators can witness a Civil War battle firsthand, and even participate directly in the "fighting."[37]

I do not mean to suggest that Crane was the first civilian novelist to describe a Civil War battle or that reading *The Red Badge of Courage* is tantamount to experiencing the realities of combat. But with greater confidence, and far greater success than other writers, he invited those who knew nothing of war to participate in the conflict. As reflected by the enormous popularity of the novel, readers were drawn to a portrait of the war that felt alive, immediate, and surprisingly real.[38] And they were enthused by the idea of a literature that thrust the reader directly into battle, allowing him or her to witness the world of the Civil War soldier personally. As one reviewer of the day expressed, "The description is so vivid as to be almost suffocating. The reader is right down in the midst of it where patriotism is dissolved into its elements and where only a dozen men can be seen, firing blindly and grotesquely into the smoke. This is war from a new point of view, and it seems more real than when seen with an eye only for large movements and general effects."[39] A review of *The Red Badge of Courage* in the March 1896 *Atlantic Monthly* struck a similar chord. "So vivid is the picture of actual conflict that the reader comes face to face with war," the reviewer remarked. "This picture [is] so vivid as to produce almost the effect of a personal experience."[40] Generations later, critics still awed at the novel's power to immerse readers in battle and to overwhelm them with sensations. Writing in 1968, one scholar almost lamented a recent reading of *The Red Badge of Courage:* "I felt suddenly blinded by the story's profuse mélange of color, choked by its omnipresent dust and smoke, and nearly shell-shocked by its roaring, deafening noise. It was sheer trauma. And this disturbed me."[41]

The sense of immediacy that grips the reader throughout the short novel owes much to the handling of narrative perspective. Through the adroit language of its third-person narrator, Crane's realist novel eschewed the "orderly and humane" verbiage and nostalgia found in most autobiographical and regimental histories of the war. And by studying Henry's thoughts and actions as they happened, rather than with the clarity of hindsight, the narrator allowed *The Red Badge of Courage* to represent the battlefield as a world of desperation, speed, and confusion:

> The throng had surged in all ways, until he lost directions and locations, save that he knew where lay the enemy.
> The flames bit him, and the hot smoke broiled his skin. His rifle barrel grew so hot that ordinarily he could not have borne it upon his palms; but he kept on stuffing cartridges into it, and pounding them with his clanking, bending ram-rod. If he aimed at some changing form through the smoke, he pulled his trigger with a fierce grunt, as if he were dealing a blow of the fist with all his strength. (174)[42]

Time and again, readers asked Crane how he had come to write such visceral battle scenes and to grasp the psychology of the common soldier. Crane's responses seemed calculated to undermine the idea that one must have participated in the war in order to write about it. The author assured others that he had never "smelled even the powder of a sham battle" and went so far as to suggest that sporting events alone might teach one what war is like. "I have never been in a battle," he reported, "but I believe that I got my sense of the rage of conflict on the football field." Although one might want to characterize such comments as youthful bravado, they in fact square with the larger message of *The Red Badge of Courage*. Both Crane's fiction and comments argued implicitly that the war and its experiences were not the exclusive realm of veterans and that it was not for them alone to describe, glorify, and censor its details. Former soldiers were correct to say that noncombatants and later generations would never know the war as they had, but for Crane—and the thousands who celebrated his work—that fact should not inhibit others from touching the war personally. Ultimately, it seems no exaggeration to say that veterans had themselves instilled in millions of Americans some desire to encounter the battlefield firsthand. Soldiers had so successfully portrayed their wartime actions as central to American identity that they had all but guaranteed that others would seek to share their experiences. *The Red Badge of Courage* marked one such attempt and inaugurated an inclusive literature of the war that at once honored and displaced the older, more exclusive narratives of veterans.[43]

The reactions of Civil War veterans in 1895 and 1896 demonstrated the unique and iconoclastic character of Crane's bestseller. One veteran assumed that the author of *The Red Badge of Courage* must have fought in the war, and famously declared: "I was with Crane at Antietam." While usually taken as evidence of the book's verisimilitude, the statement also reflected the common expectation that only a veteran would have written an account of battle "from the inside." Upon discovering that Crane had not served in the war, or been born until years after Appomattox, many veterans balked. Bvt. Brig. Gen. Alexander C. McClurg published a scathing attack on the novel in the pages of *Dial* magazine in April 1896. He complained that the British *Saturday Review* greeted *The Red Badge of Courage* "with the highest encomiums, and declared it the actual experiences of a veteran of our War, when it was really the vain imaginings of a young man born long since that war, a piece of intended realism based entirely on unreality."

Outraged at what he read to be a satire of the American soldier, the general tellingly repeated that Crane was not a Civil War veteran. "It can be said most confidently that no soldier who fought in our recent War ever saw any approach to the battle scenes in this book," he argued. "We are told that it is the work of a young man of twenty-three or twenty-four years of age, and so of course must be a mere work of diseased imagination." Yet by the end of his editorial, McClurg concluded that Crane's unhealthy mind could not alone have envisioned the combat described in the book. That was the territory of veterans, and he guessed that Union soldiers must have been behind the novel after all—not stalwart heroes, but deserters: "It must have been some of these fellows who got the ear of Mr. Crane and told him how they felt and acted in battle."[44]

Not all veterans grew irate upon learning that Crane had not participated in the war.[45] But it incensed many that the novelist had been praised for his insight into the practice of warfare. In the wake of the Spanish-American War, a sarcastic letter signed "VETERAN" appeared in the *New York Times*: "I read with interest your editorial based on the opinion of that remarkable military authority, Stephen Crane, author of the 'Red Badge of Courage.'" The author lampooned the newspaper for relying on the opinions of Crane, recently a war correspondent, in order to assess the handling of American troops in the Philippines. Having ridiculed the ideas of "this wonderful military authority," the letter writer took more seriously the opinions of the American commander in Manila, a Civil War veteran.[46] Still other veterans picked up on a different objection of McClurg's, that *The Red Badge of Courage* portrayed a Union soldier who lacked "patriotic feeling [and] soldierly ambition." "No thrill of patriotic devotion to cause or country ever moves his breast," the general complained bitterly, "and not even an emotion of manly courage." Many of his old comrades-in-arms likewise cringed at the book's "avoidance of ideology." The veteran R. L. Ashhurst protested at a Gettysburg reunion in 1896 that the novel ignored "the great and noble object of the sacrifice, [and] the noble glow of true patriotic fervor which, as we know, was the governing note and tone of the chords of the soldier's heart, and without which the story of the American soldier's deeds and endurings is but as a tale told by an idiot—full of sound and fury, signifying nothing." The historian Earl J. Hess has noted that veterans like Ashhurst were "irritated, even frightened" by Crane's novel, because "it was not sufficient to describe the true nature of battle. One also had to endow it with meaning and significance." Indeed, many veterans remembered patriotism and ideology as the crucial factors motivating them to endure the horrors of combat.[47]

It may seem odd that veterans would fault Crane for not infusing his war novel with the political and ideological issues that inspired many soldiers to fight. After all, in the immediate literary sources for Crane's fiction, veterans themselves had little to say about slavery and state's rights. The *Century* editors wrote that the "exclusion of political questions" was important to their series in order to successfully "soften controversy." The magazine remained faithful to that vision. As Blight pointed out, readers "looked in vain for any discussion of the causes or consequences of the war. Even the central question of secession remained absent. . . . [The] issues of slavery and race were resoundingly silent." Not all veterans agreed with the policies of *Century* magazine, however. For example, slavery arose as an issue in the regimental history of the 124th New York, the unit in which served men from Port Jervis, New York, the town where Crane lived from age six to eleven. At the beginning of the Chancellorsville section of the unit history, the author (and former commander of the regiment) referenced not only slavery but also the extremely volatile issue of miscegenation. He observed that while marching over Virginia soil, the 124th walked among supporters of slavery, "that vile institution." Not only were Southerners "dealers in human chattels," this veteran recorded, but they were "traffickers not unfrequently in their own flesh and blood."[48]

It is therefore unlikely that Crane avoided political controversies in *The Red Badge of Courage* simply because his sources did so. His choice appears to have been a conscious and informed one. As so many critics have pointed out, Crane signaled on the first page of the novel that the issue of emancipation would not follow his soldiers into combat. When the men in camp rush off to hear Jim Conklin's rumor of the coming battle, they leave behind the only black man featured in the book: "A negro teamster who had been dancing upon a cracker-box with the hilarious encouragement of two-score soldiers, was deserted. He sat mournfully down" (3). Crane's decision to strip away the most important political and cultural issue of the war helps explain why McClurg and other veterans found themselves so unnerved by the novel. Had the novelist indeed explored the larger issues of the conflict and commented on its cultural legacy, his work could not have maintained its intense and often unflattering scrutiny of the Civil War soldier. Even the unsavory details described in the novel—such as Henry's flight from battle—might have been interpreted as part of a tragic but ultimately redemptive national story. Had that been the case, the novel's bulldog grip on the battlefield would have weakened. But *The Red Badge of Courage* held tenaciously to the experience of combat, dragging its details into harsh light and leaving no corner of the field shrouded in glory. We see this approach to the war in chapter 5, Henry's first skirmish, where the narrator explained that among the soldiers there was "a singular absence of heroic poses" (114). Even the officers "neglected to stand in picturesque attitudes" (114).

But surely the most revealing passage in this chapter appeared just a few paragraphs earlier. There the war's causes are eclipsed by Henry's initiation into that world of violence exclusive to veterans: "There was a consciousness always of the presence of his comrades about him. He felt the subtle battle brotherhood more potent even than the cause for which they were fighting. It was a mysterious fraternity born of the smoke and danger of death" (113). Few moments in the novel more deliberately seek to crack open the world of the soldier and to grant access to the uninitiated—Henry and the civilian reader alike. And few passages more overtly distance the causes of the war from the experience of the battlefield. Indeed, because Crane deliberately excluded the names of specific historical units, leaders, regions, and causes, the novel maintained its focus on the act of fighting itself, free of contextual distractions. In his hands, even the very division between North and South collapsed within the crucible of battle. As the Cheery Soldier tells Henry, the smoke and screams of combat swelled "until I couldn't tell t' save m' soul which side I was on. Sometimes I thought I was sure 'nough from Ohier, an' other times I could 'a swore I was from th' bitter end of Florida. It was th' most mixed up dern thing I ever see" (152).

I do not agree, however, with those critics who have argued that Crane "did not think of the War as a national tragedy" and that he was never "tempted to examine its causes and consequences." As exhibited in his work *The Monster* (1899), the young author in fact maintained an acute awareness of the tensions surrounding race in American culture. And despite his overt abandonment in *The Red Badge of Courage* of the issues of slavery and emancipation, Crane inserted numerous reminders of racial violence, and white and black skin, throughout the combat sequences. For example, the "black faces" of soldiers smudged by smoke and powder appear during and after the fighting; Henry's lieutenant swings "strings of expletives . . . lashlike over the backs of his men"; and the black-faced members of the 304th fail in their bid to support the troops of General "Whiterside" (201, 196). Such subtle references to the racial dimension of the war lend support to Andrew Delbanco's argument that Crane did indeed know and care about the complexities of American history and culture. In fact, Crane might have been sympathetic to veterans' claims that no portrait of combat was sufficient unless it took into account a soldier's motivations for fighting. In chapter 19 of *The Red Badge of Courage*, Henry participates in an infantry assault noteworthy as much for its hopelessness as for its exuberance. "And because it was of this order was the reason," the narrator speculates, "why the youth wondered, afterward, what reasons he could have had for being there" (183).[49]

But no matter what reservations he may have felt, Crane left out the war's social and political causes for a purpose. When those soldiers who objected to the novel in 1895 condemned its failure to address ideology, they did so from a privileged position. Veterans already understood the complex and necessary connection between the Civil War battlefield and the war's larger meanings. For the vast majority of the reading public, however, that connection was not obvious, and perhaps unknowable. Crane himself was dissatisfied with the little he knew. Delbanco has observed astutely, "Crane somehow knew better than any American writer since Melville and Twain how experience can sear the soul's convictions. . . . Faith has to be an affair of the self, not of the fathers—and the corollary of Crane's contempt for those who claimed it lightly was his desire to experience it deeply for himself." Indeed, Crane seems to have understood intuitively that Americans could not fully appreciate the larger issues of the conflict—patriotism, ideology, faith—without first confronting the realities of the battlefield. Parades, Memorial Day celebrations, and even veterans' memoirs were not enough. Mesmerized for years by the exclusive world of Civil War combatants, the public hungered for an inclusive literature of the war that would allow it to experience vicariously what it meant to participate in the monstrous event at the center of America's national identity. The achievement of *The Red Badge of Courage* is not limited, therefore, to its having wrested the battlefield from the hands of veterans. More important, the novel also allowed Americans to explore personally the war's physical and psychological trauma—trauma that could not be divorced from the abstractions of ideology and patriotism.[50]

By experiencing the fear and fury of battle as portrayed in *The Red Badge of Courage* (and the many fictions it inspired), millions of Americans have asked the same questions posed by historian James McPherson: "Why did Civil War soldiers do it? ... What prompted them to give up several of the best years of their lives—indeed, to give up life itself in this war that killed almost as many American soldiers as all the rest of the wars this country has fought combined? What enabled them to overcome that most basic of human instincts—self-preservation?" The answers to these questions often involve issues of honor and camaraderie but just as often involve the very issues veterans emphasized in their wartime letters and diaries: patriotic devotion and cultural ideology. As borne out by the enduring popularity of Crane's novel among those who read and teach about the Civil War, an inclusive literature naturally leads the reader to a deeper investment in the war and to a more complex appreciation of the struggle. By witnessing the trauma endured by soldiers on the front lines, students of Civil War literature can better understand the cost and value of those ideals over which the nation went to war: freedom, democracy, sovereignty, union, and human rights.[51]

It would seem, therefore, that although *The Red Badge of Courage* denied the authority of veterans over the battlefield, it nonetheless initiated a literature that embraced those soldiers and their experiences. By the early twentieth century, Crane's novel had shaped expectations for writing about the war. Perhaps few readers thought of Crane upon first receiving Ellen Glasgow's 1902 novel *The Battle-Ground*. Yet the title spoke to the centrality of the soldier to any understanding of the Civil War, and Crane's influence could be found throughout the work's approach to fighting. As Sarah E. Gardner has explained, Glasgow sought to create "an unsentimental portrayal" of the war and "a deeply unsentimental portrait of battle." Because it forced readers to confront the horrors of the battlefield, "*The Battle-Ground* reads more like *The Red Badge of Courage* than like a standard Thomas Nelson Page novel." Indeed, Glasgow's reviewers praised her for eschewing romance in her battle scenes, and some saw her achievement as similar to that of Crane, another writer who never experienced a Civil War battle. "[There] is no cheap melodrama, no grandiloquence, no sentimentality," *Outlook* declared. "The events and people speak for themselves, and the author's knowledge of war conditions, although of necessity second hand, is intimate and thorough." Even well into the twentieth century, reviewers were quick to point out how and when new Civil War fictions echoed the work of Crane. For example, when James Boyd published his Civil War novel *Marching On* in 1927, one approving reviewer saw Crane's imprint on the book's content and style both. "Like Stephen Crane, [Boyd] is concerned with pictures, etched impressions, as they fall upon the now more now less sensitized surface of one man's brain." Later the reviewer quoted three paragraphs from a battle scene in *Marching On*, evidence that "Mr. Boyd's description of battle is reminiscent of the pictures in 'The Red Badge of Courage.'" Thanks in part to its debt to Crane, *Marching On* was recommended to readers as "a very fine and memorable American novel."[52]

Novelists like Boyd have not usually denied Crane's influence over their fiction. To the contrary, many popular and talented novelists of the war have cited Crane as a major inspiration for their work, precisely because of his participatory approach to the past. In a note to readers that begins his Pulitzer Prize–winning novel of Gettysburg, *The Killer Angels* (1974), Michael Shaara reflected on Crane: "Stephen Crane once said that he wrote *The Red Badge of Courage* because reading the cold history was not enough; he wanted to know what it was like to *be* there, what the weather was like, what men's faces looked like. In order to live it he had to write it. This book is written for much the same reason." As comments such as these confirm, Crane's approach to the war, what Shelby Foote terms "total immersion," resonated with authors of Civil War fiction of the twentieth and twenty-first centuries. Its influence can be found in the work of an array of writers, from Caroline Gordon and Mary Johnston to Kirk Mitchell and Charles Frazier. Undoubtedly, scores of Civil War fictions have appeared since 1895 that thrive on romance or take a removed, bird's-eye view of the war. But many of the most celebrated works have encouraged readers to themselves participate in the frantic and often inglorious world of 1861–65. Some authors follow Crane in focusing on the battlefield, while others offer an overt discussion of the ideological and political issues at stake in the fighting. No matter how closely they resemble *The Red Badge of Courage*, however, virtually all of the most memorable fictions share with it the conviction that the real war and its traumas can best be understood through lived experience.[53]

Of course, one might argue that veterans themselves deserve the credit for the thousands of fictions inspired by their actions. Not only did those men live the events reenacted by later generations, but they also created an impressive body of memoirs, remembrances, and histories that viewed the past through the lens of personal experience. Yet the literature of the war could not have matured had not a writer such as Crane arrived—one willing to unapologetically claim as his birthright the experiences of Civil War soldiers and to share that inheritance with the nation. Expressing sentiments common to millions of Americans, Crane once stated that he wanted to understand the war "as far as the books will teach it and then after that, the other things." Whether his early death came too soon for him to uncover such "other things" is impossible to say. Crane may never have reached a firm conclusion about what the Civil War meant or why it was fought. But he gave his countrymen a work of literature through which they might themselves touch a crisis still remembered as both the nation's badge of courage and fall from grace.[54]

Chapter Two

FOR WAS I NOT A SOLDIER, ENLISTED FOR THE WAR?
Female Veterans in *Gone with the Wind* and *None Shall Look Back*

By any measure, the South's literary response to the Civil War has been enormous. During the war and for decades to follow, Southerners penned thousands of manuscripts and printed millions of words in order to assess, justify, and remember secession and its aftermath. No less than Southern men, Southern white women played a tremendous role in nurturing a robust literature of the war. From 1861 through World War I and into the interwar period, Southern women authored an array of biographies, histories, diaries, memoirs, and fictions. They helped to cultivate and refine a Southern interpretation of the Civil War and ultimately shaped how generations of Americans would remember the conflict.

This chapter examines the work of Margaret Mitchell and Caroline Gordon, two Southern writers whose novels of the Civil War appeared just eight months apart. It has become commonplace to suggest that the wildly popular *Gone with the Wind* (1936) represents the culmination of the plantation legend, a claim first advanced by the critic Malcolm Cowley. But when we consider the bestseller alongside Gordon's *None Shall Look Back* (1937), we can see that Mitchell's book contributes something more to the course of southern and American literature. More deliberately and with greater success than their precursors, Mitchell and Gordon addressed and sought to resolve a long-standing tension found within Southern women's narratives of the war. That tension involves the relationship of women to the struggle, and especially to the uniformed men who fought the war and who later recounted their experiences in word and print. Were women merely the caretakers of a history that championed men and male accomplishments, or were they true participants of the war in their own right?[1]

To read *Gone with the Wind* and *None Shall Look Back* in concert, I believe, is to uncover a fascinating moment in the evolution of Civil War memory. Amending narratives that defined the war in terms of the battlefield alone, both Mitchell and Gordon declared that women, too, were veterans of the nation's greatest conflict. In doing so, they helped alter the role of the soldier's memoir in American letters, showing how that conservative genre might be used as a tool for social change.

I.

Thirty-four pages from the end of *Gone with the Wind*, Scarlett O'Hara makes what is, for her, an uncharacteristic wish—that she could "while away the afternoon" with the other women of Atlanta. Lonely, alienated from Southern society, and mourning the death of her daughter, it seems strangely appropriate that Scarlett should desire the company and comfort of those she has so often ridiculed in the past:

> Maybelle or Fanny or Mrs. Elsing or Mrs. Whiting or even that redoubtable old warrior, Mrs. Merriwether. Or Mrs. Bonnell or—or any of her old friends and neighbors. For they knew. They had known war and terror and fire, had seen dear ones dead before their time; they had hungered and been ragged, had lived with the wolf at the door. . . . It would be grim fun to laugh with Mrs. Elsing, recalling the old lady's face as she flogged her horse through Five Points the day Atlanta fell. . . . It would be pleasant to match stories with Mrs. Merriwether, now secure on the proceeds of her bakery, pleasant to say: "Do you remember how bad things were right after the surrender? Do you remember when we didn't know where our next pair of shoes was coming from? And look at us now!"

Mitchell suggested in her letters that the "whole book was written through Scarlett's eyes," but what came next seemed to transcend Scarlett's own circumstances and point of view. Indeed, it illustrated what much of the first 1,003 pages had been leading toward: "Yes, it would be pleasant. Now she understood why when two ex-Confederates met, they talked of the war with so much relish, with pride, with nostalgia. Those had been days that tried their hearts but they had come through them. They were veterans. She was a veteran too." Contrary to the narratives by men on which Mitchell was raised, *Gone with the Wind* here makes the strong assertion that women, too, "were veterans." And, as if to validate that identity, the novel assigns Scarlett one of the most excruciating wounds a true veteran might bear: her not having "cronies with whom she could refight old battles."[2]

If we take Mitchell at her word that she wrote the final chapter of *Gone with the Wind* first, then we can recognize women's veteran status as one of the objectives of the novel: a conclusion the book affirmed throughout the preceding chapters. The previous passage marks a key moment in the narrative, a hinge on which female identity in *Gone with the Wind* turns. As the narrative swings from this moment into the final chapters of the book, Mitchell revisited an earlier scene involving Scarlett and Melanie Wilkes, but now recast the women as veteran combatants. The scene is the famous one in which Scarlett shoots and kills a Yankee deserter within the walls of Tara, while Melanie, still weak from childbirth, drags her brother's saber to the top of the stairs, ready to defend her sister-in-law if necessary. There on pages 439–42, Scarlett sees for the first time that "beneath the gentle voice and the dovelike eyes of Melanie there was a thin flashing blade of unbreakable steel . . . [there were] banners and bugles of courage in Melanie's quiet blood" (441).[3]

Remembering the incident 571 pages later, however, Scarlett realizes that she had not then fully understood Melanie's soldierly nature: "[Her] mind went back through the years to the still hot noon at Tara when gray smoke curled above a blue-clad body and Melanie stood at the top of the stairs with Charles' saber in her hand. Scarlett remembered that she had thought at the time: 'How silly! Melly couldn't even heft that sword!'" (1012). But now, the narrator explains, Scarlett "knew that had the necessity arisen, Melanie would have charged down those stairs and killed the Yankee—or been killed herself" (1012). She realizes that Melanie "had always been there beside her with a sword in her hand . . . loving her, fighting for her with blind passionate loyalty, fighting Yankees, fire, hunger, poverty, public opinion and even her beloved blood kin" (1012). Scarlett's personal epiphany concerns her failure, up to this point, to recognize her love and need for Melanie. The epiphany for the reader relates instead to the military bearing of Melanie Wilkes.

Comparing the two versions of Melanie atop the stairs, we see the lady transformed. Whereas she first appears as a frail woman whose gentle exterior belies a heart of "banners and bugles," by the end of the novel she stands as a bona fide veteran inside and out. Mitchell's vocabulary deliberately closed the gap between Melanie and the legendary soldiers of the Confederacy, men whose honor and loyalty sustained them in the face of starvation and the ever-advancing Yankee columns. But why wait until the end of the novel to offer Melanie as an overtly martial figure? And why only gradually impress upon the reader the idea that the experiences of women on the home front constituted forms of fighting and sacrifice worthy of a soldier? Answers to these questions surely depend on the fact that Mitchell's first readers would have responded very differently to the idea of "female veterans" than her readers today. American audiences of the 1930s lived in a society that understood veterans as the aging, bearded men of parades and battlefield reunions or, alternatively, as the younger survivors of World War I. And during the some seventy years since the war itself, few Southern narratives had described women as true veterans.

Recent scholarship has done much to chronicle the evolution of white women's literature of the war and can help situate the literary efforts of Mitchell at the end of a long-developing tradition. In particular, historians Alice Fahs and Sarah E. Gardner have shed light on the motivations and rhetorical strategies of those women writing about the conflict between 1861 and World War II. In *The Imagined Civil War* (2001), a thorough study of the popular war literature published during the four years of fighting, Fahs made clear that early Civil War literature did not always feature men as the war's central figures. "In both the North and the South throughout the conflict," she observed, "a feminized war literature put white women center stage in the war, demanding recognition not only of women's contributions to the war effort but also, as the war wore on, of their intense suffering. In doing so, such literature did not displace the importance of men in the conflict, but it did sometimes ask for equal recognition of women's sacrifices." Unmistakably, the feminized fictions appearing in popular weeklies and magazines argued "that white women's war-related experiences constituted authentic participation in the war—and in the 'imagined community' of the nation—on par with that of male soldiers."[4]

As evidence of female participation in the conflict, writers often portrayed women as having endured prolonged emotional and physical stress. Early fictions and sketches explored the emotional strain felt by women as their fathers, husbands, brothers, sons, and beaux departed for camp and battle. These texts also depicted the aftermath of combat, with women confronting damaged bodies while nursing in hospitals and homes. Still other narratives focused on the intense pain and sorrow felt by women whose loved ones had been killed or wounded. It was not uncommon, in fact, for writers to conceive of a soldier's wound as belonging no more to the man than to his fiancée, wife, sister, or mother at home. For example, Fahs uncovered the Northern story "Wounded" from the July 1862 *Harper's Weekly*, an anonymous piece that criticized those whose limited vision blinded them to the injuries suffered by women on the home front. Describing bullets as "swift-winged messengers that kill or wound at a thousand miles instead of a thousand paces," the story's female protagonist noted bitterly that "we have no report" of the women wounded by these missiles: "They are the casualties not spoken of by our commanding generals."[5]

It should be noted that wartime literature in the South did not always follow the patterns developed in the Northern states. The extreme economic and physical constraints placed on Confederate women meant that popular women's literature did not flourish there to the same degree it did in the North. And on balance, Southerners were less willing to portray women as soldiers who, like men, actively fought and sustained wounds on behalf of the nation. "In contrast to Northern authors," Fahs observed, Southern writers "rarely claimed that women's wounds were the equivalent of men's." What cultural restrictions prevented such claims? Drew Gilpin Faust has examined how gender assumptions of the antebellum and early war periods differed between North and South. She explained that for more than a generation before the war, women's rights advocates in the North had destabilized traditional gender roles. By contrast, "emergent nineteenth-century feminism had by 1861 exerted almost no impact" in the more conservative South, "and understandings of womanhood had remained rigidly biological and therefore seemingly natural and immutable." Even if the events of the war led Southern women to question such cultural norms, most "ultimately avoided and even resisted changes that threatened to erode a self-definition and a separateness founded in the cherished prerogatives of race and class [and] gender."[6]

In her fine book *Blood and Irony: Southern White Women's Narratives of the Civil War, 1861–1937* (2004), Gardner likewise showed that Confederate women novelists did not strive to erase the line between the female patriot and the male soldier. However, Southern white women refused to play down the importance of civilian contributions. Gardner explained that some women took up writing as a way to spread Confederate propaganda and to encourage public support for the war effort, essentially becoming "pen and ink warriors." They documented the work of women in maintaining order and in healing sick and wounded soldiers sent back from the front. As with Northern literary journals, Southern publications gave rise to a literature that conceived of women as deeply committed and loyal to the war effort. In the pages of these journals, Confederate women shared with Southern men the burden of a defensive struggle waged against invading Northern armies.[7]

But by the 1890s, a booming veterans' literature had trampled feminized representations of the Civil War as nurtured by women authors and activists. Published in the same newspapers, magazines, and literary journals that once printed stories like "Wounded," the memoirs of soldiers cast the war as the quintessential masculine experience and proving ground. With rare exception, these were socially conservative texts that understood America's sectional conflict as the province of uniformed men shouldering arms and marching from one battlefield to the next. Recounting in print their bloody heroics and sacrifices, former soldiers often ignored women's wartime contributions entirely. When they did recall the service of women as nurses and seamstresses, their portraits usually took patronizing or idealized forms.

The alignment of military service with citizenship, patriotism, and progress made it increasingly difficult for women to lay claim to historical relevance. And cultural and literary developments worsened matters. Echoing Amy Kaplan's observations about the literary market of the 1890s, Fahs explained that the "new masculinization of the memory of the war dovetailed with the rise of literary realism in this period, both reflecting and reinforcing a newly masculinized literary marketplace. The cult of experience and of a 'strenuous life' permeated the pages of a wide range of realist literature at the turn of the century, from the stories of Stephen Crane to the writings of Jack London and Frank Norris."[8]

When we examine the published remembrances of soldiers, we discover a male-oriented world quite removed from that of *Gone with the Wind*. *Century* magazine's four-volume *Battles and Leaders of the Civil War* (1887–88) surely confirmed Fahs's assertion that women, in the decades following Appomattox, no longer shared equal footing with men within the national imagination of the war. In *Battles and Leaders*, writers often referred to the female gender only when describing the unsoldierly qualities of men. For example, one veteran recorded that Confederate brigadier general Humphrey Marshall "was not adapted to mountain warfare, owing to his great size; nor was he qualified to command volunteers, being the most democratic of men. Moreover, his heart was as tender as a woman's. For these reasons he could not enforce the rigorous discipline of an army." While feminized war literature of 1861–65 "valued the expression of feeling," postwar soldiers' memoirs conceived of female tenderness as a characteristic that, like corpulence, figured only as a liability during wartime.[9]

Occasionally articles by women would appear in *Battles and Leaders*, such as Constance Cary Harrison's "Virginia Scenes in '61" in Volume 1. Yet these accounts almost uniformly reinforced the differences between men and women, soldiers and noncombatants. Unlike many women writers of 1861–65, Harrison offered a limited vision of the wartime heroics of women. Nostalgically recalling the visits of young women to camp, Harrison concluded that "feminine heroism could no farther go" than for a lady to brave the coarse food of a "bright-eyed amateur cook of a well-beloved mess."[10]

By excluding women from popular memory of the war, veterans' narratives reflected how Americans chose to commemorate the conflict beyond the printed page. Beginning in the final decades of the nineteenth century, postwar veterans' organizations such as the UCV and the GAR regularly staged major celebratory events. At battlefield reunions, monument unveilings, and Decoration Day and Memorial Day parades, Americans turned out by the thousands to honor those who had fought. Often wearing faded uniforms and carrying tattered flags, the aging veterans—along with their younger likenesses cast in bronze—stood as emblems of American vitality and provided a visible connection to the country's past. Women played a crucial role in planning and overseeing these events and formed their own commemorative organizations.

Founded in the 1890s, the United Daughters of the Confederacy (UDC) became one of the most important. Undoubtedly the organization gave a voice to Southern women at the turn of the century and ensured their participation in the development of a regional and national history. But as UDC spokespersons made clear, the Daughters served predominantly as the caretakers of "the memory of the Confederate soldier" and of the "deeds of bravery, of heroism, of patriotism and of self-sacrifice that distinguished 'the men who wore the grey.'" UDC women aimed to nourish the South but not to become the equals of men. "We cannot make healthy manhood by standing in its place and assuming its obligations," one member declared. Rather, women would collect "relics and records" and do their part to preserve the heritage of the Confederacy. As David W. Blight has pointed out, UDC women functioned above all "as cultural guardians of their tribe, defenders of a sacred past." And within that past, nothing stood more worthy of celebration and excessive veneration than the Confederate veteran. Mitchell may well have had the Daughters in mind when she drew her portrait of postwar Southern women in *Gone with the Wind*. After the war, Scarlett noted with exasperation that Melanie and her female peers were "utterly silly about the Confederacy, its veterans, and anything pertaining to them" (756).[11]

Indeed, time and again Mitchell showed herself to be aware of the role women played in nurturing the memory of a masculine war. In writing of the "Old Guard" women of the Reconstruction South, her words applied just as well to UDC members of the early twentieth century: "[The] women were the implacable and inflexible power behind the social throne. The Lost Cause was stronger, dearer now in their hearts than it had ever been at the height of its glory. It was a fetish now. Everything about it was sacred, the graves of the men who had died for it, the battle fields, the torn flags, the crossed sabres in their halls, the fading letters from the front, the veterans" (876). During Mitchell's lifetime, thousands of sketches, stories, and articles were produced by UDC members for chapter logs and sometimes wider circulation. These narratives vindicated the South for its part in the war, recalled women's sacrifices at home, and above all extolled the military feats of the "Brave Defenders" in gray. Southern women also found other ways to contribute to the postwar, Lost Cause celebration. They raised money for monuments, placed portraits of war heroes in schools, housed and displayed soldiers' memorabilia, and tended to the upkeep of veterans' homes and cemeteries. And just as important, they published accounts that reinforced traditional gender roles: male actors versus female spectators.[12]

II.

It was therefore not unusual for Mitchell, like hundreds of Southern white women before her, to write about the trials faced at home by beleaguered Confederate civilians. But it was bold for her to name Scarlett and Melanie "veterans" and to bestow on them an identity so inextricably bound to the world of men. Although she published her book in the 1930s, more than ten years after the Nineteenth Amendment granted women the right to vote, she was clearly aware of the deeply rooted gender biases and distinctions that still existed in southern and American culture. Those biases help explain why Mitchell chose not to define women as veterans until after more than one thousand pages of text. To persuade readers of Scarlett's veteranhood, she would first need a great deal of space in which to create her larger portrait of the Civil War and Reconstruction.

In Mitchell's hands, the war and its aftermath existed as transformative experiences shared equally by both genders. And she worked actively to win for her female characters the same respect and honor awarded soldiers. As her narrative chronicles the increasingly dangerous path traveled by the people of Atlanta and Jonesboro, her narrator proportionately accumulates an arsenal of military adjectives with which to describe Melanie, Scarlett, and the other women who "had known war and terror and fire" (1003). The changing language of the novel, therefore, marked one of Mitchell's strategies for showing the role women played in "the most important national crisis of our history."[13]

Yet her language notwithstanding, many would argue that Mitchell did not strive consciously to change how Americans viewed the war and the roles of women within it. Especially since 1976, when Richard Harwell published the Mitchell correspondence relevant to *Gone with the Wind* and its 1939 film adaptation, critics have had reason to distance her from socially and politically minded artists. In her letters, Mitchell emphasized that *Gone with the Wind* had "no aims," no politics, and no moral to offer the public. She asked her friend Herschel Brickell: "Why will people persist in reading strange meanings into the simplest of stories? Is it not enough that a writer can entertain for a few hours with a narrative without being suspected of 'significances' or symbolisms or allegories or 'social trends'?" In light of such sentiments, and particularly Mitchell's declaration that she "didn't want to prove anything" through her novel, it becomes difficult to talk about the social objectives of *Gone with the Wind*. Even scholars who believe that Mitchell concealed her sociopolitical ideas beneath the "extraordinary plasticity" of her letters and public personality have admitted that "it is difficult to weight accurately her judgments and values." What, then, should readers make of Mitchell's treatment of women in war? Anne Goodwyn Jones, one of the most insightful and prolific critics of Mitchell, has explained that "although *Gone with the Wind* deals directly and overtly with several themes, the one issue that unites them and of which its author appears to be ironically least conscious is precisely the concern for gender." She argued that Mitchell herself saw survival as the central theme of *Gone with the Wind*, an accurate if "imprecise" assessment of what amounts ultimately to "a study of gender roles, of what it means to be a man or woman." That study, for Jones, "articulates, challenges, and finally confirms the traditional view of the nature and roles of the sexes." The novel's two most rebellious figures, in the end, return to the "old days"—Scarlett to Tara and Rhett Butler to his roots in Charleston.[14]

While I agree that gender serves as the linchpin connecting the novel's diverse themes and interests, I want to pause over Jones's conclusion that *Gone with the Wind* at last affirms traditional gender distinctions. To be sure, Scarlett and Rhett end the novel by returning from whence they came, but the experiences they undergo during the course of the story have transformed them as individuals. The novel suggests that both have achieved their veteranhood, even if Scarlett has not fought and starved with Rhett in the ranks of Johnston's army. Whether or not Mitchell set out to prove that women, too, counted as Civil War veterans, almost inevitably her fascination with gender roles led her to confront the matter. And as Mitchell's revisitation of the shooting at Tara made clear, Melanie stands as the character on whom the novel ultimately rests its conclusions about gender and war.

Why Melanie? Perhaps the issue falls on her because, unlike Mitchell's other three leading figures (Scarlett, Rhett, and Ashley Wilkes), Melanie never exists as an aberration in Southern society. As Jones pointed out, "Melanie Wilkes fits the dominant southern myth of white womanhood perfectly," even transcending "the conventional mores that define the lady." Yet rather than employ Melanie as a static icon, the novel uses her to thwart gender expectations in a way the iconoclastic Scarlett never could. From one perspective, the frail and often infirm young woman demonstrates that the masculine characteristics traditionally prized during wartime—strength, size, and endurance—matter less than those qualities available to both genders: courage and will. From another perspective, Melanie, as the quintessential lady, subverts fears that we might "unsex" or otherwise degrade women by recognizing them as participants in war. Atlanta society might believe Scarlett "unwomanly" for having entered the male sphere of business and trade, but Melanie can be both a woman and a warrior in the eyes of her culture and in the language of the novel (640). She can unapologetically stand in public "like a thin, shining blade" and look about her with "a fighting light in her eyes" (946). In this sense, then, Jones's assertion that *Gone with the Wind* affirms traditional gender norms may be correct. Part of what the novel demonstrates is that women such as Melanie, Mrs.

Elsing, and Mrs. Merriwether need not reach beyond the feminine world in order to win credibility as veterans.[15]

For readers in the 1930s, the resulting picture of the Civil War must have been both familiar and different. Mitchell's women (perhaps with the exception of Scarlett) fulfill expectations of how nineteenth-century ladies should behave and act. Yet the extreme circumstances Mitchell depicted, and the fierce courage and sense of duty exhibited by her female characters, could shock readers familiar only with narratives of men at war. Americans from outside the South—distanced from firsthand stories of starvation and enemy occupations—were at times amazed by the service and sacrifices of Mitchell's women. In 1937, the novelist assured Ruth Tallman of Lakefield, Minnesota, that her book did not exaggerate women's circumstances during the war, writing that "starvation, deprivation and suffering were the common lot of Southern women in those parts of the South where the Federal army had been." She sent Tallman "a list of books of reminiscences of Southern women which throw some light on this situation."[16]

Yet while popularizing the wartime experiences and contributions of women, Mitchell never openly decried the war as it appeared in male memoirs. And because the novel never clothed its women in uniform, nor depicted them in camp far from home, *Gone with the Wind* never flew in the face of the prevailing, masculine view of the Civil War. Some scholars would disagree. Elizabeth Young, for instance, has argued that in Mitchell's version of the war, "the best soldier for the South is a woman." It seems to me, however, that both book and author were less interested in overturning men's claims on the war than in making room for women. And to accomplish this feat, Mitchell and *Gone with the Wind* were forced to confront the published words of the war's male participants.[17]

Throughout her correspondence and public statements, Mitchell presented herself—like so many Americans of her generation—as fascinated with the men who fought the Civil War. In her letters and conversations, she recalled having been inundated in her youth with stories of military campaigns and Confederate heroes. Mitchell wrote that her mother used to sing her to sleep "with those doleful tunes of the Sixties" such as "Jacket of Grey" and "Bonnie Blue Flag," and she remembered hearing countless tales of cavalry charges and minié balls. She read the four volumes of *Battles and Leaders* and internalized the topography and personalities relevant to the war's numerous battlefields. Like many southern families with roots back to the Civil War, hers made the struggle an active part of everyday conversation. "Even now," she noted in 1936, "when John and I go to call on Father we usually find him and my brother and friends hotly arguing about what would have happened if Longstreet had only brought up his corps sooner and why Jeff Davis didn't put Hood in command at Dalton instead of waiting till the last ditches of Atlanta." The novelist had also known veterans personally, surrounded in her youth by the South's aging defenders. Mitchell recalled that as a child she "sat on the bony knees of veterans," enraptured by their stories.[18]

As an Atlanta-born woman whose family lived in the South for generations, Mitchell's interests rested primarily with those who wore butternut, but she read voraciously the memoirs of men from both sections. With the publication of *Gone with the Wind*, Mitchell went out of her way to convince others that she had mastered those memoirs' twin legacies, battles and leaders, and portrayed herself as a serious student of the Civil War. To Robert C. Taylor, she wrote, "My bibliography runs into the thousands of volumes," and she likewise informed George Ward of her having read "hundreds of memoirs, letters and diaries to get the background of 'Gone with the Wind.'" Her correspondents learned that she had been reared on military campaigns as described by old participants: "I cut my teeth on that Johnston-Sherman running fight, dug bullets out of the old breastworks when I was little, [and] climbed the steep side of Kennesaw mountain where the guns were pulled up by hand." Mitchell was aware that the voices of former Confederates and Yankees seemed to emphasize the eastern theater. Showing at once her grasp of the war's historiography and her eye for drama, she complained that "for all that's known about it, the war might have been waged exclusively in Virginia.... I got pretty sick and tired reading about the fighting in Virginia when for sheer drama the campaign from the Tennessee line to Atlanta has no equal." Mitchell knew, too, that still-living veterans would read her book with an eye for historical detail, and she sought their approval. "If I didn't get it right," she explained, "seven hundred old vets would rise up out of Soldiers' Homes and denounce me."[19]

The best-selling author also communicated with some of the leading Civil War scholars of her day, such as Henry Steele Commager, Douglas Southall Freeman, and Clifford Dowdey, male historians of male heroes. She seemed eager to demonstrate her familiarity with the war's soldiers and their remembrances. For example, she told Dowdey that "a better book there never was" than Confederate private Sam Watkins's memoir *Co. Aytch* (1882) and observed to Freeman: "Perhaps Mr. Watkins did not contribute enormously to our store of information about military strategy and campaigns, but he certainly left a record to show what the dryly humorous foot soldier thought about it all."[20]

Yet for all that Mitchell's letters proved her knowledge of veterans' narratives, as well as of the battlefields and maneuvers described therein, *Gone with the Wind* itself spends little time revering the war's military giants. Undoubtedly, the novel mentions Wade Hampton (Charles Hamilton's commander and the namesake of Scarlett's son), as well as Robert E. Lee, Joe Johnston, John Bell Hood, and the much-maligned William Tecumseh Sherman. But the story never draws these men into the immediate sphere of Mitchell's characters. Georgia's great military captain—John B. Gordon—visits the home of Ashley and Melanie during the postwar years, but the narrator never dwells on the hero's wartime feats. Nor did Mitchell, unlike so many authors of Civil War novels (both men and women), follow her male characters into the field. Rather, *Gone with the Wind* maintains its focus on women at home: Scarlett, Melanie, Pittypat, Mrs. Merriwether, and the other matrons and belles of Georgia. Men do have a place on Mitchell's home front, including members of the Home Guard, Dr. Meade and his hospitalized patients, the blockade-runner Rhett, and those soldiers on furlough. Yet what stands out so clearly is the absence of the masculine glory emphasized in so many of Mitchell's "thousands" of sources. While we hear secondhand of Ashley's distant heroics and of the Tartleton brothers' promotions, these moments seem overshadowed by what we know of their personalities and behavior at home. Although Ashley, the Fontaine brothers, and the novel's other soldiers all possess admirable qualities, they each also possess their own set of shortcomings. From start to finish, then, Mitchell presented the South's warriors—even those who sacrifice their lives for the Southern cause—as nothing more or less than human.

The refusal to exalt the military service of a soldier over his personal qualities reflected Mitchell's seeming distrust of narratives in which veterans exist as demigods inherently superior to noncombatants. In fact, in both her correspondence and fiction, Mitchell at times assumed an irreverent approach to the South's soldiers and their memory. For example, she took a flippant view of the sacred Civil War monuments erected North and South to commemorate America's veterans. "Speaking of Civil War monuments," Mitchell wrote to Sidney Howard, "you should see our Southern ones. I believe they were put out by the same company that put out the Northern ones. They are twice as ugly and three times as duck-legged!" And in an era when a soldier's wound could still symbolize the height of valor and sacrifice, Mitchell dared to present such injuries as inglorious and ironic. Writing to Dowdey and his wife, she described her grandfather's wounding at Sharpsburg by talking of his "gallantry, courage and the plain stupidity that made him stick his head up above the corn and lay his rifle across a splitrail fence. A minié ball went through the back of his head, fracturing it in two places." She later told the same story to Freeman, this time blaming Grandpa Mitchell's wounding on his "ill advised . . . curiosity." In the pages of *Gone with the Wind*, readers find a similar reluctance to glorify veterans' wounds. Rather than offer familiar, even romantic images of "empty sleeves," the novel describes Tommy Wellburn, a man wounded by a bursting shell such that his legs "spraddled in a very vulgar way" (602–3). And Scarlett mocks Rhett for lying about a chest wound in order to please young Wade: "Tell him about your dysentery," she jeered (900). Earlier in the novel, when reflecting on the body parts that Archie sacrificed for the South (a leg and an eye), Scarlett feels little sympathy or admiration: "It seemed to her that all Southern men, high or low, were sentimental fools and cared less for their hides than for words which had no meaning" (755). Both Mitchell and her novel, therefore, appeared distrustful of narratives that viewed battlefield injuries—available almost exclusively to men—as the truest sign of one's devotion to cause and country.[21]

Mitchell could also demonstrate reservations about the attention to detail found in soldiers' memoirs. She explained to Paul Jordan-Smith: "[While] in the process of checking the part of my book about the campaign from the Tennessee line to Atlanta, I was very bothered about the weather during the fighting. . . . So I reread [the memoirs of] Generals Hood, Johnston and Sherman and several other reference books but got little satisfaction." She solved her dilemma by consulting a Civil War novel authored by a woman, Mary Johnston's *Cease Firing* (1912), what Mitchell called "the best documented novel ever written."[22]

Mitchell's reference to Johnston draws attention to the link between *Gone with the Wind* and other twentieth-century Civil War novels by southern women. Among the authors of such works, few match Ellen Glasgow and Mary Johnston in terms of reputation and talent. Independent thinkers with distinct artistic agendas, these women preceded Mitchell in writing about the war in ways that differed, in part, from the prevailing Lost Cause portrait of the conflict. Gardner has traced the efforts of each to break away from the stock characters, tropes, and sentimentality of the traditional southern war narrative, and demonstrated that each writer achieved a measure of success. Glasgow's struggle against sentimental representations of the Confederate South in *The Battle-Ground* (1902) complemented the efforts of Johnston, in her novels *The Long Roll* (1911) and *Cease Firing*, to portray the gritty, unromantic, and wearying realities of combat. Neither writer shied away from the social, political, and military subjects long dominated by men, and reviewers praised Johnston in particular for her ability—despite her gender—to portray combat with unsettling detail. (At least one commentator, writing at the end of the twentieth century, argued that Johnston's work constituted "some of the finest writing about combat by any American before or since" and compared it favorably to the prose of Norman Mailer and Tim O'Brien.) However, neither woman seemed able to fully escape the romance of the Lost Cause, nor did Glasgow or Johnston erase the line between male combatants and female civilians. Indeed, both authors told the stories of traditional Confederate soldiers who enjoyed the support of white women loyal to the cause for which Southern men fought and died. In these works, both genders provided crucial and necessary contributions to the war effort, but those contributions differed widely in nature and deed.[23]

Yet there do exist moments when the works of Glasgow and Johnston appeared to ponder, if not exactly question, the prevailing male/female, soldier/civilian divisions of Civil War memory. For example, a fascinating sequence near the end of *Cease Firing* at once reinforced and challenged gender norms. In a single chapter, Johnston's heroine and hero are each wounded mortally by Yankee troops: Désirée is cornered and assaulted by drunken soldiers, while Edward Cary suffers his wound in a cavalry skirmish nearby. Importantly, Johnston took great care to show that these events happen independently; the reader understands that Désirée is a victim of rape and murder, whereas Cary is a fatality of combat. Yet the immediate juxtaposition of the two scenes, and the fact that both man and woman fight back against their uniformed killers, closes the gap between the parallel episodes. In fact, the narrative allows Cary to find and stagger to the prone Désirée before death overtakes them, granting the pair an opportunity for parting words and a final embrace: "She died. With a last effort he moved so that his arms were around her body and his head upon her breast, and then, as the sun came up, his spirit followed hers." Unable or unwilling to represent man and woman falling in combat side by side, Johnston's narrative did not declare Désirée a "veteran," nor are her wounds earned on the battlefield. But in her final embrace with Cary, we see how Johnston's novel, one that clearly impressed Mitchell for its historical accuracy, might have likewise influenced her vision of men and women living and dying together.[24]

Writing about the war even closer in time to Mitchell, Evelyn Scott published *The Wave* in 1929. Like Mitchell, Scott wrote her Civil War novel after World War I and after the Nineteenth Amendment was ratified. These monumental events influenced her work both directly and indirectly. Following Glasgow and Johnston, she aimed to produce a story that differed from the traditional southern war narrative of the nineteenth century. But unlike those women, she constructed a Modernist novel that lacked such literary mainstays as a protagonist, plot, and lucid chronology. Her approach to the war was not, therefore, a concentrated attempt to escape or upset the Lost Cause. Rather, she portrayed the Civil War as a gigantic cultural event that had, no less than World War I, produced an endless series of narratives along the strata of class, race, and gender. Within the text, "Northerners, southerners, Christians, Jews, generals, foot soldiers, combatants, noncombatants, the elderly, children, slaves, and free blacks all tell the story of the war." As Gardner observed, *The Wave* shows that all participants in the war suffered in turn, no matter what role they happened to play. The novel therefore democratized the sacrifices and contributions made during the national epic, including those of women. Yet because of its democratic approach, few readers would view the book as one that specifically reevaluates the role of women within the national memory of the war.[25]

It strikes me as regrettable that academics have so rarely examined Mitchell's novel alongside those of Glasgow, Johnston, and Scott. Undeniably, *Gone with the Wind* differs from *The Battle-Ground*, *The Long Roll*, and *The Wave* on numerous levels, but important commonalities exist as well. The authors were all interested in enlarging the standard story of the Civil War, both in the South and beyond. All sought to democratize the war such that its memory would become more, rather than less, inclusive. And all belonged to a tradition of women writers who took pains to represent themselves as responsible chroniclers of history.

Yet if Mitchell could at times value fiction by women over the narratives of former soldiers, her bestseller depended above all on the war memoirs of Southern women. When thousands of veterans began to record and publish their reminiscences during the 1880s, many women likewise took up the pen. Some women collected and prepared for publication the old letters of husbands, brothers, and fathers who served during the war. Others "caught the bug to be in print" and "just like male veterans, they sought simple recognition for their experiences." Mary Elizabeth Massey has observed that "no other event has challenged so many women to write and publish personal accounts as did the Civil War." Other scholars have suggested that by prompting women to keep diaries and journals, the war had produced a "new exploration and understanding of the self." After the war, these diarists believed it imperative that they continue writing as a means of understanding what the war meant for the future of southern womanhood.[26]

While women's reminiscences did not demand the same attention from the reading public as did those of their male counterparts, some of these texts won a wide and enduring readership, North and South. The diary of Mary Boykin Chesnut may stand as the most famous. Her wartime "diary," really written about twenty years after the Civil War, appeared in 1905; Chesnut's intelligence and narrative powers shine through her account, a work that many today consider to be a masterpiece of American literature. It is true that some Northern "women of action," those serving as nurses and teachers especially, also published successful accounts of their adventures and experiences. Louisa May Alcott's well-known *Hospital Sketches*, first published in 1863, numbers among these works. But Southern women produced the majority of women's war memoirs, and those of the Civil War South remain the most often read today.[27]

Women's memoirs alternately reinforced and questioned normative behavior for Southern ladies. Although Southern women were often reluctant to discuss "masculine" political and military phenomena in print, most believed it their right to recall for a national audience the trials, suffering, and adventures they had experienced during and after the war. If some narratives remembered women acting outside of the domestic sphere, such as those nursing wounded soldiers on the battlefield, those portrayals did not distort the past. To be sure, "the line distinguishing the home front from the battlefield was especially hazy in the Civil War South, where troops fought in backyards and the Federal army burned private homes that stood in its way." Not all women shrank from an overt analysis of masculine subject matter, however; nor did all feel obligated to write about only those events they had themselves experienced. As Gardner has suggested, many Southern women "did not entrust even their own menfolk with the telling of war," and their memoirs could combine diplomacy, ingenuity, and esprit in order to justify a discussion of topics usually left to male authors.[28]

Mitchell's familiarity with the memoirs of Southern women did not escape the attention of those readers conversant with remembrances of the war and Reconstruction. In late June 1936, she applauded one correspondent for his insight into her background research for *Gone with the Wind*. "Mr. Edwards, you are one of the very few people who are clever enough to see my source material, one of the few who realize how the back ground of my book developed. Yes, I have read most of the old memoirs I could lay my hands on. Not recently, perhaps but from my childhood. I was raised on 'Surry of Eagle's Nest' and the 'War Time Diary of a Georgia Girl' and other books of that type." Soon thereafter, she wrote to Stephen Vincent Benét with similar praise: "Do you know, you're the only reviewer who has picked up the diaries and memoirs out of my background?" No longer suggesting that she had last read these books in childhood, she explained: "Of course, I used everybody from Myrta Lockett Avary to Eliza Andrews and Mary Gay and Mrs. Clement Clay and Miss Fearn and Eliza Ripley and the Lord knows how many unpublished letters and diaries." Mitchell's enthusiasm for women's memories of the war continued long after she had finished researching her novel. She wrote a laudatory letter to George Ward, whose mother, Margaret Ketcham Ward, testified in 1883 before a Senate committee about her wartime experiences. Mitchell called the recorded testimony "the most perfect and valuable and complete picture of a long gone day that I have ever come across in ten years of research into the period of the Sixties. If I had had that book, I am sure I would not have had to read hundreds of memoirs, letters and diaries to get the background of 'Gone with the Wind.'" Apparently the wit, common sense, and charm of Ward's mother contrasted sharply, in Mitchell's mind, with the "many military histories and military memoirs of incredible dullness" she had encountered in her reading.[29]

Not surprisingly, women of Georgia authored two of the memoirs most influential to Mitchell's novel about the men and women of Atlanta and Jonesboro: Eliza Andrews's *The War-Time Journal of a Georgia Girl, 1864–1865* (1908) and Mary Ann Harris Gay's *Life in Dixie during the War* (1892). In many sections of Andrews's narrative, one can find passages that seem similar, if only superficially, to ones in *Gone with the Wind*. Andrews asserted in the introduction to her journal that the Civil War "was a pure case of economic determinism," arguing: "Our great moral conflict reduced itself, in the last analysis, to a question of dollars and cents, though the real issue was so obscured by other considerations that we of the South honestly believe to this day that we were fighting for States Rights, while the North is equally honest in the conviction that it was engaged in a magnanimous struggle to free the slave." These lines seem echoed by Rhett's controversial opinions about the true motivation of the war. "All wars are sacred," Rhett declared, "[to] those who have to fight them.... But, no matter what rallying cries the orators give to the idiots who fight, no matter what noble purposes they assign to wars, there is never but one reason for war. And that is money.... But so few people ever realize it.... Sometimes the rallying cry is 'Save the Tomb of Christ from the Heathen!' ... and sometimes 'Cotton, Slavery, and States' Rights!'" (231). Yet Andrews's journal left its strongest and most recognizable mark upon Mitchell's descriptions of the weeks and months immediately following Appomattox, when the bedraggled survivors of Lee's and Johnston's armies tramp through the Georgia countryside. The accounts of passing veterans sleeping on the parlor floor of Tara complemented Andrews's memories of homeward-bound soldiers camping in her family grove. Andrews reported, "It gives me more pleasure to feed the poor Rebs than to eat myself," a sentiment that Mitchell's Melanie shares as she happily divides her every meal with soldiers trudging homeward (508).[30]

The presence of Andrews's narrative also loomed over Mitchell's account of the racial politics of Reconstruction-era Atlanta. In a passage that paralleled the *Gone with the Wind* scenario in which Rhett kills a freedman who insults a white woman, Andrews observed: "A man of honor can hardly be expected not to shoot on the spot any wretch who should dare to insult a lady under his charge, and the consequences of reckless firing have been made so apparent that prudent people think it best to avoid difficulties by keeping out of their way as much as we can." (Rhett, not sharing Andrews's prudence, faces hanging for refusing to bend his antebellum ways to fit the shape of the postwar South.) Andrews also acknowledged the plight of former slaves who, as the "victims" of Yankee-imposed freedom, remained idle and supported themselves through theft alone. "Sometime my sympathies are very much excited by the poor creatures, notwithstanding their outrageous conduct," she wrote. "I don't know what is to become of them in winter, when fruits and vegetables are gone." These observations, along with Andrews's recollection that "it is unsafe for ladies to walk on the street," seem reflected and exaggerated in *Gone with the Wind*. Scarlett's unsympathetic views of freedmen line up with those of Andrews: "The more I see of emancipation the more criminal I think it is. It's just ruined the darkies. Thousands of them aren't working at all and the ones we have at the mill are so lazy and shiftless they aren't worth having" (639). Moreover, Mitchell's readers encounter the shantytown outside Atlanta, whose denizens, mostly black, menace and attack white women travelers.[31]

Yet in terms of evocative storytelling and imagery, Gay's *Life in Dixie* surpassed Andrews in influencing Mitchell's novel. Critics have noted that "Miss Gay's true life experiences can easily be seen in the depictions of the characters Scarlett O'Hara and Melanie Wilkes." But perhaps no episode of *Gone with the Wind* fixed as closely on Gay's memoir as did Scarlett's nighttime escape from the burning city of Atlanta. In the novel, Rhett comes to the rescue of Scarlett, Wade, Prissy, Melanie, and Melanie's newborn son by stealing a sick horse and small wagon. Piloting the three women and two boys out of the dangerous city, he then leaves Scarlett to guide the horse and wagon to Tara, a journey made treacherous by Melanie's infirmity and the threat of capture by Yankees or Confederates in need of horses. The suspense and imagery of the voyage have combined to make it one of the most famous episodes of *Gone with the Wind*, just as a parallel moment served as the climax of Gay's memoir. In her narrative, Gay captures a feeble horse and musters it into the service of a young mother and her children who need passage to the home of relations near Madison, Georgia. Risking capture or worse, Gay leads the family to safety before turning home to Decatur, appalled by the horrific destruction she finds upon the war-torn countryside.[32]

Mitchell drew numerous small details from Gay's account: as in *Life in Dixie*, the horse bears sores along its back, strains against the weight of its load, and collapses in the road. Yet while she recognized the dramatic usefulness of borrowing such pitiable details, the surreal stillness of the landscape stands out as Mitchell's most effective appropriation of Gay's account. Gay wrote that the "woods had been robbed of their beauty and the fields of their products": "Not an animate thing had we seen since we left Decatur, not even a bird, and the silence was unbroken save by the sound of the horse's feet as he trod upon the rocks, and the soft, sweet humming of the young mother to her dear little ones." In *Gone with the Wind*, there appears a nearly identical description: "They had not seen a living human being or animal since the night before.... No far-off cattle lowed, no birds sang, no wind waved the trees. Only the tired plop-plop of the horse's feet and the weak wailing of Melanie's baby broke the stillness" (398). Gay also recounted that "no vestige of anything remained to mark the sites of the pretty homes which had dotted this fair country before the destroyer came, except, perhaps, a standing chimney now and then." *Gone with the Wind* offers similarly melancholic imagery: "Every empty, shell-pitted house they had passed that day, every gaunt chimney standing sentinel over smoke-blackened ruins, had frightened her more" (398).[33]

The lines Mitchell decided not to borrow from Gay's account of her voyage, but which she seems to have internalized, concerned how the memoirist interpreted her experiences. At the end of the chapter detailing the wagon trip, Gay stated proudly: "As for myself, I labored under the hallucination that I was a Confederate soldier, and deemed no task too great for me to essay, if it but served either directly or indirectly those who were fighting my battles." Although Gay understood that she served her nation not as a uniformed soldier but in other capacities (she acted elsewhere as an unofficial spy and smuggler of supplies), she nonetheless believed her service worthy of recognition. Earlier in her memoir, Gay pressed even more firmly for her veteranhood, blurring the line between imagining herself a soldier and actually becoming one. Speaking of herself and other women at home, she asked, "Were we not soldiers, too, working for the same noble cause, and aiding and abetting those who fought its battles?" And when describing yet another memorable episode of her war years, when she and other ladies found themselves trapped in a house between the lines of opposing armies, Gay recalled that the crash of battle summoned her: "The roaring of cannon and the sound of musketry blended in harmony so full and so grand, and the scene was so absorbing, that I thought not of personal danger, and more than once found myself outside of the portals ready to rush into the conflict—for was I not a soldier, enlisted for the war?" She reported that her sentiments were shared by other women as well: "Nor was I the only restless, intrepid person in the house on that occasion. An old lady, in whose veins flowed the blood of the Washingtons, was there, and it was with the greatest difficulty that I restrained her from going out into the arena of warfare."[34]

It appears that in creating her portrait of men and women soldiering together, albeit in different capacities, Mitchell was guided by the South's female memoirists. She undoubtedly brought to *Gone with the Wind* her own ideas about the role of women in society, yet it seems that if the episodes described by Andrews and Gay left such an impression on her mind, so too did these women's attitudes toward their own experiences. Indeed, Mitchell often found ways to highlight women's participation in the South's daily struggles. After the war, Tommy Wellburn states without irony: "If we'd had our mother-in-laws in the ranks, we'd have beat the Yankees in a week.... The only reason we lasted as long as we did was because of the ladies behind us who wouldn't give up" (604). Early reviewers such as Cowley identified such passages as contributing to the novel's enormous popularity: "It is written from the woman's point of view," he wrote, "and most book buyers are women." Mitchell did not, however, write about women to boost the sales of her novel. Rather, if her novel slants toward the female perspective, it does so in the spirit of Andrews's narrative, determined to complete a picture only half-told by male memoirs: half-told not only because soldiers' memoirs focused on men rather than women, but because they focused on the war rather than Reconstruction.[35]

I find it telling that *Gone with the Wind* devotes slightly more time to Reconstruction than to the war itself—the Civil War ends on page 487, leaving another 550 pages to a world occupied by men and women struggling together to find food, protect their families, and fend off their peacetime invaders. Andrews's *War-Time Journal* similarly devoted about equal space to Reconstruction, reflecting the fact that—for Southerners and especially women—the hardships of the war did not end in 1865. Mitchell made this point explicit when Hugh Elsing observes after the war that, unlike male veterans, women will "never give up." "There's not a lady here tonight who has surrendered, no matter what her men folks did at Appomattox" (604). The novel demonstrates that women's wartime contributions and sacrifices continued unabated during Reconstruction: they still nursed sick and dying men, operated their own businesses to raise money for food and medicine, worked the fields in the absence of servants, and remained every bit the "steel-spined women on whom the South had built its house in war" (1026). Because they, unlike Southern men, neither formally surrendered nor relinquished their wartime duties, Andrews's and Mitchell's women could rightly hold up their postwar experiences as further proof of their veteranhood.

Of course some might argue that the men of *Gone with the Wind* take control of Atlanta during Reconstruction, the "nascent Ku Klux Klan" supplanting Southern women as the primary defenders of the city. After all, to Scarlett it feels as though active and violent resistance to freedmen and the Federal occupation "was an exclusively masculine affair" (790). But again, masculine affairs constitute only half the story in *Gone with the Wind*. When the Southern vigilantes skirmish with troops outside the city, they ultimately return home for rescue. There Melanie, Scarlett, India, and other women—including Belle Watling and her prostitutes—do their part to ensure that the Klansmen escape capture and avoid imprisonment and hanging. In some ways, the rescue of the Klan members represents Mitchell's portrait of the South not during Reconstruction alone, but during the Civil War as well. Mustering into action men and women both gentle and common (the planter Ashley and the convict Archie, the proper Melanie and the scandalous Belle), *Gone with the Wind* shows the whole of white Southern Atlanta working in concert to resist its enemies.[36]

Jones has noted that "Margaret Mitchell saw herself primarily not as a woman but as a southerner; and her novel not about womanhood but about the South." Yet neither Mitchell's self-image nor the view she took of her novel detracts from its progressive portrait of women in the Civil War era. For all that has been said about Mitchell's lack of self-awareness and her inability "to imagine female autonomy," *Gone with the Wind* makes a powerful statement about gender in the Civil War and, by extension, in American society as a whole. Scholars have tended to focus on Mitchell's failure to construct "a genuine female freedom" for herself and her characters, but such a freedom would seem to be out of step with her approach to gender. Mitchell's vision for women was not one of autonomy but of collaboration with men, and of veteranhood won not by one's gender but by one's courage and actions. Toward the end of the novel, Melanie searches for words to express the solidarity shared by herself, Ashley, and Scarlett through the years. After a moment's pause, she relies on language that, having so aptly described all three during the war, now seems natural to apply to their daily lives: "Why, we three have been—have been like soldiers fighting the world together" (946).[37]

III.

Writing to a friend in September 1936, Caroline Gordon expressed frustration over the smashing success of *Gone with the Wind*: "Margaret Mitchell has got all the trade, damn her. They say it took her ten years to write that novel. Why couldn't it have taken her twelve?" Gordon feared that *Gone with the Wind*, the July Book-of-the-Month Club selection and already a phenomenal bestseller, would so saturate the market that no one would read her own forthcoming novel of the Civil War. That book, *None Shall Look Back*, ultimately sold better than she expected (it was named a bestseller in some markets), yet Gordon's adversarial tone anticipated how critics would come to regard the two novels. Passing over significant similarities, many reviewers preferred to highlight the books' differences, often measure for measure. For example, in the March 20, 1937, issue of *The Nation,* Caroline Smith observed that *None Shall Look Back* was "shorter [than *Gone with the Wind*], less verbose, less reckless, less spectacular; the narrative flows less freely; the details are not so lavish; and there is more intelligence." The *New York Times* pitted the two novels against each other, noting that Gordon's "style is distinguished—vastly superior, for example, to Margaret Mitchell's." But the paper fretted that Gordon's novel lacked a strong plot and fully developed characters: "A good story, after all, is essential—as the author of 'Gone with the Wind' has most abundantly proved." As these reviews foreshadowed, before long the literary community had placed *None Shall Look Back* in a category with other Civil War novels of the 1930s that appealed to elite, educated readers rather than to Mitchell's popular audiences. Marked by the complex prose styles, irony, and symbolism of literary Modernism, these works included William Faulkner's *Absalom, Absalom!* (1936), Andrew Lytle's *The Long Night* (1936), and Allen Tate's *The Fathers* (1938).[38]

As an author who rejected sentimental fiction and claimed "to write the same kind of novel a man would write," Gordon was no doubt pleased to see her work defined against *Gone with the Wind*, what many still consider to be the quintessential female romance of the Civil War South and Reconstruction. This opposition, however, has been unfortunate. By aligning *None Shall Look Back* with highbrow fictions written by men, and thereby drawing Gordon and Mitchell apart, we have obscured their shared interest in revising the dominant, male-centric understanding of the war.[39]

If Gordon expressed disappointment over the enormous sales of *Gone with the Wind*, she was nonetheless awed by its success. "*Anthony Adverse* as a seller looks sick beside it," she wrote to Ford Madox Ford. "I don't believe any book ever sold like it before—the formula is sound, a Civil war Becky Sharp, and Lord how they're gobbling it up." Yet aside from admiring the formula and sales of Mitchell's novel, Gordon showed scant enthusiasm for the book. For her, *Gone with the Wind* was little more than "a super salesman's idea, half a dozen of the best plots in the world wrapped up, with the civil war as cellophane." By contrast, she envisioned *None Shall Look Back* as "the most ambitious novel written so far about the Civil War" and thought comparisons made between it and *Gone with the Wind* "irrelevant." Jealousy and a competitive spirit undoubtedly fueled much of Gordon's disdain for

Gone with the Wind, but other reasons lay behind the cool reception as well. Never satisfied with how Scribner's promoted her work, she felt discouraged when the popularity of Scarlett O'Hara persuaded the company to delay the publication of *None Shall Look Back*. Although she needed the extra time to revise, she believed the decision reflected her editors' doubts about her ability to compete with a "leviathan" like Mitchell. Gordon told Ford that the company felt "rather dashed now by 'Gone with the Wind'" and feared that Scribner's salesmen would now put little effort into selling *None Shall Look Back*: "The hell of it is that [rival publisher] Bobbs-Merrill tell me they know they could sell it."[40]

Beyond reasons related to the market, Gordon no doubt faulted *Gone with the Wind* for employing a "soft" sentimental style often associated with women writers and their readers—a style Gordon herself rejected out of hand. Likely viewing Mitchell as a sensationalist writer authoring fiction about women for women, Gordon saw the Atlantan as a different kind of artist from herself. Critics and biographers have generally agreed and have devoted a great deal of attention to Gordon's conservative views of gender roles, especially to how those views played into her writing. "The work I do is not suitable for a woman," she wrote to a friend. "It is unsexing. . . . Dr. Johnson was right: a woman at intellectual labour is always a dog walking on its hind legs." Such statements seem surprising when we consider that Gordon wrote professionally her entire adult life, first as a journalist and then as the author of short stories, novels, and reflections. She explained the apparent paradox by noting that although she was a woman, as a writer she was "also a freak." In the eyes of several commentators, Gordon offset her unconventional career by adopting a public persona that promoted conservative views of gender, race, and class. Whether staged or not, that persona influenced her approach to writing as well. As Katherine Hemple Prown explained, "Gordon found herself in an awkward position—an ambitious woman writer forced to rely on the patronage of a literary establishment that had been constructed on the premise that serious literature was necessarily a male creation."[41]

In order to win the respect of the establishment and prove her mettle as a writer, Gordon sought to remove any trace of her gender from the page. According to many reviewers and colleagues, such as Andrew Lytle, she succeeded: "[With] Caroline one could not tell whether her work was written by a man or a woman. This is evidence of the pure elevation of style." If writing in a hard, masculine style helped Gordon "efface her gender," so too did her decision to write about men and "masculine" subject matter. "She wrote about battles and the Civil War," Nancylee Novell Jonza noted, "because she felt no woman could do so." By taking a dim view of *Gone with the Wind*, Gordon therefore made a statement about her own writing and set herself apart from readers—especially women—who embraced Mitchell for creating in Scarlett a symbol of "female strength, power, and bloody-mindedness that is rare in twentieth-century fiction."[42]

Yet despite the stylistic differences between Mitchell's and Gordon's writing, their lives and fiction held much in common. Like Mitchell, Gordon found herself immersed in Lost Cause culture at a young age. Gordon recalled that the war infiltrated family life and childhood play. "I do not think that my childhood experiences were very different from those of any Southerner who is over thirty years old," she wrote, recollecting that she and her brothers often sang songs about Confederate idols such as Gen. Nathan Bedford Forrest. And like Mitchell, Gordon came face to face with old veterans, some of whom lived (and died) at Merry Mont, Gordon's childhood home. Beyond upbringings similarly steeped in Southern lore, Mitchell and Gordon both offered somewhat contradictory signals regarding their allegiance to traditional gender roles. Both worked as journalists as young women, in a profession then dominated by men; both published under their maiden names; and yet over time both took pains to appear outwardly deferential to their husbands and the prominent male thinkers with whom they were acquainted. Publicly, Gordon showed no interest in women's literature or in advancing the social causes of women (she argued, for example, that women should not have the right to vote). And, as we have seen, Mitchell stated time and again that her novel avoided political and social causes. Ultimately both Gordon and Mitchell seemed reluctant to address the degree to which their fiction commented directly on the contributions of American women to their nation. When read on their own terms, however, both *Gone with the Wind* and *None Shall Look Back* declare that, in affairs both public and private, women deserve the same attention awarded men.[43]

Gordon and Mitchell differed on whether a true Civil War novel must portray combat. For Gordon, it became important to capture the chaos and misery of battle in the pages of her book: "[The] novelist, like the soldier, is committed by his profession to a life-long study of wars and warriors." While that belief undoubtedly reflected Gordon's insistence on writing about the experiences of men, it also commented on the nature of her source material. Unlike Mitchell, Gordon seems to have resisted the influence of Civil War diaries and memoirs by women. Although certain details in *None Shall Look Back* suggest strongly that she read some of the same women's memoirs as Mitchell, in her correspondence Gordon tended to ridicule female remembrances. "One book has the adventures of a Union woman, spy, prostitute, psalm singer and I think nymphomaniac who seems to have had the time of her life during the war," she told her friend Sally Wood. She also mocked an account in which three "old maiden ladies in South Carolina" barely escaped being run down by a coach piloted by a drunken slave.[44]

To truly understand and write about the war, Gordon concluded, one must immerse oneself in the memoirs of veterans and, to a lesser extent, in historical works penned by men. And since the materials she investigated (and the old veterans she interviewed) focused almost entirely on military campaigns and heroes, the battleground became the most important setting of her novel. Gordon exhausted herself by reading, and attempting to master, narratives describing combat. She had earlier written about the war in her novel *Penhally* (1931) and knew that researching battles could have a transformative effect on her sense of time and place. "As for the war," she explained, "in a sense I was there. Really, I've been through it so many times in 'Battles and Leaders' I have to stop and remind myself that I was neither at Shiloh, Antietam, Malvern Hill nor Bull Run—nor sang within the bloody wood." She could almost believe that she would "sprout long chin whiskers or perhaps be put up for office in the Confederate Veterans." The Civil War, and the soldiers she revered, became a regular part of her everyday thoughts and conversation as well. Chastised for complaining about a night's dinner, Gordon's daughter Nancy protested, "Mama, I don't care what those Confederate soldiers ate." Gordon complained to Wood that "it seemed to me so unreasonable [that the girl should object to her meal] when I had just been reading about men picking blackberries as they went into line of battle."[45]

Yet for all of her research into regimental histories and veterans' personal accounts, Gordon seemed to lack confidence in her ability to pen a convincing account of the war. This fact may seem surprising in light of the accolades *None Shall Look Back* won from reviewers impressed by her ability, as a woman, to portray the surreal confusion of combat. Even those who disliked her battle descriptions were less likely to question the authenticity of those passages than to critique their duration or the abundance of technical detail. The *New York Times* reviewer, for example, admitted that Gordon's battle scenes were "admirable, graphic, blood-chilling," but believed they dominated too much of the book. A review in the *Columbus Inquirer-Sun*, in turn, observed that Gordon's "pictures of cavalry and infantry maneuvers are somewhat bewildering to the uninitiated." If Gordon numbered among the "initiated," she nonetheless depended to a great extent on the words of men. Having completed the first section of *None Shall Look Back* (then titled *The Cup of Fury*), she wrote that she was "just lifting sentences" from the memoirs and histories she read, such as the recollections of John Allan Wyeth from his *Life of Lieutenant-General Nathan Bedford Forrest* (1899). Such borrowings have left a bad taste in the mouths of some readers, who fault Gordon for taking lines and even whole paragraphs from her historical sources for use in *None Shall Look Back* and other novels. Scholars such as Veronica Makowsky have generally explained away such instances as alternately Gordon's "mistrust of her imagination" or her voracious "pursuit of the facts." Few critics wish to cast her as a lazy writer or, worse, a plagiarist. Not sharing such sensitivity, the publishers of *Battles and Leaders* complained to Scribner's that *None Shall Look Back* contained "verbatim borrowings" from their series, prompting Gordon's editor Max Perkins to step in to "soothe the publisher's ruffled feelings."[46]

Whether or not Gordon was aware of it, her wholesale borrowing from *Battles and Leaders* was not a unique phenomenon within women's literature of the war. She in fact followed in the footsteps of numerous southern women who relied on the words of men when preparing their own manuscripts for publication. The most prominent of these women were the wives and relatives of former Confederate leaders. More than twenty years after the war, both the sister-in-law and second wife of Thomas J. "Stonewall" Jackson authored accounts of the general's life and service to the Confederacy. Similarly, Varina Davis, the wife of Confederate president Jefferson Davis, published a biography of her husband. In later years, Helen Dortch Longstreet and La Salle Corbell Pickett, the wives of generals James Longstreet and George E. Pickett, also wrote several accounts of their husbands' wartime careers. Gardner has suggested that these ladies, by virtue of their connection to the Confederacy's political and military chiefs, felt licensed to write about warfare—a subject typically considered beyond the scope of acceptable womanly discourse. Yet even still, these women often relied on the published words of men when describing military maneuvers and combat. "At times, the words of men comprised entire chapters" of the books of Mary Anna Jackson and Varina Davis, "with little original writing by way of introduction or transition." Far from weakening the value of accounts by southern women, the "marshaling of lengthy passages from war records and accounts of former Confederates [helped to] bolster their claims of authority."[47]

Granted, these women usually made it clear when they were quoting from the narratives of combatants and historians, something Gordon did not do in her fiction. But like her literary predecessors, the novelist appropriated lines from veterans' remembrances in order to lend credence to her battle descriptions. And interestingly, Gordon's borrowings extended far beyond those passages concerning fighting. Her treatment of the battle of Chickamauga—generally considered the "central episode" of *None Shall Look Back*—took much of its shape directly from the third volume of *Battles and Leaders*. This fact may explain why the historical hero of *None Shall Look Back*, Confederate general Nathan Bedford Forrest, takes a backseat to the presence and perceptions of other Northern and Southern generals during the first forty-nine pages devoted to the battle. Instead of following Forrest, Gordon began narrating events from the point of view of Confederate general Daniel H. Hill, precisely because D. H. Hill authored the first article of the Chickamauga section of *Battles and Leaders*.[48]

A few comparisons between Hill's account and Gordon's novel should suffice to show how she used his words and memories. Hill recalled how he learned of his promotion to lieutenant general and of his impending transfer from Virginia to the western theater:

> I was seated in the yard of a house in the suburbs of Richmond (the house belonging to Mr. Poe, a relative of the poet), when President Davis, dressed in a plain suit of gray and attended by a small escort in brilliant uniform, galloped up and said: "Rosencrans is about to advance upon Bragg; I have found it necessary to detail Hardee to defend Mississippi and Alabama. His corps is without a commander. I wish you to command it." "I cannot do that," I replied, "as General Stewart ranks me." "I can cure that," answered Mr. Davis, "by making you a lieutenant-general. Your papers will be ready to-morrow. When can you start?" "In twenty-four hours," was the reply. Mr. Davis gave his views on the subject . . . and then left in seemingly good spirits.

On the first two pages of part 3, chapter 8, Gordon appropriated these lines almost verbatim, shifting them from the first person to the third:

[Hill] was thinking of the last time he had sat in the yard of a domestic dwelling. It had been a house in the suburbs of Richmond, his host a Mr. Poe, a relative of the poet. They had been sitting there, three or four gentlemen on a hot day, glasses in hand, when President Davis, in a suit of plain gray and attended by a small escort in brilliant uniform galloped up. . . . He called Hill to the fence, began speaking, rapidly:

"Rosencrans is about to advance upon Bragg. I have found it necessary to detail Hardee to defend Mississippi. Bragg's old corps is without a commander. I wish you to command it."

Hill was startled. He thought: *"I cannot leave Virginia."*

Aloud he sparred for a time. "How can I do that? General Alexander Stewart ranks me."

There was a curious smile on the President's face. "I can cure that by making you a lieutenant-general. Your papers will be ready tomorrow. When can you start?"

Gordon then proceeded to draw other passages and dialogue from Hill's published account, including the characterizations and words of Gen. Braxton Bragg and other senior officers near Chattanooga. Hill's comparisons between Bragg's and Lee's army also found their way into *None Shall Look Back*, such as the observation that Bragg "had no well-organized system of independent scouts such as Lee had. For information in regard to the enemy he evidently trusted alone to his efficient cavalry." Aside from the placement of punctuation and the alteration of an occasional word, Gordon here and elsewhere appropriated portions of Hill's account verbatim.[49]

Once alerted to her use of Hill's *Battles and Leaders* article, readers can easily find dozens more examples of where Gordon borrowed observations, descriptions, and dialogue from that seminal collection of veterans' remembrances. For example, her description of Federal gunboats dueling with the artillery of Fort Donelson drew heavily on an account published in the first volume—"The Western Flotilla at Fort Donelson, Island Number Ten, Fort Pillow and Memphis," by Rear Adm. Henry Walke. Walke remembered the combat in this way: "[We] saw that the other gun-boats were rapidly falling back out of line. The *Pittsburgh* in her haste to turn struck the stern of the *Carondelet*, and broke our starboard rudder, so that we were obliged to go ahead to clear the *Pittsburgh* and the point of rocks below." Gordon, in turn, wrote: "The other gunboats were rapidly falling out of line. The *Pittsburgh* in her haste to turn struck the stern of the *Carondelet* and broke its starboard rudder, so that the *Carondelet* was obliged to go ahead to clear the *Pittsburgh* and the points of rock below" (94). She borrowed many more sentences and images from Walke, and—again at Chickamauga—lifted lines and dialogue from J. S. Fullerton's article, "Reënforcing Thomas."[50]

What becomes increasingly clear as one compares the *Battles and Leaders* articles to *None Shall Look Back* is that the words of veterans influenced Gordon's portrait of the war in a wide number of ways: from her cast of characters, and the order of their appearance, to even the small details that one would expect the novelist to provide herself. This discovery seems particularly surprising in light of Gordon's correspondence: "I treated Fort Donelson in Plutarchian style, reserving my impressionism for Chickamauga." Indeed, some readers might wonder if Gordon did not in truth reserve *D. H. Hill's* impressionism for the latter battle. Why else depend on the former general for the wording to describe Jefferson Davis's suit and the dress of his entourage? Some might conclude that Gordon simply hurried the project in order to meet Scribner's deadlines. She had complained, after all, that if she "had just a little more time" she might have written a better book. But the author had already admitted to "lifting" words and details from her source material during the early stages of the writing process. It seems unlikely that she would have distanced herself from *Battles and Leaders* had she enjoyed a few weeks more in which to produce the novel.[51]

Ultimately, I believe it wrongheaded to explain Gordon's use of veterans' narratives in terms of plagiarism or a lack of imagination. But nor do I think we should chalk up the borrowings to her (genuine) reverence for the men who fought and wrote about the Civil War. Rather, *None Shall Look Back* reproduces closely the feel and verbiage of veterans' accounts in order to amend the masculine story of the war. Because Gordon's scenes otherwise sound so much like the traditional, conservative narratives of former soldiers, her progressive portrait of women often feels validated by those veterans themselves. By couching the actions of women within a battlefield narrative already imbued with the authentic words and impressions of soldiers, the novel finds an ingenious way for making a statement on behalf of female veteranhood.

At first glance, *None Shall Look Back* appears very much in tune with those memoirs of male veterans that draw a firm line between the home and the field. Once the narrative moves into the war years, for instance, the chapters more or less alternate between men at the front and women at home. The author represented the male–female scenes respectively via the experiences of Rives Allard, a Confederate scout, and his wife, Lucy, who has left Kentucky to live with her mother-in-law in Georgia. Yet rather than maintain this narrative convention still common to Civil War novels (see, for example, Charles Frazier's 1997 *Cold Mountain*), Gordon upset it by bringing women directly onto the battlefield and into direct contact with the army. During the course of part 3, chapter 16, a section devoted to the aftermath of Chickamauga, an exhausted Rives suddenly encounters his wife moving among the bloody heaps of dead and wounded: "Rives looked up, saw the wagon first and then the woman moving toward it. Tall and in black. She came with an odd, hobbling motion but that was because of the canteens, slung one on each side and one across her back. . . . She saw him and stopped short, the still moving canteens bobbing back and forth on each side of her. . . . She cried 'Rives,' and was in his arms" (267). The sudden appearance of Lucy on the field shocks not only the husband but also the reader: after forty-two pages that describe the battle wholly in terms of men, living and dead, the arrival of a woman seems disorienting and alarming. Once the initial surprise passes, we learn that Lucy—whom we last saw at home, collecting cane in a quiet swamp—arrived on the field the night before in the company of her mother-in-law and servants. They had spent the morning bringing morphine and water to the wounded and had carried injured men, by wagon, to a makeshift hospital.[52]

Gordon seems especially interested in forcing the horrific realities of the battlefield on Lucy and Mrs. Allard, so as to bring them face to face with the world of Rives and his comrades. Lucy labors under the weight of soldiers' gear; she hears the moans, shrieks, and prayers of the dying; she smells the gas rushing from the intestines of a dead horse. And of course the physical consequences of battle assault her vision: upturned earth slick with blood and vomit; flies infesting the wounds of the dead; bodies nearly obliterated by musketry and exploding shells. In fact, once Rives enters the house where his mother oversees the care of wounded men, we learn that the revulsions of the hospital *overtake* those of the field: "The man threshing about on the bed, moaning, had an enormous arm, swollen darkly red and blistered, where it was not hidden by scraps of filthy bandage. The odor from it was living evil. It crouched about the bed on angry feet, made forays into the room. Rives thought: Nothing like this on the battlefield. He stepped back" (271).

Although Rives seems willing to step back and let his wife and mother do their work, not all men are as accepting of the women's contributions. Before long, an army surgeon appears at the house to assert masculine command, telling Mrs. Allard that the unofficial hospital "is most irregular" and announcing in "a loud, irate voice" that she has "no authority" (271). But *his* authority fades once he discovers the vast number of wounded and dying men inside the house, and he seems somewhat embarrassed to learn that the women "were the first people on the field" to offer medical attention to the troops (271–72). Seemingly unable to provide better care for the men than Mrs. Allard, the doctor soon vanishes from the narrative, leaving the women to experience this part of the field on their own. The appearance of the surgeon may in part reflect Gordon's concern that readers, particularly men, might have misgivings about her writing women into a narrative that had, to this point, followed quite closely the words and arrangement of the *Battles and Leaders* articles related to Chickamauga. Yet knowing from her research that women did serve as nurses, in connection with the army or with women's associations, Gordon overcame any self-doubts and represented Lucy and Mrs. Allard as rightful participants in the story of the battle. We see this confidence in a later chapter, when Rives muses over the makeshift hospital: "He wondered if his mother and Lucy were still at the Parkins' house.... The field hospitals must be in operation now. There would be no more work for ladies' associations. He grinned, thinking of his mother. You could not set her down as belonging to one of those associations. She was a host in herself.... A 'captain' the negroes called it" (283). Here, via the consciousness of a bona fide soldier, Gordon removed Mrs. Allard from women's associations (both literal and figurative), and considered her, if with a tinge of irony, in terms of military rank.

In many ways the centerpiece of *None Shall Look Back*, the portrait of Lucy and Mrs. Allard at Chickamauga pleased Gordon more than any other episode of the novel. She later transformed it into a short story titled "The Women on the Battlefield," one she hoped to publish in the *Southern Review*.[53] While working to revise the book, Gordon also mentioned the chapter to Ford. She expressed confidence about her picture of women at war, though the creative process had strained her severely. Gordon complained: "So much of my energy had to go into mastering [military] manoeuvres—and the writing on the whole is poor.... I had to use every device I ever heard of or could invent—the material I had was so complicated and resistant to handling." By writing of camp and war she felt at once exhilarated and exhausted, the same sensations felt by her female characters as they struggled on the "masculine" battlefield. The cumulative effect of the experience, however, seemed to justify the effort. Having described so many campaigns and battles, and imagined so many wounds and deaths, she felt and acted like a veteran herself, able to list the engagements in which she participated. "I am pretty well soaked in gore by this time," she acknowledged, "having treated of the siege of Fort Donelson, the battle of Chickamauga, the battle of Okolona, the battle of Brice's Cross Roads as well as a few cavalry skirmishes."[54]

Gordon found other ways, too, to undermine Americans' prevailing view of the Civil War as an affair between men. In her chapters describing wartime at the Allards' Kentucky and Georgia plantations, Gordon's women assume tasks hitherto unimaginable for proper ladies. Like Mitchell's women, the female Allards take to performing physical labor: working in the fields and foraging in the woods and swamps. And when the family perceives that some of its own slaves have grown dangerous, Lucy's Aunt Cally announces that she "would keep a good fire going and would sit up all night. 'Stand guard,' she put it, striking a military attitude" (140). Indeed, soon all of Gordon's women come to think of themselves as soldiers responsible to their nation and comrades: "Terrible things were happing every day now—men that they knew were being killed in battle or suffering tortures in prison. The chief thing was to keep your head, not to forget the duty that you owed to others" (134). And as with Mitchell's novel, *None Shall Look Back* demonstrates that the Confederate home front could be synonymous with the fighting front. The novel not only depicts Yankee soldiers looting and burning the homes of Southerners, including the plantation house of Lucy's grandfather, but also portrays fighting near homes occupied by women and children. Throughout one such episode, Mrs. Allard, Lucy, and her sister-in-law Mitty sit in stolid silence as bullets whine about the house and smoke drifts over the roof. When a slave girl weeps in fear, Mrs. Allard clips her on the head. "Aren't you ashamed of yourself," she asks, "crying like that, when men are over there wounded and dying?" (214). Clearly, the expectations for womanly behavior have changed with the arrival of war.

Anticipating their later role on the field at Chickamauga, the Allard women soon leave the embattled house to care for the wounded. Like a soldier helping an injured comrade from the field, Lucy thrusts her shoulder under the arm of one wounded man and helps him up a slope to the house. Only after the man dies, spread out on an upstairs bed, does Lucy permit herself to rest. Both she and the dead soldier have performed their duties well, and Lucy can weep on the porch, tears of sorrow and exhaustion rather than of "womanly" fear (219).

More than *Gone with the Wind*, Gordon's novel reflects explicitly its indebtedness to the words and memories of those men and women who lived through the war. In a late scene in *None Shall Look Back*, two Confederate prisoners at Johnson's Island meet in a cell to contemplate the odds of escaping the Federal prison. Ned Allard finds himself speechless when he learns that his cousin, Spencer Rowe, has decided to make a near-suicidal prison break. "Ned did not answer. Spencer began moving about the cell, straightening his papers. He picked up the copy book containing his 'Memoirs' and handed it to Ned with a smile. 'If you're exchanged and get home in any kind of shape take that along. They might like to know how I employed my time.' He snapped the rubber band that held the book shut" (294). As expected, we learn later that Federal sentries shoot Spencer to death on the prison wall. But by passing on his memoirs he has ensured that his experiences will survive: at last exchanged, Ned carries the book back to the family and community in Kentucky.

For Gordon, the transmission and preservation of wartime experiences bordered on the sacred, and *None Shall Look Back* therefore registers a great deal of anxiety about lost memories and lost voices. At the close of chapter 10, the young lieutenant George Rowan rushes off to battle with plans for a memoir in his head: "As he ran back to the camp fire he was thinking that after the war was over and he had leisure he might collect his impressions into a book. 'In Tent and Saddle' might do for a title or perhaps 'Bugle and Bayonet' would be better. He might even look up the Indian legend [about the Chickamauga], put in something about 'the bloody river'" (242). But the chapter ends tragically. George, as the reader has guessed from the novel's dark foreshadowing, dies from a sharpshooter's bullet, never penning the memoir he had planned.

Indeed, Gordon's near-obsession with throat wounds seems connected to her fear, as a storyteller, of losing one's voice. The image of the damaged larynx recurs time and again in *None Shall Look Back*. The dying Captain Linton, carried to the Allards' home, can produce only a "whistling sound" when he tries to speak (214). Although overtly referencing the bullet lodged inside his body, Gordon's choice of words conveyed that the true horror of Linton's condition relates to his inability to communicate with those around him: "He put his hands to his chest. Something was inside, trying to get out. It was tearing him to pieces" (215). As time runs out on the captain, the struggle to speak becomes all the more furious: "Then she heard a strangled cry from the bed. Captain Linton was sitting up. His head shook from side to side. His poor hands kept tearing at his throat" (216). That Lucy will sponge the officer's face, hold his head, clasp his hand, but "dare not touch his throat" reflects her sense that the human voice remains one's most personal and sacred attribute (216). Yet the scene also provides a warning of what can happen when we do not act to help others communicate their sentiments. When the doctor arrives, "he put out a stubby forefinger, seemed about to touch the man's throat, but the finger came back and he got to his feet, shaking his head. 'In a coma now,' he said" (216). The opportunity for intervention gone, the soldier's final words and unspoken memories go forever lost.

That the novel means for this lesson to apply to women as much as men becomes clear in another scene, when Rives, captured as a spy, learns of a great commotion outside the prison where he is held: "A little girl playing in the yard of a house opposite the jail building had been fired upon by a soldier. The bullet struck the child in the throat, wounding her severely" (202). One of Rives's cellmates watches through a window as a doctor works on her wound: "He turned to Rives, shaking his head and laying his hand on his throat, 'Must have clipped the jugular,' he said. 'I knew a fellow once got hit like that. They sewed him up all right, but all he could ever say after that was "Hobble Gobble." Yep, if that kid over there comes through, expect she'll be in the same fix. Hobble Gobble'" (203). Like Rowe and Linton, the wounded girl faces death, or—somehow more horrible— the lifelong inability to speak more than gibberish. It seems telling that the plight of the little girl should figure within *None Shall Look Back* as one of the most distressing and memorable episodes. Not only does the scene belie the author's claim that her writing concerned itself with the struggles of men rather than women, but it also unearths her deep discontent with the war's written legacy. Though she undoubtedly "wrote about men called to be heroes," Gordon also wrote about women who through their words and actions soared above the absurdities of "Hobble Gobble."[55]

Near the close of the novel, General Forrest's brother Jeffrey falls in battle, also shot through the throat: "His eyes seemed glued down, his face was the color of greenish wax. The bright blood came from a wound in the neck" (318). Yet rather than let precious moments slip away, Nathan Forrest speaks on behalf of his brother, demanding "in a loud, passionate voice" that the bugler sound the charge (318). To a great extent, *None Shall Look Back* similarly aims to speak loudly and passionately on behalf of those women whose voices were lost after the war, whose experiences fell by the wayside when the nation set about writing and remembering its greatest conflict.

IV.

In 1951, Flannery O'Connor thanked Gordon for providing commentary on the manuscript of *Wise Blood* (1952). "There is no one around here," she wrote of her residence in Georgia, "who knows anything at all about fiction.... Sidney Lanier and Daniel Whitehead Hickey are the Poets and Margaret Mitchell is the Writer. Amen. So it means a great deal to me to get these comments." Gordon undoubtedly appreciated the young woman's words. Having long stood in the shadow of Mitchell, it must have been gratifying that O'Connor—whom she considered "a real novelist" and "a rare phenomenon"—should praise her expertise while rebuking the author of *Gone with the Wind*. O'Connor's note also reflects the critical distance that had grown between Gordon and Mitchell during the nearly fifteen years since *Gone with the Wind* and *None Shall Look Back* saw publication. As scholars such as Richard Dwyer have demonstrated, Mitchell's novel at first enjoyed considerable praise from America's literary establishment before falling into disrepute. J. Donald Adams claimed that the novel, "in narrative power, in sheer readability, [was] surpassed by nothing in American fiction." Similarly, the *New York Sun* asserted that in "emotional power (and no American writer has approached Miss Mitchell in this respect) and in its picturing of a vast and complex social system in time of war, *Gone with the Wind* is most closely allied to Tolstoy's *War and Peace*." But after the novel won the 1937 Pulitzer Prize for fiction, and after the film version enraptured the American public and won eight Academy Awards, *Gone with the Wind* quickly sank in reputation among men and women of letters. Academics seemed to be put off by the novel's sheer popularity, revealing "their elitist ideological biases against the nonacademic majority of the American public as consumers of convenience, comfort, and mindless diversion." Dwyer quoted Bernard De Voto's 1938 *Saturday Review* editorial, which concluded: "*Gone with the Wind* is important as a phenomenon but hardly as a novel.... Its author has no eye and no feeling of human character, and its page by page reliance on all the formulas of sentimental romance and all the effect of melodrama is offensive. The size of its public is significant; the book is not."[56]

By contrast, over the years the far less popular *None Shall Look Back*, no doubt aided by Gordon's connection to her academic husband Allen Tate and his fellow Agrarians, won grudging respect from scholars. Though initial reviews had been mixed, twenty years later the historian Robert A. Lively included *None Shall Look Back* on his list of the fifteen "Best Civil War Novels." Lively relegated *Gone with the Wind*, despite its prizes and sales, to a second tier of thirty "Other Representative Civil War Novels." By the time O'Connor wrote to Gordon, therefore, commentators had begun to reach a consensus. *None Shall Look Back* counted as quality fiction, whereas *Gone with the Wind*—as stated as late as 1991 by the editors of *Classics of Civil War Fiction*—stood merely as "a monumental distraction" from any "serious" discussion of American literature. More recently, Gardner has portrayed *None Shall Look Back* as a Modernist Civil War novel, stylistically innovative in the tradition of Scott's *The Wave* and therefore removed from the straightforward narrative of *Gone with the Wind*. Faced with the novels' clashing artistic and political allegiances, the historian followed earlier critics in remarking less on the similarities of the works than on their "profound differences."[57]

Critics aside, it is not surprising that Gordon never identified Mitchell as a kindred spirit. To do so would have required her to admit to what others had already concluded about her work: that despite her claims to the contrary, Gordon's writing often did focus on womankind and its struggles. My own view is that the differences between *Gone with the Wind* and *None Shall Look Back* can help us better understand what they have in common, and what they achieve together. Mitchell and Gordon may not have been the first Civil War novelists to imbue their female characters with soldierly virtues, but timing and effective narrative strategies enabled them to surpass their precursors in doing so. These novels together mark the late 1930s as the moment during which both mainstream and highbrow fictions of the war could voice aloud what many southern white women had intimated, less boldly or less successfully, for more than seventy-five years. Women were true participants of the war, they proclaimed, and had an equal share in forging a new South and a new American nation.

What cultural circumstances made audiences receptive to this message? Women's suffrage no doubt played a role, as did the growing presence of women in the work force during the early twentieth century. Similarly, World War I opened the eyes of millions of Americans to the contributions of women and civilians on the home front during times of war. I do not mean to overstate the significance of this moment for Civil War literature, however. Male "gods and generals" continued to dominate memory of the war, and Gordon's dependence on *Battles and Leaders* indicated that masculine narratives still weighed heavily on the minds of those women who wrote about the conflict. Moreover, of the hundreds of Civil War fictions appearing after 1937, most continued to privilege the battlefield exploits of men over the actions of women at home. Even the experience of World War I had not shattered traditional gender norms in America. The historian Maurine Weiner Greenwald has argued that World War I did less to liberate American women than to provide short-term opportunities for women laborers, and even those opportunities were staunchly opposed by many trade unions. In related studies, other scholars have shown that although women served as nurses abroad and volunteered at home with the Red Cross and other agencies, the line between the American soldier and civilian (a line then as wide as the Atlantic Ocean) remained intact.[58]

Nonetheless, the worldwide conflict did prompt many American men and women to recall previous wars, the Civil War especially. For example, UDC members compared their charity work during World War I with the work of Southern women between 1861 and 1865. Americans from other regions likewise volunteered at home, preparing medicine, food, and supplies for shipment abroad. As they did so, it was difficult not to notice the dramatic differences between the relatively calm home front of World War I America and the chaotic, desperate Southern home front portrayed in Civil War stories and novels. Southern women, as depicted in those narratives, endured war-related suffering, starvation, and violence entirely unknown to most U.S. citizens reading at home in 1917.

For readers of Mitchell and Gordon in the 1930s, then, it may not have seemed inappropriate for Scarlett, Melanie, or Lucy to wear the label of "veteran." Of course, few commentators then or now would argue seriously that the experiences of the female civilian were the same as those of the Civil War soldier. The fact remains that as traumatic as the Southern home front could be, the experiences of those who survived it were simply not equivalent to those of the men who endured the unspeakable psychological and physical distress of fields such as Antietam, Chickamauga, and Gettysburg. But because former soldiers had so successfully defined participation in the war in terms of battlefield experience, it only followed that women would in time seek to enlarge the definition of the term "veteran." Many readers of *Gone with the Wind* and *None Shall Look*

Back probably accepted declarations of women's veteranhood not as literal statements of fact but as a rhetorical device designed to make the point that women, too, had a hand in the nation's greatest struggle. But whether or not the fiction of Mitchell and Gordon persuaded readers to redefine their definition of military service, it is telling that their first audiences did not criticize them for blurring the line between soldiers and civilians, men and women. A rapidly changing society, influenced by war, social reform, and international politics, permitted new ways of looking at the past.

In terms of literary contexts, the significance of *Gone with the Wind* and *None Shall Look Back* rests a great deal on these works' unconventional treatment of the soldier's memoir. For decades, women writers had venerated the words and memories of men, even if they at times chafed beneath the sexist language and subject matter therein. By moving away from this tradition, Mitchell and Gordon helped mark a turning point in the reception and cultural usage of soldiers' narratives. To be sure, these novelists anticipated and encouraged many of the strategies with which later writers would approach the words of veterans. As Mitchell worked to humanize the Confederate veteran and lower the volume of his voice, Gordon added to, amended, and edited the genre of the soldier's narrative. The pair together showed how a conservative literary genre might be refashioned, cut, and parceled in support of a progressive social agenda. Of course, neither woman seemed willing to pen a novel that rejected outright the standard version of the war, one that they had themselves internalized. Helen Taylor pointed out that although *Gone with the Wind* trumpets the "courage not of soldiers but of women," always "the absent soldiers and battles are present, in the words of letters and lists of the dead." Gordon, too, adhered closely to the Civil War familiar to her readers of 1937 (and still today), making Confederate leaders part of her narrative and following her lionized male characters into combat. Most notably, both felt it necessary to militarize the women in their novels, conforming to the world of battles and leaders. But even while making those concessions, Mitchell and Gordon opened the door for later writers to confront, appropriate, mold, and satirize the memories of veterans—and by doing so, advance new cultural perspectives.[59]

In 1953, for example, O'Connor published "A Late Encounter with the Enemy," a satire of southern cultural memory that bears the influence of both Mitchell and Gordon. The story features Gen. Tennessee Flintrock Sash, a Confederate veteran who, at one hundred and four years old, "didn't remember that war at all." "People were always asking him if he remembered this or that—a dreary black procession of questions about the past. There was only one event in the past that he cared to talk about; that was twelve years ago when he had received the general's uniform and had been in the premiere [in Atlanta]." Clearly the story mocks the nostalgic fanfare that accompanied the 1939 premiere of the film version of *Gone with the Wind*, but it also shares Mitchell's irreverence for the South's defenders and their recorded memories. Contrary to the iconic image of the Civil War veteran as a virtuous and articulate commentator on America's sacred past, General Sash is a "shriveled," egotistical, and lecherous coot who "had forgotten history" altogether: "He heard the words, Chickamauga, Shiloh, Johnston, Lee . . . these words meant nothing to him. He wondered if he had been a general at Chickamauga or at Lee." Displayed with sword and uniform at the movie premiere and later at a graduation exercise, the general exists as a hollow reminder of "the old traditions" he has himself long forgotten. When in his final moments the past suddenly reemerges and rushes in upon his psyche, the old warrior grows terrified and tries to flee: "He recognized it, for it had been dogging all his days. He made such a desperate effort to see over it and find out what comes after the past." The scene echoes General Forrest's epiphany in *None Shall Look Back*, the realization that death "had been with him, beside him all the time and he had not known" (375). Indeed, O'Connor suggested that a failure to escape the past is tantamount to a kind of cultural death. Death grips General Sash before he can escape history, let alone contemplate the future—a reflection of the static southern society O'Connor saw around her in the years following World War II.[60]

"A Late Encounter with the Enemy" would no doubt have shocked audiences had it appeared in the late 1930s, as readers were then accustomed to noble portraits of the war's participants. But in part because the novels of Mitchell and Gordon had gone before, O'Connor could twenty years later envision General Sash as a comic figure whose grotesque personality is matched only by his tragic and all-too-human struggle with the past. The way was open for women writers to claim the words and remembered deeds of veterans as their American inheritance and to adapt them to fit their unique perspectives and agendas.

The achievement of Mitchell and Gordon depended on issues of region as well as gender. Critics have remarked on "Mitchell's ability to transform a southern story of the Civil War into a national story[, succeeding] where generations of southern white women authors had failed." The fiction of

Gordon likewise offered up southern womanhood as a badge of honor for American women of all regions. Even those readers who have never set foot in the South can celebrate the stories of Scarlett O'Hara and Lucy Allard for showing American women to be every bit as central to the nation's history as men. When we consider that these novels appeared just months apart, it seems plausible that circumstances might have turned out differently. Perhaps had *Gone with the Wind* been a measure less popular, and *None Shall Look Back* a bit more so, the novels might have been read for their commonalities rather than their differences.[61]

Yet aside from the reception history of the pair, why have scholars not made more of how *Gone with the Wind* and *None Shall Look Back* argue on behalf of female veteranhood? Most obviously, each novel's treatment of women, read alone, leaves less of an impression than when the books are read in succession. Later generations, reading Mitchell's and Gordon's books separately, could miss or ignore the authors' treatment of gender altogether. Thematic and stylistic factors have also influenced the reception of these works. Taylor's girlhood experiences probably mirror those of hundreds of thousands of readers of *Gone with the Wind* who found it easy to focus on the ordeals of romance rather than on women's service during the war: "Cheerfully skipping what I found to be boring political and social details, I concentrated hard on the central love triangle of Scarlett, Ashley and Rhett, which I found endlessly satisfying." Similarly, most reviews and commentary on Gordon's novel dwell not on gender but on her portrait of battle and history, and on her use of a roving omniscient narrator.[62]

Perhaps, too, the progressive agendas of Mitchell and Gordon have often gone unnoticed due to these writers' inability to imagine black men and women as veterans. While both make a solid case for white women's contributions to the war effort, and while both depict black servants struggling alongside their white companions, neither bestowed on black characters the same soldierly qualities awarded whites. There does exist a poignant scene in *Gone with the Wind* where Scarlett offers Gerald's faithful servant, Pork, her father's gold watch—a reward for his extraordinary service during wartime (721). Yet Mitchell's narrative never declares Pork a veteran nor offers him to readers as a martial figure. More strikingly, in *Gone with the Wind* and *None Shall Look Back*, black women garner little recognition for their contributions to the nation. For all the hardships endured by Mitchell's Mammy and Dilcey and Prissy, or by the black women in Gordon's novel, neither author represented these figures as true veterans.

Moreover, while both writers had read postwar reminiscences by women, neither appears to have relied on the published words of black women who lived through the war. At least one black memoirist, Susie King Taylor, offered words in step with the gender principles found in the novels of Mitchell and Gordon. In her *Reminiscences of My Life in Camp with the 33d United States Colored Troops, Late 1st S.C., Volunteers* (1902), Taylor wrote: "There are many people who do not know what some of the colored women did during the war. . . . These things should be kept in history before the people. There has never been a greater war in the United States than the one of 1861, where so many lives were lost,—not men alone but noble women as well." Ultimately, Taylor's vision seems too progressive and democratic to fit the agendas of Mitchell and Gordon. As southerners who embraced their society's traditional hierarchies regarding race, they were unwilling to imagine the same nobility for blacks as for whites. Undoubtedly, had their novels argued for the veteranhood of southern blacks, and criticized rather than promoted racism, their efforts on behalf of white women would have won—and deserved—more attention.[63]

But while we might condemn these works for the handling of race therein, we can nonetheless acknowledge their role in helping to launch a conversation still underway in the twenty-first century. Scholars such as Catherine Clinton lamented during the late 1990s that historians and filmmakers of the war too often ignored the role of women in the struggle. Weary of "testosterone-laced legends" and "the macho hot buttons that have kept Civil War literature a popular staple of the past century," Clinton argued that by "fully representing women in their prize-winning epics, historians would build a better future for all our children." In a somewhat different vein, several historians wrote books and articles during the early twenty-first century about women who had literally become soldiers during the Civil War. Works of scholarship such as *All the Daring of a Soldier: Women of the Civil War Armies* (2001), *They Fought Like Demons: Women Soldiers in the Civil War* (2003), and *She Went to the Field: Women Soldiers of the Civil War* (2003) revealed that a small number of women, Union and Confederate, disguised themselves as men in order to serve as combatants. Although estimates typically place the number of women in uniform between 240 and 400, as compared to the some four million men who served, the female veteran has become a disproportionately high-profile figure in Civil War memory.[64]

Aside from historians and their readers, writers and filmmakers have also taken an interest in portraying women as active participants in the war.

Ann Rinaldi, the popular author of young adult fiction, published her book *Girl in Blue* in 2001. The story follows the adventures of a sixteen-year-old Northern girl who masquerades as a man in order to join a Michigan regiment. And in 2003, a news service reported that writer-director Catherine Hardwicke hoped to cast a well-known star for the forthcoming *Soldier Girl*, a Civil War film that offers "a true story of a girl who disguised herself as a man for two years to fight in the war for a cause she believed in." Neither Mitchell nor Gordon portrayed such cross-dressing female soldiers in their fiction, and it seems unlikely that either would have found such characters especially compelling. But we can nonetheless link these authors' insistence on a female veteranhood to the still-developing scholarly, literary, and cinematic studies of women's participation in the Civil War.[65]

It is significant that Mitchell and Gordon refused to accept in full the prevailing, masculine story of the war. They and like-minded writers understood the past's relationship to the future of their community and nation. By wedding the battlefield to the realities of the female experience, these women helped ensure that future generations would not forget the sacrifices made by American women of any period. It seems almost certain that we will continue to perceive of Mitchell and Gordon as two very different writers, perhaps with good reason. Yet by contending with the words of their forebears, and constructing complex portraits of women in the Civil War, both writers became veterans in the continuing war for American memory.

Chapter Three

THE EGGSHELL SHIBBOLETH OF CASTE AND COLOR TOO
Civilian Narrators in *Absalom, Absalom!* and *The Unvanquished*

When we consider how often the works of William Faulkner grapple with the Civil War and its legacy, it should surprise us that the writer had so little to say about the Confederacy's oft-mythologized troops.[1] After all, the Mississippi-born author "was growing to manhood" during the years between 1890 and 1920, when the Lost Cause civil religion "flourished especially."[2] The Myth of the Lost Cause functioned substantially—one might say predominantly—as a military phenomenon. As Gary W. Gallagher has observed, the Lost Cause explanation for Confederate secession and defeat "drew strength from the pages of participants' memoirs, from speeches at veterans' reunions, from ceremonies at the graves of soldiers killed while serving in Southern armies and other commemorative events, and from artwork with Confederate themes." As a "public memory of the Confederacy" that positioned "wartime sacrifice and shattering defeat in the best possible light," the Lost Cause placed courageous Confederate soldiers at center stage.[3] Yet in sharp contrast to other southern writers of the early- and mid-twentieth century, Faulkner played down the cultural role of uniformed Confederates in his fiction and public statements. Soldiers in gray exist as distant, often shadowy figures in his writing; those we do see up close shed their uniforms quickly and "are largely incommunicative about their War experiences."[4] To be sure, Faulkner appeared to go out of his way to *silence* veterans, to remove their voices—and hence their interpretations of the conflict—from the postwar society he portrayed. The Confederate soldier's memoir, so clearly a source and reference for scores of others who wrote about the war, seems to have left few traces in Faulkner's pages.[5]

What should we make of the fact that the premier writer of the twentieth-century South draped a mantle over the postwar literary and oratorical efforts of veterans? Contrary to the conclusions of many critics, Faulkner remained fascinated by the military side of the Civil War his entire life. Moreover, the figure of the Confederate soldier played an important role in his family and community history. As Thomas L. Connelly and Barbara Bellows pointed out, Faulkner "lived in the last generation that saw the Confederate veteran as a reality," a generation that often romanticized that figure as a symbol of traditional values standing in opposition to the twentieth-century "commercial and cultural Americanization of Dixie." Yet if Faulkner realized that veterans had shaped southern life to a remarkable degree, he also believed that a martial understanding of the war could severely limit one's vision of American history and culture. Indeed, for all its drama and bloodshed, the battlefield existed for Faulkner as only the loudest and least evocative representation of the nation's Civil War.[6]

Of course, it was the issue of race that gave the war its most enduring meaning—morally, legally, and culturally. During the 1930s, the racial legacy of the Civil War and Reconstruction could be found wherever one looked. Among other phenomena, the war left its imprint on Jim Crow laws and practices throughout the South, the Scottsboro case in Alabama, congressional filibusters over antilynching legislation, and Depression-era racism against black workers. Yet for all these reminders that race was essential to the Civil War and its aftermath, in the popular imagination the story of the war remained one of a grand "military competition between brave people for no particular reason other than the honor of it all." In writing *Absalom, Absalom!* (1936) and *The Unvanquished* (1938), Faulkner sought to restore race and race relations to the story of the Civil War and to help revise nearly seventy years of narratives about the conflict. He had not yet entered public debates about such subjects as integration and civil rights, but as has been said of him in another context, these novels "suggested he was thinking about the present while he talked of the past." By showing that race was central to *the* foremost crisis in American history, Faulkner prompted American readers to likewise acknowledge the centrality of race to their own experiences.[7]

Faulkner's writing suggests that only by de-mythologizing the South's Civil War can we understand its relevance to American culture and life in the twentieth century and beyond. To combat the legacy of the Lost Cause, the author sought to demilitarize not only the image of the Confederate soldier but also the very telling of the war, transferring the responsibility of narrating and interpreting the conflict to civilians such as Rosa Coldfield, Bayard Sartoris, and Virginia Du Pre. More than soldiers who experienced the war in the field, these narrators could grapple with what Faulkner identified as the true cause of the conflict and its moral center: racism and institutionalized slavery.[8]

I.

In order to understand the intricacies of Faulkner's two most important novels about the Civil War, *Absalom, Absalom!* and *The Unvanquished*, one must first consider his views on the Southern past and its symbols. Louis Rubin Jr. has explained that Faulkner "knew that understanding what happened in the past is a matter of interpretation" and that any valid interpretation required "a moral as well as [an] analytical" component. The novelist's genius "led him to see that the best way to both chronicle and judge that history was to let it be discovered and interpreted by an observer, one who would be near enough to it to be involved emotionally, yet distant enough from it to view it in moral perspective."[9] While Rubin did not take up the issue of Civil War veterans explicitly, his observations go a long way toward explaining why Faulkner did not turn to former soldiers for insight into the war they fought. Of course some veterans did have the ability to step back, years later, and consider the conflict in "moral" terms. Albion Tourgée, a veteran of the Union army and a postwar journalist, essayist, and author of *A Fool's Errand* (1879), argued that Americans should remember "not the battles, the marches, the conflicts,—not the courage, the suffering, the blood, *but only the causes that underlay the struggle and the results that followed from it.*"[10] The vast majority of former soldiers, however, could not or would not extricate their vision of the war from their experiences on the battlefield. Many of them—including black veterans—saw the courage and carnage of battle as a metaphor for the racial struggle underlying the conflict. Thousands more veterans ignored the war's moral and political issues altogether, focusing entirely on its military figures and events.[11] Consider, for example, the final passage of *Notes of a Private* (1909) by John Milton Hubbard, one of the two veterans' memoirs housed in Faulkner's private library:

I have concluded to conclude this book with the following conclusions:

1. That it is an everlasting pity the war was not averted because of the great mortality of good citizens on both sides, the backset given to the morals of the whole country, the sectional feeling engendered and likely to endure for a season, and the loss of wealth and prestige by the Southern people.
2. That the victors in a civil war pay dearly for their success in the demoralization of the people at large by having so numerous an element supported by the government; in the rascally transactions connected with army contracts; and in the enlargement of that class of pestiferous statesmen (?) who have been aptly described as being "invisible in war and invincible in peace."
3. That the most peaceful of Southern men can be readily converted into the most war-like soldiers, when convinced that they have a proper grievance; can march further on starvation rations and in all kinds of weather, and will take less note of disparity of numbers in battle than will any other soldiers on earth.
4. That the South, in the war period, was essentially a country of horseback riders, and her young men furnished the material out of which was formed, when properly handled, regiments of cavalry that were practically invincible, even when confronting an adversary of twice or thrice their own strength.
5. That Forrest's men demonstrated the fact that Southern cavalrymen, fighting on foot, can meet, with good chances of victory, a superior number of veteran infantry in the open field.
6. That in cavalry operations, the most essential thing is a bold and dashing leader, who will strike furiously before the enemy has time to consider what is coming, and with every available man in action.
7. That Nathan Bedford Forrest, by his deeds in war, became an exemplar of horseback fighting, whose shining qualities might well become the measure of other deeds on other fields when war is flagrant.
8. That there is not an instance recorded where so large a body of defeated soldiers returned so contentedly to their former pursuits, "beating their swords into ploughshares and their spears into pruning hooks"; yes, thousands of them going into the fields to plough and plant with the same horses they rode in battle.

9. That the unpreparedness of both sides at the beginning of the war emphasizes the necessity for a thorough preparedness of our united country for any emergency, that is to say, that while Uncle Sam needs not to be strutting around "with a chip on his shoulder," and his hat cocked up on the side of his head, he should be able to say to "the other fellow" that he is rich in men and munitions and, moreover, has the finest navy that floats.[12]

At least seven of Hubbard's nine conclusions deal explicitly with military operations or with the nature of the men who fought the war; nearly all ignore the social and political issues of the conflict, and none takes up the issues of racism and slavery. In these respects, Hubbard's memoir resembled the only other Civil War remembrance in Faulkner's library at Rowan Oak, the far more famous and ostentatious *I Rode with Stonewall* (1940) by Henry Kyd Douglas.[13] Belonging as they do to the Lost Cause school of Civil War interpretation, both memoirs devoted considerable space to honoring the resilience and courage of the common Confederate soldier and to championing the military genius and personal character of Confederate leaders such as Robert E. Lee, Thomas J. "Stonewall" Jackson, and Nathan B. Forrest. By contrast, in his own fiction Faulkner set out to recover what was lost during the Lost Cause celebrations of the late nineteenth and early twentieth centuries: an understanding of the complex role that race played, both politically and morally, in the rise and violent demise of the Confederacy.[14]

Few scholars have commented on Faulkner's decision *not* to embrace the military dimension of the Lost Cause, but those who do tend to agree with the conclusion of Daniel Aaron: "The War did not interest him much—only its aftereffects." Katherine Arn Clark elaborated on this point in her account of *The Unvanquished:* "Faulkner simply ignores it [the Civil War]. He canvasses no issues, airs no explanations, goes into no sources or causes, describes no real battles, rehearses no facts, figures, dates, statistics, gives no numbers of wounded or dead, and just barely follows the progress of the War." From the perspective of Aaron and like-minded critics, Faulkner's supposed disinterest in the Civil War paid dividends for his art, insofar as it allowed him to escape the siren song of the Lost Cause and hence "read the War's meaning not in its heroes and battles but in the consciousness of a people."[15]

Some might wonder whether Faulkner avoided writing about the war, and Confederate soldiers in particular, because of his *own* failure to see combat during World War I. As biographers and essayists have shown,

Faulkner created an elaborate, often comic mythology about his exploits as an aviator with the Royal Air Force (RAF). Although he spent only five months as a cadet in the Canadian RAF before returning home with no combat experience, the "veteran" impressed his Mississippi neighbors with war stories, a fake limp, and tales of a silver plate in his head. Biographer Joseph Blotner explained that Faulkner would eventually "make it clear that he had not crashed in combat," but his "having flown military aircraft in wartime was still too much a part of his personal myth to be surrendered." Did a lifelong insistence on his veteranhood arise from Faulkner's jealousy of those men who did serve in battle? Moreover, could that jealousy explain why he did so little to champion the figure and voice of the Southern soldier or to conceive of the Civil War in military terms? It may well be true that Faulkner's feelings of inferiority colored his literary portrait of soldiers, even those from an earlier era. But we should ultimately reject this explanation for the limited military presence in his Civil War fictions. No matter how intimidating or shaming Faulkner may have found the image of the Confederate hero, the fact remains that his works also eschew other major tenets of the Lost Cause and its white supremacist version of southern history. Absent, inarticulate soldiers represent only one part of his literary and historical vision.[16]

Far more erroneous is the claim that Faulkner simply had little interest in the Civil War. The author knew the details of his great-grandfather's military career in all its phases and dwelled on his ancestor's connection to renowned Confederate leaders. He boasted to Malcolm Cowley, for example, that his great-grandfather was "a part of Stonewall Jackson's left at 1st Manassas that afternoon" and that the family possessed "a citation in James Longstreet's longhand as his corps commander after 2nd Manassas." As a child, Faulkner and his playmates regularly uncovered relics of the war—rifles, bayonets, sabers, and once a broken horse pistol that William restored to working order and, to the chagrin of his mother, fired into the neighborhood. Surely not all encounters with the visual and verbal reminders of the Confederate past were so explosive, but Faulkner's early fascination with the Civil War clearly became a lifelong interest. Those who knew the famed writer personally understood that the war fired his imagination like little else. Late in life, while living in Virginia, Faulkner made frequent road trips to nearby battlefields, following the military movements of 1861–65 and leaving his car to survey the historical markers and monuments. Faulkner's brother John, near the end of his reminiscence *My Brother Bill* (1963), turned to the subject of the Civil War: "As I think back on Bill, the picture that keeps recurring is [that of] Bill in his mud-splashed gray Plymouth, tracing out the course of battles on those Virginia fields. He was an avid reader of the histories of the War Between the States. He was as well versed in most of them as any professor.... I only wish I could have seen through his eyes what he saw as he followed those Virginia battle markers."[17]

Of course, some might ask whether it matters that Faulkner knew a great deal about the fighting if he did not, in fact, write about it. Could it be that he simply distanced a personal interest in battles and soldiers from the world of his fiction? Faulkner's 1944 letter to Harold Ober reveals something of his rationale for *not* describing the fighting that so fascinated him. "War is bad for writing," he explained. "This sublimation and glorification of all the cave instincts which man had hopes that he had lived down, dragged back into daylight, usurping pre-empting a place, all the room in fact, in the reality and constancy and solidity of art, writing." Faulkner seemed to fear that a representation of combat would consume his narratives about the war, laying bare the dark and primitive side of human nature and utterly blotting out the cultural and historical context of the fighting described. Something of this nature had occurred in the stories and poetry of Ambrose Bierce, a veteran so "choked on the blood of the Civil War" that he rarely considered the political and social issues that inspired it. Faulkner sought to avoid this phenomenon just as urgently as he did its reverse—narratives that cast the war as a romantic adventure on a grand scale. Yes, John Faulkner probably exaggerated when claiming that his brother knew as much about the conflict as "any professor," but William well understood the ways by which others had told the story of the sectional and social struggle. He learned a great deal from Civil War fiction, memoirs, and histories, and the limitations of those works encouraged him to explore neither the carnage nor the glory of 1861–65, but rather that period's meaning for his region and nation.[18]

In order to explore the meanings of the South's Civil War, Faulkner deflected attention away from the figure and voice of the Confederate veteran. Many twenty-first-century readers take up his fictions without ever balking at the limited space those works devote to soldiers in gray. This absence is striking, however, when we consider the southern fiction and verse contemporary with the writing Faulkner produced. Representing a wide range of literary talent, popularity, and style, some of the nineteenth- and twentieth-century authors who made the Rebel soldier a major presence in their writing include Donald Davidson, Clifford Dowdey, Shelby

Foote, Ellen Glasgow, Caroline Gordon, Mary Johnston, Andrew Lytle, Evelyn Scott, Mary Lee Settle, and Allen Tate. Not only did Confederate troops march through the pages of southern literature, but the words and memories of individual soldiers often echo there as well. Faulkner's literary peers drew frequently on veterans' memoirs, borrowing dialogue, imagery, period detail, and historical interpretation. And outside the pages of their imaginative writing, these authors also demonstrated a mostly genuine reverence for those who fought the war. Johnston dedicated her 1911 masterpiece *The Long Roll* to her father, a Confederate veteran, as well as to her relation Gen. Joseph E. Johnston, one of the South's premier military commanders. She and others also celebrated the anonymous Confederate foot soldier, whose wartime actions demanded attention and respect long years after Appomattox. In a 1931 letter, Gordon recalled how Lytle made "an impassioned speech" on Confederate Memorial Day, after which he addressed three ancient veterans, guests of honor at the occasion, with somber words: "Gentlemen. . . . You have not fought in vain." If it seems scarcely imaginable that Faulkner could have delivered a similar speech, or so addressed living veterans, this is largely because he seldom treated southern history—and especially the Civil War—in the heroic mode.[19]

Nor did he celebrate Southern symbols associated with the war and its combatants. Asked in 1957 to name which elements of southern tradition and heritage he hoped his grandson would or would not maintain, Faulkner replied in a way that would have unsettled Lost Cause adherents: "I hope of course that he will cope with his environment as it changes. And, I hope that his mother and father will try to raise him without bigotry as much as can be done. He can have a Confederate battleflag if he wants it but he shouldn't take it too seriously." In this brief response, Faulkner revealed an allegiance to social and moral progress, tellingly punctuated by his dismissal of the oft-revered standard. It seems unlikely that the writer here meant to be flippant. He clearly recognized the power of the flag to evoke the Southern past—a complex past marked by heroism, religiosity, and individualism but marred by violence, racism, and intolerance. By dismissing the flag as a child's toy, he made the iconoclastic suggestion that the South should mature beyond the legacy of the men who carried it during four years of war.[20]

Faulkner's linking the flag to juvenile play would seem to support the argument, advanced by some critics, that the author envisioned the war itself "as a game played by children . . . the product of a basically childish mind." But the reference truly does less to disparage veterans than to illustrate Faulkner's strategy of moving battlefield heroics into the wings of southern memory. Even when his interviewers asked specifically about the men who fought the war, Faulkner redirected the conversation toward the actions and voices of civilians—particularly women. "Yes. I remember a lot of them," Faulkner said in 1958 when asked about the veterans he encountered as a youth. "I was five-six-seven years old around 1904–5–6 and 7, old enough to understand, to listen. They didn't talk so much about that war, I had got that from the maiden spinster aunts which had never surrendered. But I can remember the old men, and they would get out the old shabby grey uniforms and get out the old battleflag on Decoration, Memorial Day. Yes, I remember any number of them. But it was the aunts, the women, that had never given up." To hear Faulkner tell it, veterans existed in turn-of-the-century Mississippi as bland, silent reminders of a bygone era. They showed little interest in reminiscing about old victories and defeats and left the job of remembering and interpreting the war to women. The point is not that Faulkner misled his audience (no doubt many veterans truly *were* reluctant to discuss their experiences) but that he time and again presented civilians as the most prominent and captivating representatives of the war.[21]

The same phenomenon occurs in his fiction. The twelve-year-old Bayard Sartoris narrates *The Unvanquished* rather than his war hero father, Colonel Sartoris, and the character there committed most passionately to the Confederate cause is Drusilla Hawk, a young woman. Moreover, in *Flags in the Dust* (1973), Aunt Jenny makes clear that Southern women endured more hardship and psychological damage during the war than men: "Do you think a man could sit day after day and month after month in a house miles from anywhere and spend the time between casualty lists tearing up bedclothes and window curtains and table linen to make lint and watching sugar and flour and meat dwindling away ... and hiding in nigger cabins while drunken Yankee generals set fire to the house your great-great-grandfather built and you and all your folks were born in? Don't talk to me about men suffering in war."[22]

It seems therefore appropriate that although Faulkner admitted that his great-grandfather stood as the "prototype" of his fictional Col. John Sartoris, Col. William Clark Falkner's affinity for writing failed to manifest itself in the character he inspired. Like Falkner, Colonel Sartoris (a) raises, pays for, and leads a regiment of Mississippi volunteers; (b) finds himself voted out of his own command and thereafter puts together a cavalry unit;

(c) builds his county's first railroad after the war; (d) wins election to the state legislature; and (e) is shot to death by his former railroad associate. Yet Falkner also published poetry, a travel narrative, and several novels—works in which political and social ideas would sometimes arise. For example, his novel *The White Rose of Memphis* (1881) contained reflections on the recent war, its causes, and the future of a reunited America. Such literary accomplishments (and social commentary) seem beyond the reach and temperament of the colonel's counterpart, John Sartoris.[23]

I believe we might rightly overlook this discrepancy between a historical figure and a fictional one were it not for the fact that Faulkner obscured consistently the literary and oratorical achievements of former soldiers like his great-grandfather. This phenomenon is encapsulated in an episode from *Sartoris* (1929). When Old Bayard asks one veteran, "What the devil were you folks fighting about, anyhow?" the man's answer is unsettling in its simplicity: "Be damned ef I ever did know."[24] As Thomas C. Leonard has observed, Faulkner's warriors "endure or fight back, but they lack the ability to make sense of it all."[25]

In *Requiem for a Nun* (1951), too, the author drew attention away from veterans' powerful voices in American culture. There Faulkner described a group of elderly veterans who, to celebrate the unveiling of a new monument at Confederate Decoration Day in 1900, "tottered into the sunlight and fired shotguns at the bland sky." Though now as bland as the sky above, the old soldiers momentarily stir the crowd by offering a re-creation of the famous Rebel yell: "[Their] cracked quavering voices in the shrill hackle-lifting yelling which Lee and Jackson and Longstreet and the two Johnstons (and Grant and Sherman and Hooker and Pope and McClellan and Burnside too for the matter of that) had listened to amid the smoke and the din." But Faulkner undercut the thrill of the moment by referring to this inarticulate yell as the war's "epilogue and epitaph." Collapsing the space between the battle cry of 1861–65 and its re-creation in 1900, the scene effectively silences veterans' voices between the end of the war and the beginning of the twentieth century—the very years during which Civil War veterans penned countless narratives that articulately explored the war and helped to define an image of the American nation.[26]

From one perspective, therefore, Faulkner appeared to defang the Lost Cause by depicting its monuments, flags, and living relics as having grown dull and powerless by the turn of the century. As the narrator of *Requiem for a Nun* observes, "the old deathless Lost Cause had [by 1900] become a faded (though still select) social club or caste, or form of behavior when you remembered to observe it." Even the power of the legendary Rebel yell had diminished, no more potent than "the blasts of blank shotgun shells." Yet from another perspective, by deftly ushering aside the important postwar presence of veterans, Faulkner revealed his deep concern that twentieth-century southerners could *not* forget the Cause, even if they wanted to. This aspect of Faulkner's work appears at the beginning of *Absalom, Absalom!* where we see Quentin Compson haunted by the past of Jefferson, Mississippi, and the South at large: "His childhood was full of [names]; his very body was an empty hall echoing with sonorous defeated names; he was not a being, an entity, he was a commonwealth. He was a barracks filled with stubborn backward-looking ghosts still recovering, even forty-three years afterward." Surely not all southerners of Quentin's generation shared this paralyzing obsession with the past, but the passage well captures the nightmare side of the Lost Cause. "Lost things are always prized very highly," Shelby Foote has said in reference to the Myth, an explanation that seems an understatement when applied to Quentin, who looks backward not only because he prizes what was lost but also because he has no capacity to look forward. The novel seems to suggest that Quentin is the true legacy of the Lost Cause—a consciousness so devoted to memory of a mythic Confederacy that it ceases to function as anything but a "barracks" for the ghosts of those who fought and then re-fought the war, over and over, in memoirs and public memory.[27]

The same anxiety about the Lost Cause exists in Faulkner's most famous passage regarding the war, one quoted so often that it has become nearly a cliché to include it in any discussion of southern memory. In the novel *Intruder in the Dust* (1948), Gavin Stevens remarks in one "impossibly long sentence" on the enduring legacy of Pickett's charge:

> For every Southern boy fourteen years old, not once but whenever he wants it, there is the instant when it's still not yet two o'clock on that July afternoon in 1863, the brigades are in position behind the rail fence, the guns are laid and ready in the woods, and the furled flags are already loosened to break out and Pickett himself with his long oiled ringlets and his hat in one hand probably and his sword in the other looking up the hill waiting for Longstreet to give the word and it's all in the balance, it hasn't happened yet, it hasn't even begun yet, it not only hasn't begun yet but there is still time for it not to begin against

that position and those circumstances which made more men than Garnett and Kemper and Armistead and Wilcox grave yet it's going to begin, we all know that, we have come too far with too much at stake and that moment doesn't need even a fourteen-year-old boy to think *This time. Maybe this time* with all this much to lose and all this much to gain: Pennsylvania, Maryland, the world, the golden dome of Washington itself to crown with desperate and unbelievable victory the desperate gamble, the cast made two years ago; or to anyone who ever sailed even a skiff under a quilt sail, the moment in 1492 when somebody thought *This is it:* the absolute edge of no return, to turn back now and make home or sail irrevocably on and either find land or plunge over the world's roaring rim.

Scholars and cultural historians have read this passage in a number of ways. Douglas T. Miller viewed these lines as reflecting Faulkner's tendency to promote "the storybook version of Southern history." Earl J. Hess saw Faulkner's words as "the ultimate expression of Pickett's charge as a turning point of the war," the crucial moment—according to postwar mythmaking—after which Northern victory became inevitable. Carol Reardon believed that the Mississippi-born author used the charge at Gettysburg to reflect on the seemingly "demarcative" moments in human history. Tony Horwitz admired Faulkner for here capturing "the nostalgic might-have-been that [has] lingered in Southern imagination" since the war. Taking matters further, Lloyd A. Hunter cited Faulkner's words as an example of how Confederates and their descendents believed "that the Lost Cause was never genuinely lost"; one could always revisit and exalt the point immediately before the long collapse of the South's nationhood. By far, the individual whose interpretation has enjoyed the widest currency is Shelby Foote. In Ken Burns's 1990 PBS documentary *The Civil War*, Foote paraphrased the famous passage and then summed up its meaning by saying that "every southern boy" can "go back in his mind to the time before the war was going to be lost and he can always have that moment for himself."[28]

While these readings together suggest a wide range of nuances, they more or less all share the affirming notion that the war's mythologies could and can provide comfort. In particular, the words of Horwitz, Hunter, and Foote concentrated on how Faulkner's passage reflects on the generations of southerners who took solace in a fabled past before the fall. Living in a modern South that lacked the glow of the mythologized antebellum and early war periods, southerners devoured soldiers' memoirs and erected monuments to Confederate heroes in an attempt to find their way back to a better age. Yet commentators have tended to ignore the grim reverse of the *Intruder in the Dust* passage, that while a youth can "whenever he wants it" stand among Pickett's command before two o' clock on July 3, 1863, that fantasy only serves to emphasize the wreckage and anxieties of the postwar South, a world that "doesn't even need a fourteen-year-old boy" to evoke it. It therefore seems that one of our most familiar literary passages about the Civil War may comment as much on the burden of the war's mythos as on its recuperative power. By so glorifying the Southern soldiers who met their gallant destruction at Gettysburg, Lost Cause architects all but required that later generations devalue their own courage, way of life, and moment in time. Moreover, they insisted that their descendents act as the (at times unwilling) caretakers of Confederate memory.

Francois Pitavy has noted that Faulkner's interest nearly always lies not "in the instant so much as in its outraged repetition or its externalization."[29] Why, then, should Faulkner obscure the men and the memoirs that had inspired the "outraged repetition" of Pickett's charge among generations of southerners? Part of the answer lies in Faulkner's belief that after the war former soldiers "were obsolete." "Southern men," he told a classroom audience in 1958, "were the ones that couldn't bear being—having lost the war. The women were the ones that could bear it because they never had surrendered. The men had given up and in a sense were dead and even generations later were seeking death."[30] Surely we might dispute Faulkner and argue that Confederate soldiers never gave up, that their postwar writing began the Lost Cause not as a backward-looking movement but as one determined to shape the future of southern and American memory.[31] Yet, for Faulkner, the celebration of dead and defeated soldiers was usually just a celebration of death and defeat. Available to "every southern boy" of succeeding generations, the Lost Cause led many to prize death during the war over life in the present. This notion seems borne out in *Absalom, Absalom!* when the Canadian Shreve McCannon asks Quentin with exasperation: "What is it? something you live and breathe in like air? a kind of vacuum filled with wraithlike and indomitable anger and pride and glory at and in happenings that occurred and ceased fifty years ago? a kind of entailed birthright father and son and father and son of never forgiving General Sherman, so that forever more as long as your children's children produce children you wont be anything but a descendent of a long line of colonels killed in Pickett's charge[?]."[32] Here Shreve well captures the self-destructive, martial culture that so haunts Quentin and his fellow southerners. They are descended not from those who fought the war, survived it, and endured, but rather from men killed gloriously during Pickett's charge. Indeed, in some respects, Quentin exists as only the most recent addition to the "long line" of men who perished in the war.

There can be no doubt that the Southern past haunted Faulkner as it did Quentin; he at one point commented, "Ishmael is the witness in *Moby-Dick* as I am Quentin in *The Sound and the Fury*." But unlike his alter ego, Faulkner could find relief in the memories of civilians who lived through the South's most tumultuous period and who narrated their experiences for the benefit of later generations. Yes, like veterans their tales might romanticize the feats and sacrifices of Confederate troops (consider Aunt Jenny's stories about the Carolina Bayard in *Sartoris*), but civilians could reflect on the past from an unvanquished position—one where life and human endurance overshadow death and martial sacrifice. The idea that women and children on the home front had never formally surrendered (and hence had made peace with neither the Yankees nor the notion of defeat) clearly struck a chord in Faulkner. In *The Unvanquished*, he wrote that "the men had given in and admitted that they belonged to the United States but the women had never surrendered." Outside of his fiction, he told affectionately of the "old undefeated spinster aunts that children of my time grew up with" and recalled how a relation of his had walked out on a screening of *Gone with the Wind*: "She had paid good money to go there, but she wasn't going to sit and look at Sherman." Faulkner admired this aunt not for her refusal to be reconciled with former enemies but for her dignity and her will to remain autonomous. These same qualities characterized the "family annals" that were passed down to Faulkner by men and women who experienced the war on the home front. Ultimately, these storytellers, more than his great-grandfather or other Confederate heroes, lie behind *Absalom, Absalom!* and *The Unvanquished*. By looking closely at how each of these novels reflects the narrative power of the South's civilians, we can best come to terms with Faulkner's vision of the war and its role in endowing "the Southern story of race relations" with "broad human significance."[33]

II.

Had any southern writer preceding or contemporary with Faulkner chosen "The Unvanquished" as the title for a Civil War novel, he or she would almost surely have been alluding to the white South of the Lost Cause. Yet in the hands of Faulkner, "the unvanquished" refers not to those who promote the Cause, or even to southern society as a whole, but to anyone—white or black—who possesses the will to endure and to prevail. The white narrators of *Absalom, Absalom!* and *The Unvanquished* possess an indomitable spirit, a spirit that can at times span the racial divide and allows them to connect with similarly "undefeated" characters of color. Such connections are often brief and almost always exist in spite of the racism, ignorance, or naïveté of the participants. But they are meaningful connections, nonetheless, and set Faulkner's world apart from typical Confederate narratives—memoirs and fictions in which the subject of race relations is lost beneath the haze and din of battle.

Historian Joel Williamson has argued in his book *William Faulkner and Southern History* (1993) that race "was central, integral, and vital" to Faulkner's writing. His novels "remain, probably, the ultimate indictment not merely of the injustice of the racial establishment in the South in and after slavery, but of its capacity for the often subtle, always brutal reduction of humanity, both black and white. Simultaneously, however, these novels offer the contrary capacity of humanity at large to survive and transcend the most devastating afflictions." As Williamson suggested, Faulkner understood both the failings and the triumphs of America as necessarily multiracial in character. I do not mean to argue, however, that Faulkner was himself free of racist beliefs. Although his fellow southerners often grew angry over what they took to be his liberal views on the proper place and treatment of African Americans, Faulkner was also criticized by "outsiders who thought he hadn't gone far enough." Surely some of his public statements about civil rights sounded reactionary, offending those who listened. During the late 1950s, for example, he told student groups at the University of Virginia that perhaps "the Negro is not yet capable of more than second-class citizenship. His tragedy may be that so far he is competent for equality only in the ratio of his white blood." Even while holding white Americans responsible for perceived deficiencies within the black race, Faulkner's comments could turn ugly, such as when he compared the nation's unassimilated black population to "five hundred unbridled horses loose in the streets."[34]

In step with such intransigent statements, *The Unvanquished* adheres to a southern literary tradition that denied African Americans equal space and a narrative voice. The family and experiences of the white narrator, Bayard Sartoris, dominate the plot of all seven sections of the novel.[35] Accordingly, many scholarly treatments of the book have focused on Bayard to the exclusion of the important black characters, namely Ringo, Loosh, and Louvinia. By the end of the novel, it would indeed seem that the title refers to the narrator. "It is Bayard who is 'the unvanquished' one," Clark argued: "'Unvanquished' by the expectations of his community, 'unvanquished' by the role that is forced upon him, 'unvanquished' by the stereotypical notions surrounding the romantic heroic legend of his own father." Few would dispute that the novel functions overtly as a traditional coming-of-age story, a narrative about the emerging self-awareness of a white southerner destined to help shape the culture and community of the postwar South.[36]

Yet although Faulkner demonstrated an allegiance to certain regional and racist traditions, *The Unvanquished* offers a more complex vision of the Civil War and race relations than it may at first seem to. Careful readers have been quick to point out that in the treatment of the slave Ringo, Bayard's boyhood friend and companion, and in the portrait of slaves "moving along the roads at night toward their 'homemade Jordan,'" Faulkner departed from the novelists of the 1930s who made "little or no effort to view the war of slavery from the Negro's point of view." Ringo's presence is so strong in the early chapters of the book that Bayard often narrates using the words "we" and "us" rather than "I." Moreover, Bayard often appears far less tangible than his companion. "The boy who is the main actor in this novel is at first shadowy and indistinct," one commentator observed, "not a strong personality. We form no clear picture of him. He is overshadowed by his Negro playfellow and intimate friend, Ringo." For critics who read the novel exclusively as *Bayard's* story, this phenomenon "illustrates confusion in the novel's focus." One scholar bemoaned the amusing sequence involving Granny, Ringo, and the forged requisition papers for army mules. "[The] whole episode probably runs on too long in relation to Bayard's story. He is not even a major participant in these events, his place being taken by Ringo."[37]

I do not believe that Bayard's story is compromised by the presence of Ringo. If anything, I would argue that the reverse is true. Throughout the first half of the novel, Ringo stands as the most compelling, charismatic, and interesting of the characters. It is therefore regrettable that we do not hear Ringo tell in his own voice of his childhood and adolescent experiences. At moments in the narrative, it almost seems that Faulkner *wanted* to turn the novel over to Ringo but felt bound by convention, or his own biases, to maintain a white storyteller.[38] I nonetheless admire his decision to create in Bayard a character who, via his youth and temperament, can see in his black companion a reflection of himself—and therefore freely acknowledge his friend's considerable intellect and wit. Early in the novel, the boys are nearly at one with each other. As Bayard explains, "That's how Ringo and I were. We were almost the same age, and Father always said that Ringo was a little smarter than I was, but that didn't count with us, anymore than the difference in the color of our skins counted."[39]

Such passages emphasize the system of exchange that exists between Bayard's story and the story of the black characters. Soon after the novel opens, for example, Faulkner upset the racial divide separating Bayard from Ringo. Narrating from an unknown point in his adulthood, Bayard recalls: "Ringo and I had been born in the same month and had both fed at the same breast and had slept together and eaten together for so long that Ringo called Granny 'Granny' just like I did, until maybe he wasn't a nigger anymore or maybe I wasn't a white boy anymore, the two of us neither, not even people any longer: the two supreme undefeated like two moths, two feathers riding above a hurricane" (7). It seems no accident that Bayard here characterizes himself and Ringo—two boys whose similarities transcend race and even their respective roles as people—with the word *undefeated*. As we have seen, Faulkner used this same term elsewhere to describe "spinster aunts" who never surrendered; used here, *within* the context of the war, "undefeated" refers to Bayard's and Ringo's ability to transcend the limitations of the war itself. Not actual combatants, they are free to change race, name, and nationality: "The arrangement," Bayard explains, "was that I would be [Confederate] General Pemberton twice in succession and Ringo would be Grant, then I would have to be Grant once so Ringo could be General Pemberton" (7). It would seem, therefore, that the boys remain "undefeated" by virtue of their *distance* from the battlefield and the fact that they wear civilian clothing rather than the blue or gray. Yes, the boys play at war and assume the identities of soldiers, but their relationship—one where black spills into white—overshadows the war's military dimension. The Civil War here exists as a tool to illustrate their shared, multiracial experience. It functions as the hurricane that buoys the boys up like "two feathers," temporarily freeing each from the cultural restraints of the earth.

In *The Unvanquished*, therefore, the relationship between white and black Americans eclipses the physical war as fought in the fields and waters of Virginia, Tennessee, and Mississippi. We see this development early in the novel. Coming upon the miniature version of Vicksburg that Bayard and Ringo have constructed out of wood chips, dirt, and well water, the slave

Loosh stoops down and sweeps the chips "flat." "There's your Vicksburg," he tells the boys (5). At face value, Loosh's action reflects his belief that Grant has captured the crucial city, and that Union troops will soon occupy the countryside.[40] In a deeper sense, however, his action sweeps aside the military dimension of the war itself, calling attention instead to Loosh and to the role that slavery and emancipation play in the conflict. Admittedly, the boys reconstruct the miniature Vicksburg after the interruption, but Faulkner and Loosh have together ended the novel's interest in large-scale engagements and famous generals. For example, when Colonel Sartoris returns home for a brief stay, Bayard and Ringo expect to hear tales of "Forrest and Morgan and Barksdale and Van Dorn; the words like Gap and Run which we didn't have in Mississippi even though we did own Barksdale" (15). But instead of telling of Confederate heroes or describing "the cannon and the flags and the anonymous yelling," the Colonel sends the boys to bed (15, 17). Bayard's waking and sleeping thoughts thereafter focus not on Lost Cause heroes but on his anxieties concerning Loosh. The boy tells Ringo of a dream in which his father warns him to study Loosh closely: "Father said to watch Loosh, because he knows. . . . That he would know before we did. Father said that Louvinia would have to watch him too, that even if he was her son, she would have to be white a little while longer. Because if we watched him, we could tell by what he did when it was getting ready to happen" (20–21). Loosh therefore acts as the figure through which Bayard, and the reader, come to study and anticipate the future—the future of the war, the family, and the South itself. Moreover, he prompts Bayard and the reader to consider how race cannot itself determine human thought and behavior. Louvinia, though black, can "be white" in mind and action. And Bayard, though white, might in time sympathize with Loosh's aspirations for change.

Indeed, if the novel develops a clear connection between Bayard and Ringo, it also develops a complex connection between Bayard and Loosh. Bayard's fascination with Loosh arises not only from his fear of the slave's physical size and "knowledge" of the future but also from the man's intense desire for freedom. Bayard at first believes Loosh has "been drinking" when he flattens the boys' model of Vicksburg (4) but soon discovers a less mundane reason for the man's red eyes: "[He wore] that look on his face again which resembled drunkenness but was not, as if he had not slept in a long time and did not want to sleep now" (22). Unlike the stereotypically content and loyal slave of Lost Cause narratives, Loosh has awakened to the possibilities of freedom. He eagerly awaits the arrival of Northern troops and the autonomy they promise to bring. By the end of the novel, Bayard too seeks freedom from cultural expectations regarding his class, gender, and family. His childhood obsession with Loosh therefore reveals something of his own embryonic will to remain "undefeated."

Faulkner conflates the two characters in an episode directly preceding the first appearance of Northern soldiers at the Sartoris property. Overheard by Bayard and Ringo, Loosh makes an excited announcement to the other slaves upon his return from a secret voyage toward Corinth: "Ginral Sherman gonter sweep the earth and the Race gonter all be free!" (23). When Bayard rushes to relate the news to his grandmother, ostensibly to warn her, his own excited words spill out in a way that collapses the distance between himself and Loosh:

> We ran into the room where Granny was sitting beside the lamp with the bible open on her lap and her neck arched to look at us across her spectacles. "They're coming here!" I said. "They're coming to set us free!"
> "What?" she said.
> "Loosh saw them! They're just down the road. It's General Sherman and he's going to make us all free!" (23)

Though amusing and ironic, this episode is a revealing one. By placing the words of Loosh in Bayard's mouth, Faulkner suggested that, for both characters, the war represents the opportunity for dramatic social change.[41]

Of course, some readers might object to the use of black slavery as a metaphor for the social conventions that confine white southerners. No matter how restrictive the customs that surround Bayard, he never shares with Loosh the dehumanizing and psychologically damaging experience of slavery. Yet while Faulkner surely used the story of Loosh to comment on (and lend meaning to) Bayard's struggle to break free of cultural traditions, he also understood the difference between figurative and institutionalized slavery. In a passage that strikes hard against the content of Lost Cause memoirs and conventional southern literature, Faulkner allowed Loosh to assert his autonomy and justify his decision to assist and follow the Union troops: "I going," he tells Granny, "I done been freed; God's own angel proclamated me free and gonter general me to Jordan. I dont belong to John Sartoris now; I belongs to me and God" (75). When Granny argues that Loosh has sinned by showing the Yankees where the Sartoris silver is buried, Loosh speaks with dignity and arresting logic: "You ax me that?" Loosh said. "Where John Sartoris? Whyn't he come and ax me that? Let God ax John Sartoris who the man name that give me to him. Let the man that buried me in the black dark ax that of the man what dug me free" (75). Not only does Loosh here remove himself from the "faithful slave" stereotype that occupied "a more or less official status in the Confederate myth," but he also departs from the figure of the greedy, oversexed, and mindless runaway so often vilified in sensational southern novels as a product of Yankee intervention within southern culture.[42]

Loosh's poignant critique of a society where human beings exist as property reflects Faulkner's decision to offer a demilitarized portrait of the war. Where, among accounts of cavalry maneuvers and naval battles, might the figure of Loosh have appeared to voice the aforementioned sentiments? Could the voice of a single slave hope to compete with the sheer volume of the Rebel yell, or with reminiscences of roaring cannon and cursing generals? Even narratives penned by Northern veterans who fought with Negro regiments usually understood the black experience in terms of combat alone. Rather than dwell on the "contraband" slaves whose sheer number and offers of assistance reflected a deep zeal for freedom, Union memoirists usually reflected on the "stubborn bravery" of black troops under fire. Black veterans who wrote about the war could themselves let memories of combat obscure the larger story of the African American experience. David W. Blight points out that Joseph T. Wilson's work *The Black Phalanx* (1888) recounted the military sacrifices of black troops, from the Revolutionary War through the Civil War, in order to "deliver a vigorous defense of black manhood and devotion to country." Similarly, in his essay "Colored Soldiers in the Union Army" (1887), George Mike Arnold sought to "overcome the black soldier's invisibility in the nation's memory." Both Wilson and Arnold emphasized black military service largely in order to justify emancipation, but the attention to arms could obscure the courage of black noncombatants, especially women, who likewise risked everything for freedom.[43]

Immediately after Loosh and Philadelphy leave the Sartoris property for their "Jordan," readers encounter the chapter "Raid," Faulkner's most evocative representation of the racial struggle underlying the Civil War. Countering the notion that black Americans played a passive role in the struggle, Faulkner here illustrated slaves taking action to free themselves.

Moreover, he explained those actions in terms of the universal impulses of all humankind. Early in the chapter, Bayard connects Ringo's obsession with the railroad to the growing search among African Americans for movement and change:

> It was as if Ringo felt . . . that the railroad, the rushing locomotive which he hoped to see symbolized it—the motion, the impulse to move which had already seethed to a head among his people, darker than themselves, reasonless, following and seeking a delusion, a dream, a bright shape which they could not know since there was nothing in their heritage, nothing in the memory even of the old men to tell the others, "This is what we will find"; he nor they could not have known what is was yet it was there—one of those impulses inexplicable yet invincible which appear among races of people at intervals and drive them to pick up and leave all security and familiarity of earth and home and start out, they dont know where, empty handed, blind to everything but a hope and a doom. (81)

At first reading, Bayard's assessment of the black search for freedom sounds nearly like a critique. Here the "darker" impulses of African Americans seem questionable indeed, inspiring man, woman, and child to seek a "reasonless . . . delusion." For every glimmer of hope, there exists the equal possibility of "doom." Yet Bayard's point of view actually reflects an amazing degree of impartiality. An adult narrator looking back on past events, he reserves judgment and never maligns Loosh, Philadelphy, or the other slaves he encountered on the road near Hawkhurst. Nor does he accuse them of having betrayed their masters and assisted the enemy. Rather, Bayard seems almost in awe of their determination and sense of purpose. Encountering scores of slaves moving toward the river in an effort to join the Union army and to achieve their freedom, he observes: "We might not have been there. We did not even ask them to let us through because we could look at their faces and know they couldn't have heard us" (103). These men and women seem beyond social critique; nothing about them invites Bayard to think of them as slaves, and little in his description calls attention to their station in life. His observations instead reflect on the universal and timeless quality of the slaves' blind exodus, removed from any particular people, race, time, setting, or conflict. In fact, we should notice the similarity, in both language and subject matter, between this passage and the Pickett's charge passage from *Intruder in the Dust*. Both begin by discussing the actions of a specific people, at a specific moment in time, but then expand to address a universal human impulse: to approach "the absolute edge of no return [and] sail irrevocably on and either find land or plunge over the world's roaring rim" (*Intruder in the Dust*, 195); to "leave all security and familiarity of earth and home and start out . . . blind to everything but a hope and a doom" (*Unvanquished*, 81).[44]

How should we react to the fact that Faulkner's work would invite us to blur the distinction between the Confederate war (symbolized by Pickett's charge) and the desperate African American bid for freedom? And what should we make of the paradoxical connection between a people gambling to preserve slavery and a people gambling to free themselves from that same institution? We might conclude that Faulkner meant to complicate any easy understanding of the South, depicting its various peoples as fundamentally similar despite their physical and cultural differences. Yet if it seems that the *Intruder in the Dust* passage, by winding backward to 1492 and the legendary edge of the earth, will forever sustain itself by virtue of its link to the larger mythologies of the Western world, then the *Unvanquished* passage signifies something even larger. In Faulkner's work, the temporary nearly always gives way to the universal and the timeless. The symbols and mythic figures of the Lost Cause, particular to a specific culture and race, cannot hope to compete with the more universal struggle for freedom that lay behind the Civil War. We therefore see that Faulkner's treatment of the conflict—even when reflecting elements of the Lost Cause—ultimately finds the slave's pursuit of freedom more meaningful than the pursuit of Southern independence.

Bayard's narrative, in fact, breaks down the Lost Cause story as rehearsed by Southern memoirists and novelists. He can state, for instance, that for all the childhood excitement of hearing war stories that featured Southern names and nearby places, the fact remained that "old men had been telling young men and boys about wars and fighting before they discovered how to write it down. . . . Because wars are wars: the same exploding powder when there was powder, the same thrust and parry of iron when there was not—one tale, one telling, the same as the next or the one before" (94). Contrary to Lost Cause rhetoric that would have Americans forever understand the Civil War as "*the* War," Bayard acknowledges that it will go down in history as just one among many vast and destructive armed conflicts. Faulkner himself noted in *Requiem for a Nun* that the sons of Confederate veterans had "already died in blue coats in Cuba" by 1900, and he lived through several of the twentieth century's major wars. The writer was not, therefore, fascinated with the Civil War because of its violence, courage, and national risks—elements nearly all wars have in common. Rather, aside from its relationship to his own family and region, "the racial equation" of 1861–65 captured his attention as "the most urgent moral issue involved in that past." As reflected in the voice of a civilian narrator who witnesses and participates in the war's racial struggles far more than in its military episodes, *The Unvanquished* subordinates mythology about heroes in gray to the "inexplicable yet invincible" impulses that propel races of men to risk everything for a better existence.[45]

At the end of the novel, the connection between Bayard and Loosh remains intact. Bayard remains unvanquished insofar as he has rebelled against a society that would have him shed the blood of his father's murderer, yet has still found a way to maintain the respect of his peers. (George Wyatt tells him: "I wouldn't have done it that way, myself. I'd a shot at him once, anyway. But that's your way" [250–51]). Less visible, but similarly undefeated, are the Looshes of southern society—those who remain within that oppressive culture but who understand that the war had not yet ended. The Yankees had failed to carry them all to a promised land, and the place of blacks in southern society remained a subservient one, but African Americans had signaled their willingness to stand up and act out their own latent impulses. For Faulkner, who believed ardently that black men and women would have to re-create their own role in the South, the journey to "Jordan" represents something closer to a triumph than a folly.[46]

III.

If critics have at times referred to *The Unvanquished* as "Faulkner Lite" because of its relatively direct plot and chronology (Faulkner himself thought it his easiest book to read), *Absalom, Absalom!* ranks among his most complex.[47] Narrated by multiple characters who freely invent plot, action, and dialogue while telling the story of Thomas Sutpen and his family, the novel also employs a detached third-person narrator and a complicated temporal scheme. Interestingly, Faulkner wrote *Absalom, Absalom!* at the same time he wrote and published the short stories later adapted for *The Unvanquished*. If the two novels diverge in terms of presentation and marketability, they nonetheless share a civilian's perspective on the Civil War.

As with the story of Bayard and Ringo on the home front, here the war exists as a distant phenomenon—one represented primarily by the names of faraway battles, imagined scenes of Henry and Charles Bon in camp, and a "citation for valor in Lee's own hand" brought home by Sutpen.[48] But even more so than in the later novel, in *Absalom, Absalom!* Faulkner used that civilian vantage point to challenge the most basic tenets of the Lost Cause. Time and again the novel questions the noble principles of the Confederate war, the quality of its people, and even the mythic ability of its leaders. Richard Gray explained the differences between the two novels by arguing that Faulkner "was using *The Unvanquished* as a kind of safety-valve, a means of indulging in forms of closure and feelings [of] nostalgia that he simply could not and would not entertain in *Absalom, Absalom!*"[49] While even Faulkner himself may have underappreciated the complexities of Bayard's story, he certainly saw *Absalom, Absalom!* as the more important achievement.[50] During the revision process, he told screenwriter Dave Hempstead, "I think it's the best novel yet written by an American." His serious approach to the novel did not, apparently, leave room to entertain the romance of Confederate mythology.[51]

A comparison between the two novels reveals the far harsher handling of the Lost Cause in *Absalom, Absalom!* In *The Unvanquished*, Bayard recalls a late war "sermon" delivered by Brother Fortinbride, a wounded veteran-turned-minister: "He never talked long. There wasn't much anybody could say about the Confederate armies now; I reckon there is a time when even preachers quit believing that God is going to change His plan and give victory where there is nothing left to hang victory on." Though not effusive in his praise for the South and its sacred cause, the veteran nonetheless offers his auditors the Myth's standard response to Northern victory. Fortinbride "just said how victory without God is mockery and delusion, but that defeat with God is not defeat. Then he quit talking" (136). These words, delivered in a church no less, reflect what for many southerners became "a civil religion that helped them link their sense of loss to a Christian conception of history."[52] By contrast, in *Absalom, Absalom!* we find the Lost Cause turned on its head. Rather than work as the basis for a civil religion that defines a culture, the basic features of the Myth function in the novel as nothing more than liabilities, damning the Confederacy to loss after loss.[53]

> [It] was '64 and then '65 and the starved ragged remnant of an army . . . retreated across Alabama and Georgia and into Carolina, swept

onward not by a victorious army behind it but rather by a mounting tide of the names of lost battles from either side—Chickamauga and Franklin, Vicksburg and Corinth and Atlanta—battles lost not alone because of superior numbers and failing ammunition and stores, but because of generals who should not have been generals, who were generals not through training in contemporary methods or aptitude for learning them, but by the divine right to say 'Go there' conferred upon them by an absolute caste system; or because the generals of it never lived long enough to learn how to fight massed cautious accretionary battles, since they were already as obsolete as Richard or Roland or du Guesclin, who wore plumes and cloaks lined with scarlet. (276)

Here the noble ancestry of knightly Southern generals, so often glorified and exaggerated in romantic treatments of the Confederacy, appear as a partial explanation for the nation's defeat. Obsolete, incapable of negotiating the vicissitudes of modern warfare, and drawing authority from a "caste system" rather than true prowess and power of mind, the generals themselves doom Southern arms at least as much as do failing ammunition and inferior numbers.[54]

Faulkner also challenged other attributes of the Lost Cause, such as the tendency in southern narratives to exalt the Christian virtues of Confederate soldiers, what Alan T. Nolan has called "The Saints Go Marching In" legend. Rosa Coldfield undermines this element early in the novel, when she describes the "demon" Sutpen: "Oh he was brave. I have never gainsaid that. But that our cause, our very life and future hopes and past pride, should have been thrown into the balance with men like that to buttress it—men with valor and strength but without pity or honor. Is it any wonder that Heaven saw fit to let us lose?" (13). Some might argue that Rosa errs in conflating Sutpen's dubious morality with that of Southern society and its cause. Yet as Donald M. Kartiganer has argued, "Thomas Sutpen is, in his basic intentions and in the fundamental characteristics of his methods, an image of the pre–Civil War Southern plantation owner." While Sutpen's primitive brutality seems to distance him from other men of property, "Faulkner is quick to indicate the basic brutality in the whole plantation system. If Sutpen horrifies the community, it is largely because he is a pure, naked version of its own deepest principles, the incarnation of those values and attitudes that enable a slave system to survive." As with his critique of officers of high birth and breeding, in the figure of the mountain-born

Sutpen, a scoundrel masquerading as a gentleman, Faulkner cut away at the virtues of mythic Southern gentility.[55]

In fact, to the degree that he represents Southern respectability as a veneer stretched thin over the violence and brutality of slavery, Faulkner showed that the Lost Cause itself works to mask the disturbing realities of Southern culture. As he was aware, many postwar apologists characterized the Confederacy in righteous terms; a line engraved on several postwar monuments read: "Never was there a land so white and pure and fell so free of sin."[56] Yet even if proponents of the Lost Cause took such rhetoric to heart, it would seem that their words belied an unspoken (and perhaps unconscious) admission of mythmaking. After all, no one could deny that millions of enslaved black men, women, and children existed within the Confederacy, that mythic "land so white." Indeed, a major motivation for the rise of the Lost Cause was the wish to forget not only the centrality of slavery to the war but slavery itself. Masking memory of a hostile and inhumane institution, narratives of the Southern past often portrayed black men and women as faithful servants, not slaves. Indeed, as reflected in the previously mentioned monument engraving, it even became possible—through the transformative power of memory—to claim that the South never sinned, never lost its purity, and never required black labor to make white gentility possible.

Departing from the mythic fold, Faulkner examined openly the South's guilt over slavery. In section 4 of "The Bear," as published in *Go Down, Moses* (1942), Ike McCaslin argues that white society had poisoned his region by introducing slavery to the land: "'Dont you see?' he cried [to the black man]. 'Dont you see? This whole land, the whole South, is cursed, and all of us who derive from it, whom it ever suckled, white and black both, lie under the curse? Granted that my people brought the curse onto the land: maybe for that reason their descendants alone can—not resist it, not combat it—maybe just endure and outlast it until the curse is lifted.'"[57] In *Absalom, Absalom!* Faulkner similarly shattered the Lost Cause portrait of a sinless white society. Indeed, the voices in the novel often admit to the evils inherent in human bondage. The narrative identifies the war as "a stupid and bloody aberration in the high (and impossible) destiny of the United States," brought on not by a national dispute concerning states' rights but "maybe instigated by that family fatality which possessed, along with all circumstance, that curious lack of economy between cause and effect which is always a characteristic of fate when reduced to using human beings for tools, material" (94). Mr. Coldfield later supports the idea that the South had to suffer for its use of human tools, predicting "that day when the South would realise that it was now paying the price for having erected its economic edifice not on the rock of stern morality but on the shifting sands of opportunism and moral brigandage" (209).[58]

The price of such moral brigandage seems especially clear when viewed from the civilian point of view. In *The Unvanquished,* Aunt Louisa identifies the "highest destiny of a Southern woman" as that of a "bride-widow of a lost cause," suggesting that sorrow and loss will help to define Southern womanhood long years after the war (191). Although some Southerners could find a frame of reference with which to interpret their losses, in *Absalom, Absalom!* the conflict often seems alien and illogical to civilians on the home front. Rosa Coldfield's father, for example, sees the war as little more than a colossal waste of the South's valuable resources. A merchant and Methodist steward who hides from Confederate service, he objects "not so much to the idea of pouring out human blood and life, but at the idea of waste: of wearing out and eating up and shooting away material in any cause whatever" (65). Combined with his dismay over the dependence on slave labor in the South, Coldfield's point of view strays far from any romantic, military vision of the Confederate war effort. He understands the conflict primarily as an economic disaster, one that destroys not only the "edifice" of slavery but also the South's store of food and materiel.

Yet if *Absalom, Absalom!* strikes out against Confederate mythology and its vision of the war, what should we make of the fact that one of its primary narrators, Rosa Coldfield, stands as a prolific source of Lost Cause mythmaking? We learn that only one year into her father's "voluntary incarceration" in his attic, where he hid from the Confederate provost marshal's men, Rosa had already compiled a massive portfolio of "odes to Southern soldiers" (65). Numbering "a thousand or more" and written feverishly "at two oclock in the morning" (65), her odes are works of devotion "in which the lost cause's unregenerate vanquished were name by name embalmed" (6). Several critics have read Rosa simply as a "patriot-poetess of the Confederacy," a romantic writer whose work reflects the "curse and glory of her own legendary South."[59] Few seem to understand that by recording the names of "vanquished" men, Rosa seeks and achieves an impressive degree of cultural power. Witness, for example, the striking contrast between the awakened and unvanquished Rosa and the defeated soldiers she writes about, men powerless in their "embalmed" and lifeless state. The distinction is an important one. Whereas most narratives of the Civil War insist that generals and battles shaped the civilian experience (particularly that of women), here Faulkner suggested that the reverse could also be true—that the civilian commanded the power to record, interpret, and shape understanding of the war's military dimension. And by doing so, the noncombatant might stake a claim to authority and social relevance. The novel underscores this point by observing, ironically, that the county's foremost Lost Cause poet should be Rosa, "a woman whose family's martial background as both town and county knew consisted of the father who, a conscientious objector on religious grounds, had starved to death in the attic of his own house" (6). It would seem that in Faulkner's world, civilians require no martial connections whatsoever to understand and interpret the war—in fact, the *further* one stands from the battlefield, the deeper one's "bitter and implacable reserve of undefeat" (6).

Rosa therefore occupies a uniquely authoritative position in *Absalom, Absalom!* For unlike Quentin and Shreve and Mr. Compson, she alone experienced and remembers the war. As a result, her voice functions as the all-important connection between the past and the present, demanding the same attention (and even reverence) typically afforded the old soldiers who took up the pen and the podium. Of course, many scholars have in turn frowned upon Rosa as a narrator, character, and institution. Some have dismissed her insights altogether. "At best, Rosa is an utter snob," Kartiganer declared, "at worst, she represents precisely that kind of weak-minded hatefulness which is the life-blood of a society built along strict class lines, or any society where the idea of status quo becomes the highest good." As this assessment suggests, just as critics see Rosa as toeing the line of the Lost Cause, they often also believe her incapable of thinking in iconoclastic ways. Admittedly, it can be difficult to reconcile the racist and conservative Rosa to her statements falling outside the range of conventional southern rhetoric.

Such difficulty surely applies to Rosa's famous admission, prompted by the touch of Clytie: "*But let flesh touch with flesh, and watch the fall of all the eggshell shibboleth of caste and color too*" (112). Kartiganer observed that Rosa is here "uttering a wisdom that is quite beyond her capability," a statement with which other commentators have agreed. But rather than dismiss this moment in the novel as an aberration, I believe we must judge Rosa's entire narrative in light of her words concerning relationships that cross "caste and color too." Her epiphany, an understanding that divisions of race and class are just "*devious intricate channels of decorous ordering*"

(112), is made all the more powerful by the fact that we *know* she is a racist. No matter how fleeting, that moment's realization paralyzes her and throws into doubt the divisive cultural constructions on which she depends. She can and does return to those constructions, of course, but neither she nor the reader can again trust their value and integrity.[60]

Rosa's ability to see beneath the racism of her society—even if briefly, even if against her will—should complicate our understanding of the story she tells. Too many readers take at face value Rosa's early statement that she "saw Judith's marriage forbidden without rhyme or reason or shadow of excuse" (12) and hence determine that the old woman remains oblivious to the powerful role of race within the Sutpen story. With regard to Rosa's view of Henry shooting Charles Bon, his own half-brother, Kartiganer asked: "[Who] can doubt that, had she known the truth of the potential incest and miscegenation, she herself would have urged Henry to shoot him?"[61] Similarly, Cleanth Brooks argued that Rosa "clearly does not understand what happened" between Henry and Charles Bon and concluded that she knows nothing of Bon's possible black ancestry.[62] But her understanding of the Sutpen family history, as of the war itself, is far from simple.[63] For example, if we know that her writing dwells on military themes unrelated to slavery, we also know that Faulkner chose never to reproduce her Lost Cause poetry or share the contents of her folios. Ironically, then, Rosa's most important narrative role in the novel occupies ground outside of the "poems, ode eulogy and epitaph" that she publishes in the Jefferson newspaper (6). We see her true narrative achievement unfold within the pages of Faulkner's novel itself, with her determination to explain the downfall of Sutpen's Hundred. Admittedly, the novel does not always make the woman's motivations clear. Mr. Compson suggests that "the real reason" Miss Rosa tells her story to Quentin relates to the fact that "your grandfather was the nearest thing to a friend which Sutpen ever had in this county. . . . She may believe that if it hadn't been for your grandfather's friendship, Sutpen could never have got a foothold here. . . . So maybe she considers you partly responsible through heredity for what happened to her and her family through him" (8). This conjecture may hold real merit, but it explains Rosa's motivations only if we consider her story in the narrowest of terms. If we accept that "Faulkner's purpose as historical novelist [was] to reveal the past of his community," then we must accept that Rosa seeks to relate the story of Sutpen and his family not merely to account for "what happened to her," but to account for what happened to the South itself.[64]

Rosa appears to have realized that her literary devotion to Southern arms has prevented her from telling the story of how the white South's moral failings destroyed it from within. To make amends, she grows determined to communicate with younger generations. She tells Quentin:

> Because you are going away to attend the college at Harvard they tell me. . . . So I don't imagine you will ever come back here and settle down as a country lawyer in a little town like Jefferson. . . . So maybe you will enter the literary profession as so many Southern gentlemen and gentlewomen too are going now and maybe some day you will remember this and write about it. You will be married then I expect and perhaps your wife will want a new gown or a new chair for the house and you can write this and submit it to the magazines. Perhaps you will even remember kindly then the old woman who made you spend a whole afternoon sitting indoors and listening while she talked about people and events you were fortunate enough to escape yourself when you wanted to be out among young friends of your own age. (5)

Quentin puzzles over these words for a long while, knowing that the woman could simply write and publish the history on her own. Though he eventually accepts his father's rationale for why Rosa summoned him, Faulkner suggested that Quentin's first reaction hits closer to the mark, when he understands Rosa's story as having meaning for those well beyond the boundaries of Jefferson: "*It's because she wants it told* he thought *so that people whom she will never see and whose names she will never hear and who have never heard her name nor seen her face will read it and know at last why God let us lose the War: that only through the blood of our men and the tears of our women could He stay this demon and efface his name and lineage from the earth*" (6). Quentin may here uncover not only Rosa's reasons for telling her story but also Faulkner's. By relating how and why the transgressions of Sutpen brought about the murder of one son by the other, both Rosa and Faulkner can illustrate how the purging of slavery—what the novel calls the "disease" and "sickness" of the South (7)—required the blood and tears of thousands of men and women.

If *The Unvanquished* connects Bayard to Loosh through their mutual refusal to conform to social expectations, Faulkner drew a similar connection between Rosa and Charles Bon—one that grows clearer as the novel progresses. Early in *Absalom, Absalom!* Mr. Compson explains to Quentin: "Years ago we in the South made our women into ladies. Then the War came and made the ladies into ghosts. So what else can we do, being gentlemen, but listen to them being ghosts?" (6–7). By the end of the novel, however, it has become clear that Rosa has denied her identity as a phantom. (Indeed, that role seems instead occupied by the men who fought the war and who, like Henry Sutpen in his final days at Sutpen's Hundred, seem quietly to haunt the vestiges of the Old South.) As Shreve observes in a late conversation with Quentin, Rosa has rebelled against convention by digging up the past. "All right. You dont even know about her. Except that she refused at the last to be a ghost. That after almost fifty years she couldn't reconcile herself to letting him lie dead in peace. That even after fifty years she not only could get up and go out there to finish up what she found she hadn't quite completed, but she could find someone to go with her and bust into that locked house because instinct or something told her it was not finished yet" (289–90). Charles Bon, too, refuses to let the status quo go unchallenged. Unwilling to be confined by social symbols and ceremonies, at one point Bon ridicules the idea of a marriage ceremony, one of the most traditional and commonplace of social rituals: "Ah. That ceremony. I see. That's it, then. A formula, a shibboleth meaningless as a child's game, performed by someone created by the situation whose need it answered . . . a ritual as meaningless as that of college boys in secret rooms at night, even to the same archaic and forgotten symbols?" (93). It would therefore seem that both Rosa and Charles Bon, sharing a common disdain for "shibboleths," seek to expose and undermine the cultural barriers that distance one man from the next. Granted, Rosa only assails these barriers late in life. (In her career as a Lost Cause poet, she had of course *reinforced* the South's symbols, ceremonies, and hierarchies.) And she never sheds entirely her society's prejudices. Nonetheless, her changing allegiances afford her the credentials necessary to initiate the telling of Charles Bon's story.

In the logic of the novel, Sutpen's "black" son becomes the key to the entire narrative. Because his mother may have had black ancestry, Charles Bon becomes a threat to Sutpen's "design" when he seeks to marry Sutpen's daughter Judith. Shreve comments shrewdly on the central place of Sutpen's oldest son within the family story: "So it took Charles Bon and his mother to get rid of old Tom, and Charles Bon and the octoroon to get rid of Judith, and Charles Bon and Clytie to get rid of Henry; and Charles Bon's mother and Charles Bon's grandmother got rid of Charles Bon" (302).

The constant repetition of Bon's name alone reflects his importance to the novel's narrative structure, but his personality also plays a crucial role in the story, representing "the force of a new time, a new kind of order to be contrasted with the prevailing ethic of Thomas Sutpen." Showing something of his father's resolve to act on one's impulses (but doing so for the sake of ideology rather than personal gain), Charles Bon seeks Judith's hand in marriage. While perhaps doing so with a martyr's sense of self-satisfaction, his words and actions seem designed to awaken others to the prejudices that grip them. When Henry refuses to shoot Bon in camp, objecting "*You are my brother,*" the latter famously says: "*No I'm not. I'm the nigger that's going to sleep with your sister. Unless you stop me, Henry*" (286). With these words, Charles Bon means to challenge his half-brother, to open his eyes to the fact that his community and nation would prefer any taboo to miscegenation. As he states, "*So it's the miscegenation, not the incest, which you cant bear*" (285).[65]

The reader, of course, knows, just as Bon does, that Henry *will* shoot down his own brother. And that knowledge raises the dramatic stakes all the more: we understand that fratricide, too, is less taboo than the threat posed by "just 'a little spot of negro blood—'" (247). Here Faulkner appeared to once again reflect on the nature of the Civil War, a conflict portrayed increasingly during the twentieth century as a war between brothers, fought over the issue of race. Yet in Faulkner's hands, race existed as the foremost cause of the war (more than states' rights or the economy) precisely because it was the most *human* of causes, influencing the actions of men and women no matter what their color. His characters may indeed remain racist, violent, and morally flawed, but like Rosa they can at moments realize that common humanity supersedes social divisions, that "*there is something in the touch of flesh with flesh which abrogates, cuts sharp and straight*" through man's artificial hierarchies (111). These moments of abrogation, no matter how rare, are what at once inspire and affirm Faulkner's vision of the Civil War.

IV.

The ending of *Absalom, Absalom!* set in 1909, encapsulates Faulkner's demilitarized approach to the war. Having broken into the dilapidated Sutpen's Hundred with the help of Quentin, Rosa confronts the frail and dying Henry Sutpen where he lies in a second-floor bedroom. The meeting represents more than just a reunion of old relations; it also constitutes a meeting between Faulkner's civilian narrator and the exiled soldier whose voice she has displaced. Blight pointed out that published accounts of the war often "were collaborative family creations where wives, daughters, and sons fashioned a war record and a story for their veteran of choice." Almost always laudatory and devotional in nature, these accounts stood as literary monuments to aging and deceased men. In the logic of the late nineteenth-century South, then, Rosa could publish florid verse about fallen heroes from her family and community, but it was not her place to illuminate and criticize the immoralities of Thomas and Henry Sutpen. Because Henry was a veteran who fell wounded at the battle of Shiloh and who served and starved with the Confederate army, the story of Sutpen's Hundred was *his* to tell. He reserved the right to cast aspersions on Sutpen, and to evaluate Bon, because both were fellow soldiers during the war. Who might better understand the merits and faults of a soldier than his comrade-in-arms? Yet during the long years when so many real-life veterans had assessed the war and its personalities in print and oratory, Henry instead hides from the law and lives in shame. His silence creates a narrative vacuum ultimately filled by Rosa and her initiates from later generations.[66]

Interestingly, Faulkner never narrated the meeting between the sick and dying Henry and the aging Rosa. Seen from Quentin's perspective, Rosa emerges from the second-floor room wearing a wide-eyed expression that he interprets as conveying neither shock nor fear, but perhaps "triumph" (296). When Quentin himself makes his way into the room, he is overawed to discover above the bed linen the "wasted yellow face" and "wasted hands" of the seventy-year-old Henry. Although the youth does not himself feel triumph, the dialogue that follows makes it clear that Rosa *has* triumphed over Henry in at least one way: that she has become the narrator of his family's history.

> [Quentin asks:] *And you are——?*
> Henry Sutpen.
> And you have been here——?
> Four years.
> And you came home——?
> To die. Yes.
> To die?
> Yes. To die.
> And you have been here——?

> Four years.
> And you are——?
> *Henry Sutpen.* (298, italics in original)

Here we understand that Henry—incapacitated, concealed from the outside world, and appearing "as if he were already a corpse"—offers nothing in the way of an articulate voice (298). As reflected in his exchange with Quentin, he can at best assert his identity, name, and resignation to death. Henry lacks the narrative power to relate more than the most basic of facts and can only reflect on the war in the most tangential of ways, repeating the words "four years" in a manner that calls to mind the conflict's long duration. Destined to die in the blaze that will consume Sutpen's Hundred three months later, the old veteran exists almost entirely as an inert symbol of the tortured Southern past. His voice can neither compete with Rosa's nor shape the thinking of later generations. Not Henry's words, then, but a civilian's—and the imaginative detective story they inspire[67]—are what lead to Quentin's famous and ironic assessment of his relationship to the South: "'I dont hate it!' . . . *I dont hate it. . . . I dont. I dont! I dont hate it! I dont hate it!*" (303).

Perhaps some would respond to Quentin's confused anguish with sympathy and wonder whether Henry, given the opportunity, might have imparted a more nurturing vision of the South. But Faulkner cherished such "anguishes" of life, those which threatened "the fragile web of flesh and bone and mostly water" that comprises mankind.[68] Unlike the Lost Cause mythos that had reduced Quentin to a life among phantoms, Rosa's story forces the youth to grapple with the flesh and blood of his community. He comes to confront in its full complexities the issue of race, what Faulkner called, late in life, "simply and primarily a moral problem that has but one answer."[69]

Should we view this final portrait of Henry Sutpen as indicative of a callous view of Confederate veterans on Faulkner's part? Admittedly, it is tempting to see Faulkner's fiction as consistently lampooning or disgracing those who wore gray. That argument has been made most strongly by Clark, who believed Faulkner went "so far as to suggest that the so-called Southern cause was little more than the grand folly of foolish and immature males who may have seen themselves as saviors and heroes, but who were really the destroyers of their society and nearly destroyers of their country." She found the details of Faulkner's work particularly damning of Confederate "heroes." For example, because Faulkner depicted Colonel Sartoris as having a small physical stature in *The Unvanquished*, he must have aimed to comment on the soldier's "moral littleness" (113). "Faulkner does this consistently," Clark elaborated, "[and he] picks the absurd, the petty, the trivial episodes to represent its heroes. . . . He does this in *Light in August*, with Gail Hightower's great-grandfather, who was killed while robbing a henhouse during the War." Similarly, Lynn Levins has interpreted Faulkner's treatment of Confederates in *Flags in the Dust* and *Sartoris* as foolish rather than heroic: "By the extreme foolhardiness of a quest after anchovies, by the humiliating fact that the Carolina Bayard was shot in the back by a cook, Faulkner undercuts Aunt Jenny's [romantic] telling of the tale."[70]

These unromantic episodes, read in isolation, would seem to illustrate the author's wholesale attack against the defenders of the South. Yet because the Civil War and its participants so fascinated Faulkner, I believe it wrongheaded to see him as determined to portray Southern soldiers as simply immoral or foolish. His uniformed Confederates succeed and fail as do any other characters in Faulkner's fiction and deserve and receive the same balance of satire and admiration as any noncombatant. We see this phenomenon in *The Unvanquished*, where Uncle Buck can—in the same public speech—shout out that Colonel Sartoris is both a cunning military hero and "a coward and a fool" (53). Faulkner's world is complex enough to allow that *both* versions of Sartoris might and do coexist. If his flawed Confederates suggest anything, it would be that the Lost Cause had committed a grave disservice by so sanitizing and sanctifying the South's defenders. While *The Unvanquished, Absalom, Absalom!* and *Requiem for a Nun* silence those men who fought the war, these works reach out to them as well. Distancing veterans from the myths they helped create after 1865, Faulkner's fiction represents a significant attempt to rescue the humanity of the Confederate soldier from the cold marble and bronze of the Lost Cause.

Chapter Four

Each Man Has His Own Reason to Die
The Triumph of the Individual in *The Killer Angels*

In January 1993, Bantam Books published a paperback edition of Joshua Lawrence Chamberlain's 1915 memoir, *The Passing of the Armies*. Early in his introduction to the text, historian James M. McPherson explained how Chamberlain, a brevet major general in the Union army, has become one of "the best-known figures" of the Civil War: "Chamberlain's modern fame springs from his role as protagonist in Michael Shaara's *The Killer Angels*, a gripping epic of the battle of Gettysburg that won a Pulitzer Prize and has become a favorite assigned reading in college Civil War courses throughout the land. Sharing the spotlight in the novel with the likes of Robert E. Lee and James Longstreet, Chamberlain comes across to the reader as more heroic and human than either."[1] Nothing in this passage will surprise readers familiar with the widespread popularity of *The Killer Angels*. Millions of Americans have viewed the war and its personalities through the lens of the 1974 novel and the books and films it has inspired. The reputation of the once-obscure Chamberlain has soared; at least one scholar credited Shaara "with giving his country a legendary hero all its own" and with making the Maine professor and soldier "the largest commercial subject in the Civil War community."[2] What might surprise readers of McPherson's introduction, however, is what happens once the focus turns to the historical Chamberlain rather than Shaara's version. Aiming to enlarge his reader's knowledge beyond the fictional account of Gettysburg, McPherson explained that Chamberlain "went on to become one of the most remarkable soldiers of the Civil War—indeed, in all of American history."[3] Yet readers of *The Killer Angels* already know as much, because Shaara said so in his afterword, and with nearly those exact words. Though wounded, the novel states, Chamberlain went on "to become one of the most remarkable soldiers in American history."[4] McPherson likewise used other phrases from the novel's afterword, and again followed Shaara's language closely in noting that "Grant selected him [Chamberlain]—out of dozens of generals who ranked him—for the honor of receiving the Army of Northern Virginia's formal surrender."[5]

Should it matter that Shaara's words and emphases have influenced those of McPherson, arguably the foremost living historian of the Civil War era? I believe even those who answer "no" to this question might think twice on realizing that McPherson followed Shaara—on the issue of Chamberlain's role at Appomattox—into the complex world of Civil War myth. In *A Place Called Appomattox* (2000), William Marvel pointed out that "Chamberlain was the only original source of the claim that he commanded the surrender ceremony; he offered no witnesses or documentation, and none has been found." Marvel further explained that while the hero of *The Killer Angels* "undoubtedly was present" at the ceremony, he was "evidently not in formal command, and he certainly was not designated for that service by General Grant."[6] Rather than clarify the relationship between Shaara and McPherson, and between fiction and history, these observations muddy the waters all the more. Indirectly, the analysis by Marvel shows us that *The Killer Angels*, influenced by Chamberlain's mythmaking in *The Passing of the Armies*, has in turn influenced McPherson's "historical" account—an account meant by Bantam Books to introduce Chamberlain's narrative. As confusing as this circle of myth, fiction, and history may seem, it nonetheless suggests something about why *The Killer Angels* stands as the most popular Civil War novel published during the last fifty years. Though undoubtedly well crafted and narrated, Shaara's novel owes its tremendous success to the fact that it both reflects and perpetuates the words, interpretations, and mythologies of Civil War veterans. Carefully uniting elements from different veterans' traditions and individual memoirs, Shaara created a story that interprets the war in a way attractive to Americans of the late twentieth and early twenty-first centuries.

I.

The Killer Angels has appealed to a wide range of readers. A favorite among Civil War enthusiasts and the reading public at large, it also draws praise from academic historians. Elsewhere naming it his "favorite historical novel," McPherson explained: "It is a superb re-creation of the Battle of Gettysburg, but its real importance is its insight into what the war was about, and what it meant." Carol Reardon appreciated the work as "a tautly drawn psychodrama," and Stephen B. Oates lauded it as "the best Civil War novel ever written, even better than *The Red Badge of Courage.*" Oates's words in particular capture the place of *The Killer Angels* atop the mountain of Civil War fiction. Especially since the early 1990s, many readers have argued that Shaara's novel compares favorably to the Civil War works of Stephen Crane, Ambrose Bierce, William Faulkner, and other well-known writers. Indeed, the 1994 compilation *Three Great Novels of the Civil War,* edited by Marc Jaffe, gives *The Killer Angels* top billing over MacKinlay Kantor's *Andersonville* (1955) and Crane's *The Red Badge of Courage* (1895).[7]

By examining how *The Killer Angels* situates itself in relation to other literature and fictions of the war, we can better understand its relationship to veterans' narratives. Shaara chose to narrate the story of Gettysburg from the shifting point of view of seven of the battle's participants and witnesses, both North and South. Though not a wholly innovative approach (one thinks immediately of Shelby Foote's 1952 novel *Shiloh*), the decision sets *The Killer Angels* apart from the hundreds of Civil War romances, short stories, and novels told from the perspective of one side, Union or Confederate. Philip Beidler has noted that if readers in 1974 found this approach "quirky," they nonetheless embraced it as an "ingenious expedient for conveying the human dimension of the battle." This observation would have pleased Shaara. As he made clear in the "To the Reader" section that begins the novel, humanity stood as his primary subject. Unlike those fictions that gloss over individuals in their effort to capture the epic sweep of the war, *The Killer Angels* stays close to the men who did the fighting.[8]

Shaara made this point by associating his novel with an earlier work already well known to most readers, *The Red Badge of Courage.* Claiming *The Killer Angels* was written "for much the same reason" as Stephen Crane's novel, he suggested that his book was interested primarily in "what it was like to *be* there" (vii). The comparison also allowed him—even before the novel opened—to assert his work's objectivity. Those readers familiar with *The Red Badge of Courage* might remember it as a story seemingly uninterested in the political and moral dimensions of the war. For many Americans, Crane's classic exists as a nonpartisan narrative. And at first blush, *The Killer Angels,* which depicts the thoughts and actions of men from both sides of the conflict, seems similarly neutral in its approach.

Yet despite these similarities, readers familiar with both novels have reason to doubt Shaara's claim that he wrote his for much the same reason as Crane. For instance, some might wonder why Shaara told his story from the perspective of elite officers rather than common soldiers: four of the seven are generals, six are commissioned officers, and none is an enlisted man. Why not focus on privates, such as Crane's Henry Fleming? Might not this approach have allowed Shaara to better "live" the battle (vii), away from the distractions of strategy, officer in-fighting, and towering political and military personalities? Moreover, why should a narrative meant to explore "what men's faces looked like" (vii) require the foreword Shaara offered, in which he contextualized the battle, provided background on the novel's major characters, and commented on the religion and literacy of the two armies (ix–x)? Certainly Crane included nothing of the sort in *The Red Badge of Courage*. (Crane not only refused to provide background but also maintained Fleming's virtual anonymity for a good portion of the book.) Admittedly, Shaara might have defended his choices in any number of ways, one being that his characters—Chamberlain and Gen. Lewis A. Armistead in particular—lend insight into both the realities of battle and the big picture unrealized by privates. The fact that these officers understand the significance of Little Round Top and the Angle, respectively, intensifies the novel's portrait of the desperate fighting experienced there.[9] And perhaps Shaara believed that readers would require background on the war, and the men involved, in order to imagine Gettysburg. After all, even those who admire *The Red Badge of Courage* have argued that Crane's novel fails to provide enough in the way of context. Yet no matter what we might speculate about the rationale behind Shaara's decisions, the fact remains that his first words to the reader, "This is the story of the Battle of Gettysburg" (vii), seem emblematic of a different kind of book than Crane's, which never once names the battle it describes.

Perhaps a more substantial objection to Shaara's linking his novel to *The Red Badge of Courage* concerns these works' differing approaches to the past. As Shaara suggested, Crane's novel aims not to interpret the war but to re-create, as nearly as possible, the sights, sounds, and fear of a Civil War battle. In this sense, *The Red Badge of Courage* operates as a work of literary reenactment, a haphazard and even dangerous endeavor insofar as its author abandons the comfort and familiarity of his own historical moment. Crane and his protagonist find themselves swept along by the traumas of the past, frequently lost in the fog and desperation of battle. By contrast, neither *The Killer Angels* nor its author ever forfeits control, no matter how traumatic the subject matter. Unlike Crane, Shaara strove to contain the confusion and largeness of the battle and war. "I have condensed some of the action," he informed the reader, "for the sake of clarity, and eliminated some minor characters, for brevity" (vii). He admitted, too, to changing the men's verbiage: "I have changed some of the language. It was a naïve and sentimental time, and men spoke in windy phrases" (vii). Perhaps few would fault Shaara for altering the soldiers' language, but we might wince at his explanation for doing so, which seems to condescend to the past: "I thought it necessary to update some of the words so that the religiosity and naiveté of the time, which were genuine, would not seem too quaint to the modern ear. I hope I will be forgiven that" (vii). The fact that readers *have* forgiven him suggests that Shaara knew something about the modern mind as well as the "modern ear." Issues of religiosity aside, he knew he would not raise the ire of many readers by twice calling nineteenth-century Americans "naïve" in the space of two sentences. As a writer of popular fiction, Shaara's fingers were pressed firmly to the pulse of the American public. Time and again he exploited his readers' foregone conclusions about the Civil War era, one being that nineteenth-century Americans lived in a simpler and more unaffected time.

By altering, compressing, simplifying, and updating the past, Shaara positioned himself at the opposite end of the spectrum of historical fiction from Crane. That is, his work functions as an interpretation rather than as a reenactment. Throughout *The Killer Angels*, men interpret their experiences, ruminating over the purpose of the war and the role Gettysburg will play in deciding its outcome. To a large degree, these moments and conversations reflect the author at work, sifting through different historical schools of thought. Indeed, Shaara's genius ultimately lay in his role as an effective arbiter of competing postwar versions of the conflict and in his ability to maintain a convincing aura of objectivity. For the same reason that he aligned his novel with one more different than similar, Shaara also disguised the nature of his sources. He meant for *The Killer Angels* and its origins to seem, like *The Red Badge of Courage*, unbiased: "There have been many versions of that battle and that war. I have therefore avoided historical opinions and gone back primarily to the words of the men themselves, their letters and other documents" (vii).

Of course, anyone familiar with Civil War diaries, papers, and published letters knows that one cannot separate "historical opinions" from the words of soldiers. One certainly cannot distance such opinions from the *postwar* writing of veterans, documents often written for the very purpose of establishing or challenging historical and political positions. Although Shaara failed to acknowledge his use of postwar memoirs, his novel demonstrates his familiarity with the published narratives of Edward Porter Alexander, Chamberlain, Jubal Early, John Bell Hood, James Longstreet, and British foreign observer Arthur James Lyon Fremantle. His novel also strongly suggests his having read Volume 3 of *Century* magazine's *Battles and Leaders of the Civil War* (1887–88). That volume devotes 196 pages to the Gettysburg campaign, consisting primarily of accounts by officers who participated in the battle. Numerous details and exchanges in *The Killer Angels* indicate Shaara's familiarity with more obscure veterans' memoirs as well. At times, his sources leave their mark quite clearly in the novel. Stephen Cushman has observed, for instance, that Shaara not only relied heavily on Longstreet's account of Gettysburg but also used the words of the general "sometimes almost verbatim."[10] The novel also reproduces word for word some of the descriptions and dialogue found in "Through Blood and Fire at Gettysburg," Chamberlain's record of his regiment's fight on Little Round Top.[11]

Far short of avoiding the opinions voiced by such works, Shaara marshaled them into the service of his own interpretation of 1861–65. It was one that differed, in focus if not in spirit, from the prevailing understanding of the war. By the 1970s, readers had for more than thirty years absorbed narratives that drew attention to the complex and volatile role of race within the nation's history and culture. The fiction of William Faulkner anticipated or ran parallel to works by other artists who identified race relations as central to the American identity. These writers included some of the most prominent of the twentieth century, among them James Baldwin, Langston Hughes, Carson McCullers, Flannery O'Connor, William Styron, Richard Wright, and Eudora Welty. Beyond the realm of fiction and poetry, other social phenomena brought race fully to the forefront of the national consciousness. Riots, protests, marches, and legal battles over institutionalized racism became commonplace as the civil rights movement gathered momentum during the 1950s and 1960s. Mirroring the growing media focus on race during these years, American school textbooks increasingly advanced an "emancipationist vision" of the Civil War.[12] A handful of scholars have traced this phenomenon in educational materials, charting representations of African Americans in textbooks published from the 1960s through the 1970s and beyond. With growing frequency, "black abolitionists, Civil War soldiers, Reconstruction officials, and twentieth-century civil rights workers marched into textbooks that students read across the country."[13] Not all discussions of the war hinged on slavery, to be sure. But far more than members of previous generations, baby boomers and their offspring understood America's central crisis in terms of race—a struggle to end human bondage and set free the nation's enslaved people.

Undeniably, this vision tapped into fundamental, patriotic values shared by millions of Americans at the end of the twentieth century. Yet the emancipationist interpretation of the Civil War did not satisfy the needs of all Americans. Surely it explained the importance of the Civil War for African Americans since 1865, but what was the legacy of the war for *other* Americans? Had white soldiers truly fought the war to destroy or protect slavery? And what did the outcome of the war mean for men and women generations removed from slavery? In an effort to answer these questions, Shaara distilled his interpretation of the war from several competing postwar traditions. The message of *The Killer Angels* can be clarified in a few statements: (a) Roughly speaking, the North and the South stood for two different and incompatible worldviews: the North for democratic equality and individuality, the South for a variation on European aristocracy; (b) the Civil War took place because the North could no longer abide Old World emphases on class and pedigree in America; and (c) although both sides fought with valor and devotion, the North's victory at Gettysburg, and thereafter in the war, sounded the death knell for a Southern aristocracy already rife with internal conflict.

Laid bare, this summary may at first seem surprising. No one can doubt, after all, that *The Killer Angels* depicts men who discuss aloud the issues of states' rights and slavery, two of the most common explanations for secession and the outbreak of war. During one such conversation, the narrator probes Longstreet's rather un-Southern thinking about the role that human bondage plays in the conflict: "The war was about slavery, all right. That was not why Longstreet fought but that was what the war was about" (271). Yet the novel itself never endorses such a blunt or standard view of the Civil War. In fact, Shaara indicated early on that his work might challenge the assumptions his readers bring to the text: "You may find it a different story than the one you learned in school. There have been many versions of that battle and that war" (vii). By collapsing both emancipation and states' rights into his larger version of the conflict, Shaara acknowledged the power of each interpretation without taking sides. He used veterans' narratives in a similar way. Judiciously employing the familiar claims and myths advanced by former soldiers, he strengthened his vision of the Civil War as America's purging of European aristocracy.

II.

While no one tradition enjoys free reign in the pages of *The Killer Angels*, the Myth of the Lost Cause spreads its tents wide. As described in the last chapter, former Confederates developed the Myth after the war in an effort to validate Southern secession and explain Southern defeat. Simplifying some aspects and personalities of the war, and exaggerating the importance of others, the Lost Cause straddled the divide between truth and fiction. The tenacity of its proponents, and the Myth's romantic allure, together paid dividends. By the turn of the century, Lost Cause architects such as Jubal A. Early had succeeded in influencing how future generations would understand and interpret the Civil War, both within and beyond the former boundaries of the Confederacy. In an essay on the postwar literary and oratorical efforts of Early, Gary W. Gallagher provided a concise description of the claims made by the former lieutenant general and like-minded veterans: "(1) Robert E. Lee was the best and most admirable general of the war; (2) Confederate armies faced overwhelming odds and mounted a gallant resistance; (3) Ulysses S. Grant paled in comparison to Lee as a soldier; (4) Stonewall Jackson deserved a place immediately behind Lee in the Confederate pantheon; and (5) Virginia [and by extension, the eastern theater] was the most important arena of combat." In a brief but insightful analysis, Gallagher showed that *The Killer Angels* and the 1993 film *Gettysburg* (based on the novel and coscripted by Shaara) would "by turns delight and upset Lost Cause adherents." Followers of the Myth, he suggested, would approve of Shaara's focus on the eastern theater, Gettysburg, and the morale and valor of the Army of Northern Virginia. They would grumble at the novel's portrait of Lee "as an aging and ill lion, blindly insistent on attacking [at Gettysburg] despite ... advice to the contrary."[14] These observations do more than demonstrate that Lost Cause thinking influenced at least a portion of Shaara's presentation. They also help us see that the Myth, and its method of compressing the war's scope and meanings, remained viable in the latter half of the twentieth century. Realizing the surviving potency of many of the "reductions" popularized by Early, J. William Jones, Fitzhugh Lee, and others, Shaara borrowed them in order to narrow the war to a struggle between democracy and aristocracy.

The Killer Angels begins its series of reductions by excluding everything outside of the eastern theater. Shaara built his novel on figures associated inextricably with the East—Lewis A. Armistead, John Buford, Joshua Lawrence Chamberlain, Robert E. Lee, and James Longstreet. Other famous personalities from the eastern theater appear or find mention in the novel: John Brown Gordon, Winfield S. Hancock, Thomas J. "Stonewall" Jackson, George B. McClellan, George G. Meade, George E. Pickett, and James E. B. "Jeb" Stuart. Although it makes sense that these men think and talk about the battles in which they participated (such as Fredericksburg, Antietam, Chancellorsville, and Thoroughfare Gap), these names further emphasize the Virginia and Maryland campaigns fought by the Army of Northern Virginia and the Army of the Potomac. The novel virtually ignores events and figures in the West. We read nothing of Braxton Bragg, Ulysses S. Grant, Albert Sidney Johnston, Joseph E. Johnston, and William Tecumseh Sherman. Moreover, soldiers' campfire conversations in *The Killer Angels* include talk of European figures and sentiment but never turn to the battles and troops in the West.

For most readers, Shaara's focus on the East may pass wholly unnoticed.[15] This phenomenon owes much to the fact that school history books traditionally devote little attention to the war's trans-Mississippi and western contests. Most general histories of the Civil War, as well as films and television programs, do little more to present a balanced portrait of the war's landscape. To a great measure, Lost Cause authors shoulder the responsibility for the uneven treatment. In the years following Appomattox, veterans of the Army of Northern Virginia launched a determined campaign to preserve memory of their wartime leaders and service. Beyond newspaper articles and commemorative speeches, former Confederates found the *Southern Historical Society Papers* a welcome forum in which to record the history of events and soldiers in the East. Thomas L. Connelly noted that the Southern Historical Society, although styling itself as a Southwide organization, was "devoted to the idolization of Lee and his army. In its first year [1876], the *Papers* printed twenty-nine articles on Lee and the Virginia army, and five on military affairs elsewhere.... By 1878 there were rumblings of displeasure in other parts of the South over this imbalance."[16]

When veterans of other Confederate armies tried to draw attention away from the East, their efforts brought little success. Western-oriented journals such as the *Annals of the Army of Tennessee*, the *Southern Bivouac*, and the *Confederate Veteran* failed to capture the interest of readers and historians to the degree that the *Southern Historical Society Papers* did.[17] One might explain the faint response in several ways. The eastern location of the Union and Confederate capitals—Washington, D.C., and Richmond—no doubt accounts for a great deal of the attention awarded that region. Moreover, during the conflict, much of the world genuinely did look to Virginia "as the crucial arena of the war." It therefore makes sense that the postwar spotlight would likewise fall on the East. Yet it also appears that efforts to shift attention westward failed because Lee's former troops had already popularized a version of history imbued with tenacious myth. For example, Early and his comrades distorted the truth when acknowledging that a Confederacy existed outside the eastern theater "only when convenient to explain southern failures in Virginia." We might posit manifold reasons for why Americans of the late nineteenth century found this condensed and limited version of the Civil War landscape so attractive—one being the simple need to manage, organize, and cope with memories of four years of upheaval, destruction, and bloodshed.[18]

Yet before we identify Shaara as having made intentional use of Lost Cause traditions, I think it wise to consider the alternative. Is it possible that Shaara emphasized the East simply because he agreed with veterans and scholars who argued that the eastern theater, primarily Virginia, functioned as the true "cockpit of the war"?[19] Might he have remained altogether unaware of his use of Lost Cause emphases? On the one hand, these questions have merit. After all, why should we assume that Shaara, elsewhere the author of science fiction and sports fiction, understood Civil War mythmaking any better than his readers? It would be easy to read the novel as yet another example of how Lost Cause writers managed to guide the minds and pens of later generations. On the other hand, to argue that *The Killer Angels* uses Civil War mythology unaware requires that we deny the sophistication of the narrative and its author. Such an argument could not ultimately bear scrutiny. The novel's shifting viewpoint functions as merely one dimension of its complexity.[20] The more one studies the novel, in fact, the more one appreciates its numerous intricacies—and Shaara's own sleight of hand. Although cloaked by the somewhat folksy persona he affects in his "To the Reader" page, Shaara revealed himself—from start to finish—to be an astute student of Civil War historiography. And like all good storytellers, he remained very much aware of how his predecessors told the same tale.

Such predecessors included not only memoirists but also historians such as Douglas Southall Freeman, a man whose influence on Civil War history cannot be overstated. In his classic *Lee's Lieutenants: A Study in Command* (1942–44), Freeman began each of his three volumes with a *Dramatis*

Personae. There he provided a colorful yet tersely written account of each of the major personalities discussed in the text to follow. In his foreword, Shaara lifted this technique and style rather shamelessly, often repeating or elaborating on the content of sketches by Freeman. But Shaara did not imitate Freeman's work slavishly. For instance, in the Longstreet section of Freeman's *Dramatis Personae*, readers learn that the general nearly went ten months without fighting an offensive battle: "This experience may have spoiled him, may have led him to think that if he chooses a good position and remains there, an impatient enemy will attack and give him all the advantage of the defensive." To this observation Freeman added ominously, "Nobody seems aware of this at the time." The corresponding sketch of Longstreet in *The Killer Angels* reads: "He has invented a trench and a theory of defensive warfare, but in that courtly company few will listen" (xi). Though subtle, Shaara here parted with Freeman by portraying the *comrades* of Longstreet as unwise, not the general himself. Such interpretive shifts demonstrate that Shaara's novel is less derivative of the works of Freeman and other authors than in conversation with them. The same is true of the book's relationship to veterans' narratives. Just as Shaara chose when to follow or depart from the work of Freeman, so too did he know when to adhere to, or stray from, the strategies of Lost Cause architects.[21]

Having reduced the war to the eastern theater, *The Killer Angels* next reduces that entire theater to the battle of Gettysburg. In his foreword, Shaara described the sentiments of Northern troops facing the Confederate invasion: "They think this will be the last battle, and they are glad that it is to be fought on their own home ground" (x). Colonel Chamberlain reiterates this idea shortly before leading his 20th Maine toward Gettysburg: "I think if we lose this fight the war will be over" (33). Southern characters also suspect that the coming battle at Gettysburg will be decisive. "The whole war could be damn well over soon," Pickett complains in a moment of dramatic irony, "and my boys would have missed it" (64). And when preparing his division leaders for the third day's assault on Cemetery Ridge, Longstreet drives home the importance of the coming action: "Gentlemen, the fate of your country rests on this attack" (315). Lest we think that these men misread the writing on the wall, Shaara showed that General Lee himself believes Gettysburg will decide not only the East but the entire conflict. "This is the great battle," he muses on the eve of July 1. "Tomorrow or the next day. This will determine the war" (152).

In light of so many declarations of Gettysburg's significance, even readers familiar with the battles fought before and after July 1863 might be persuaded that Gettysburg encapsulates them all. After describing the Confederates' failed July 3 assault on the Union center, Shaara left no doubt that, despite another two years of bitter fighting to come, the war is over. The Confederacy has lost. In camp, Lee says to Longstreet, "We will do better another time." His lieutenant's brief reply is dark: "I don't think so . . . I don't think we can win it now" (360). Shaara concluded the novel with a quotation from Winston Churchill: "Thus ended the great American Civil War, which must upon the whole be considered the noblest and least avoidable of all the great mass conflicts of which till then there was record" (367). After absorbing this postscript, few readers would believe that *The Killer Angels* deals with a single battle among many. Indeed, the novel places the entire Civil War between its covers.

Shaara's treatment of Gettysburg reflects the enormous stature and importance granted the battle by Lost Cause writers. As the bloodiest engagement of the war, and the South's deepest incursion into Northern soil, Gettysburg would have garnered special attention even without the help of postwar mythmaking.[22] Yet former Confederates elevated the Pennsylvania campaign to legendary proportions. As William Garrett Piston noted, "The events at Gettysburg were much more than a battle. They entered the Southern psyche and afforded an explanation for the loss of the war."[23] Postwar writers conceived of Gettysburg as the climax of the conflict, the "High Water-Mark of the Confederacy," the battle that doomed the South to a drawn-out and agonizing defeat. In his popular 1903 memoir, John B. Gordon left no doubt that the war hung in the balance during early July 1863: "Victory to Lee meant Southern independence. Victory to Meade meant an inseparable Union. The life of the Confederacy, the unity of the Republic—these were the stakes."[24]

This point of view no doubt took root in the late 1860s, when in hindsight Americans realized that Confederate fortunes in the East generally declined after Gettysburg. Yet it was not until the 1870s, particularly with the establishment of the influential *Southern Historical Society Papers,* that the battle became key to the commemoration of Robert E. Lee and his Army of Northern Virginia. Connelly explained that the "Lee Cult," wishing to portray "their hero as invincible on the battlefield," felt it necessary to account for his failure at Gettysburg—"the most prominent blemish on Robert E. Lee's reputation."[25] By assigning blame for the lost battle to a number of subordinates, notably Ambrose Powell Hill, Ewell, Stuart, and especially Longstreet,

Lee's supporters could claim that the commanding general did not err at Gettysburg. Longstreet's availability as a scapegoat began in the late 1860s. Lee's "old war horse" fell out of favor with the postwar South for a number of reasons, including his membership in the Republican Party, his friendship with Ulysses S. Grant, and especially for his willingness to criticize in print the generalship of Robert E. Lee.[26] Unable to endure attacks against Lee, who by the 1880s stood as the South's greatest hero and who was sometimes regarded as a saint, Lost Cause advocates blamed the failures of Gettysburg on Longstreet. Gallagher summed up their claims: "If only Longstreet had obeyed Lee's orders more expeditiously, they insisted, Gettysburg would have been a great victory and Confederate independence a reality."[27] This staple of Lost Cause ideology, known as the "Longstreet-lost-it-at-Gettysburg" theory, maintains much of its force today.[28]

The Killer Angels acknowledges the efforts of the Lee Cult to discredit Longstreet. In the afterword, Shaara described Early as "the Southern officer most involved in trying to prove that Longstreet was responsible for the loss at Gettysburg" (372). In fact, *The Killer Angels* allows the pair's postwar animosity to guide its presentation of the men's wartime relationship. In an early chapter told from Lee's perspective, the reader understands that "Longstreet cannot stand" Early (146), reinforcing what we learn in the foreword, that "Longstreet despises him" (xiii). And Shaara's Early smirks at Longstreet's reticence to take the offensive, advising Lee that the First Corps should fight on July 2 only if Longstreet "can be induced to attack" (147).[29] Considering Shaara's positive portrait of "Old Pete" as a tough, somber, but compassionate soldier, it is not surprising that the author had little good to say about Early and his views. Shaara noted that Lee removed Early from command of the Second Corps in 1865, "because of complaints against him by citizens he ha[d] offended" and pointed out that Early later became "the central figure in the infamous Louisiana lottery, which cost thousands of Southerners thousands of dollars" (372). It may seem that by telling much of the novel from the perspective of Longstreet, and by conflating Early's postwar arguments with a corrupt lottery, Shaara ultimately rejected Lost Cause mythology altogether.[30] But the novel shows itself to be aware of the complexities of the Lost Cause, and of how it extended beyond the postwar feud between Early and Lee's second-in-command.

Indeed, some Lost Cause writers found it possible to emphasize the importance of Gettysburg and the quality of Lee without attacking the performance and character of Longstreet. Few former Confederates knew and admired Lee more than Walter H. Taylor, a staff officer of Lee's throughout the war and a minor character in *The Killer Angels*. In his 1878 memoir, *Four Years with General Lee*, Taylor called it a "great injustice" that critics of Longstreet should claim "he had orders from the commanding general to attack the enemy at sunrise on the 2d of July, and that he disobeyed these orders." Taylor also published a letter he wrote to the former commander of the First Corps. "I regard it as a great mistake on the part of those who, perhaps because of political differences, now undertake to criticise and attack your *war* record," he told Longstreet. "Such conduct is most ungenerous."[31] Another member of Lee's staff, Charles Marshall, likewise steered clear of attacking Longstreet in his published papers. Marshall criticized Longstreet's failure to keep Lee apprised of the army's store of ammunition but suggested that the general's delays on July 3 owed more to the enemy than to his own disposition.[32] Showing his familiarity with Marshall's papers, Shaara correctly identified the true target of the staff officer's ire at Gettysburg, the missing cavalry under General Stuart.[33] "Marshall was furious with the absent Stuart," the novel notes, "[and he] was ready to draw up court-martial papers" (83). Fair treatment of Longstreet aside, however, Taylor and Marshall often fit "firmly within the Lost Cause interpretive tradition."[34] Both men, for instance, emphasized and at times exaggerated the numerical disadvantages facing the Southern army. And in their memoirs both devoted more attention to Gettysburg than any other campaign or episode of the war.[35]

How can the fissures and countermarches within the Myth of the Lost Cause improve our understanding of *The Killer Angels*? I want to suggest that by understanding the fragmented traditions facing Shaara, we can better understand his tendency to polish some pieces of the Myth while abandoning others. Even if his novel at times sides with Longstreet, he could still take up and make use of other fragments of the Lost Cause. Indeed, he sometimes put to use elements that grew unintentionally from the efforts of Lost Cause architects. In the foreword to *The Killer Angels*, for example, Shaara wrote that Lee marched North "knowing that a letter has been prepared by Jefferson Davis, a letter which offers peace. It is to be placed on the desk of Abraham Lincoln the day after Lee has destroyed the Army of the Potomac somewhere north of Washington" (xi). The notion that Lee and his troops marched north in order to deliver the final blow for Southern independence has long occupied the popular mind. That idea likely began with former Confederates, albeit not always by design. In a letter published in the August 1877 edition of the *Southern Historical*

Society Papers, Early argued: "If we could have gained a decided victory north of the Potomac, it would have done more to produce a financial crisis at the North and secure our independence than a succession of victories on the soil of Virginia."[36] Other Southern writers echoed the idea that a victory on northern ground might have spelled the end of the war. "If [the fighting on July 3] should be favorable to us, the war was nearly over," the artillerist Alexander wrote in *Battles and Leaders,* "if against us, we each had the risks of many battles yet to go through."[37] Yet neither Early nor Alexander argued that the destruction of the Union army, and the end of the war, stood as the immediate purposes of the Pennsylvania campaign. As twenty-first-century scholars have pointed out, Lee "fully understood that one campaign could not make or break a huge, complex war effort." He instead ventured northward to "siphon" Union troops from Virginia, relieve the state and its resources from Federal occupation, and disrupt the Union army's summer campaign against Richmond. Lee may have hoped to "strike an effective blow" against the Army of the Potomac but would have been surprised by postwar talk that he went north to finish the war.[38] From Shaara's point of view, however, it apparently made good sense to follow this errant branch of Lost Cause mythmaking, adopted since the 1870s by many Americans and Europeans. By doing so, he heightened the drama of his story and further emphasized the decisive nature of Gettysburg. From first to last, *The Killer Angels* makes clear that *this* battle determines everything.

Shaara followed another staple of the Lost Cause by reducing the entire South to a single state: Virginia. In *The Killer Angels,* Virginia figures as the foremost state not only of the Southeast but also of the entire Confederacy. This role may not seem strange, considering that the Old Dominion furnished the Confederacy with its capital, Richmond; its most famous general, Lee; and the name of its premier army, the Army of Northern Virginia. Moreover, battles raged in Virginia more often than in any other state, further accounting for its prominence. Yet for all of these factors, it is surprising how Virginia and her sons dominate Shaara's portrait of Lee's army at Gettysburg. With the exception of Longstreet, all of the novel's major Southern characters hail from Virginia. Generals Hood, James Johnston Pettigrew, and Isaac R. Trimble represent Texas and North Carolina, but they play minor roles rather than commanding the action. And while regiments from Mississippi, Alabama, and Texas appear briefly in the novel's description of the July 2 fighting, they are easily buried by an avalanche of references to Virginia. Planning strategy before the second day of the battle, Lee's thinking betrays the novel's view of his home state: "Virginia is here, all the South is here. What will you do tomorrow?" (152). Virginia does not stand apart from the rest of the South so much as stand for it.

Shaara's emphasis on Virginia makes sense in light of the origins and efforts of Lost Cause writers. In *Ghosts of the Confederacy: Defeat, the Lost Cause, and the Emergence of the New South,* Gaines M. Foster devoted considerable attention to how Virginia-born veterans gained control of postwar historical societies and publications, memorial organizations, and monument associations.[39] Lost Cause advocates, nearly all Virginian by birth, soon crafted a version of the war that offered few accolades to Confederates from other states—even those operating within the command structure of the Army of Northern Virginia. Taking the Virginians Lee and Jackson as their heroes, veterans of the Old Dominion produced voluminous articles, speeches, and books intent on proving the centrality of Virginia and its soldiers to Confederate memory. Even if most Southerners failed to carry the state's banner, by the 1880s the Confederate celebration nonetheless emphasized many of the ideas introduced by Virginians during the previous decade. As Connelly and Barbara Bellows have suggested, "one could make a strong argument that the principal driving force behind the entire Lost Cause mentality came from Virginia."[40]

In *The Killer Angels,* the emphasis on Virginia seems to derive in part from Shaara's having read Longstreet's 1895 memoir, *From Manassas to Appomattox: Memoirs of the Civil War in America.* In those pages, Longstreet lashed out at his postwar tormentors, that "clique of Virginians" who "so dominated" Civil War writing. In his account of the Pennsylvania campaign, the aging general at times paused to counter the arguments of his detractors, whom he lampooned as "Knights of the quill." These plumed knights of aristocratic and elitist Virginia, Longstreet made clear, operated under a heavy state bias. He noted, for example, that Gen. William N. Pendleton's postwar lecture tour made Longstreet a scapegoat at Gettysburg while ignoring the shortcomings of generals Ewell and Hill, "both Virginians, and not under the political ban." A few pages later, Longstreet again commented on his critics from the Old Dominion: "The Virginia writers have been so eager in their search for a flaw in the conduct of the battle of the First Corps that they overlook the only point into which they could have thrust their pens." Readers might find dubious Longstreet's claim that his First Corps began its attack on July 2 "too soon" rather than too late. Yet the passage reflects its author's open contempt for Virginia veterans who found that they must tarnish the reputation of other states in order to burnish that of their own. Indeed, Longstreet seethed at postwar claims—such as those of Gen. Fitzhugh Lee—that the Confederates would have won Gettysburg were Stonewall Jackson alive and facing the Union right. Longstreet chalked up much of Jackson's immense reputation to exaggerated statements by Virginians, statements that siphoned glory from other deserving soldiers. In appraising Jackson's performance at Sharpsburg, he admitted that the general "made a brave and gallant fight in the morning, losing 1601 officers and men." But Longstreet then went on the offensive, contrasting Jackson's work against that of Gen. Daniel H. Hill, a native of South Carolina: "General Jackson left the field at seven o' clock in the morning and did not return until four o'clock in the afternoon. . . . But D. H. Hill was there from the first to the last gun, losing from his division 1872 officers and men. Jackson had the greater part of the two divisions. *But Hill was not a Virginian, and it would not do to leave the field for refreshments* [emphasis added]."[41]

Having fired a venomous (and in this case unfair) barb at Jackson, his promoters, and their prejudices, Longstreet reserved another for Early, his chief opponent among the "latter-day knights." He noted that "General Early has been a picturesque figure" in the Virginians' attempts to deride the First Corps and accuse Longstreet of treason: "The subject was lasting, piquant, and so consoling that one is almost inclined to envy the comfort it gave him in his latter days." Early here appeared as a quixotic figure whose obsession made him more pathetic than credible or dangerous.[42]

Narrating six chapters from Longstreet's point of view, Shaara put to use the general's vision of Virginians as anachronistic, modern-day "knights." The impulse to conflate Virginia with the past shines through that character's musings about Lee, Stonewall Jackson, and other Virginia soldiers. "They come from another age," Longstreet thinks. "The Age of Virginia" (269). Indeed, *The Killer Angels* teems with descriptions of Lee and his Virginians that hearken back to chivalrous times. At one point, Shaara described Confederate gentlemen riding "through soft green rounded hills, a sunny morn, a splendid air, moving toward adventure as rode the plumed knights of old" (90). Such images also capture Virginia's aristocratic character, one of the emphases of Lost Cause writers. By the 1870s, they had established, in both northern and southern newspapers, the "national stereotype of Virginia as the center of antebellum Southern culture."[43] More than any other state of the antebellum South, they argued, Virginia could boast of a fine pedigree, a rich history, and genteel rural and urban societies. Shaara emphasized these qualities time and again. When viewing a column of Mississippi troops, Longstreet recalls a joke about that state's ferocity in battle: "'You men of Virginia are gentlemen. But those people from *Mississippi.*' Longstreet grinned. [He had heard] the same thing about Hood's Texans" (210–11). As this passage suggests, on those rare occasions when Shaara did characterize other Southern states, the effort seems intended to highlight Virginia's aristocratic nature and connections to the Old World.

By presenting Virginia as a synecdoche for the South, Shaara freed himself from accounting for the idiosyncrasies of each Confederate state. More important, it enabled him to represent the entire South as an aristocratic society with strong ties to European culture and ideals, even if the region's younger states—such as Mississippi and Texas—lacked the blue blood and society of the Old Dominion. Standing as one of Shaara's key compressions of history, the focus on Virginia allows his novel to best represent the Civil War as democratic America's triumph over Old World aristocracy. Of course, Lost Cause writers surely identified the Confederacy as a democratic nation and perhaps would chafe under Shaara's portrait of their country. Yet by emphasizing the aristocratic and chivalrous qualities of Virginia officers, these men had opened the door for the novelist to cast the South as a quaint, old-fashioned community rooted more in Europe than America.[44] Embedded within the timeworn focus on the eastern theater and Gettysburg, this vision of the Confederacy has gone unnoticed—and unchallenged—by most readers.

III.

Of all the novel's characters, the English colonel Arthur James Lyon Fremantle does the most to connect the South explicitly to the Old World. Joined by the Austrian Fitzgerald Ross and the Prussian Justus Scheibert, Fremantle acts as a foreign observer in Lee's army. While the presence of Europeans in the Confederate camp itself suggests a Southern tie to England and the Continent (see 164), Shaara drove home the point by sharing Fremantle's musings. Sitting at breakfast on July 2 amid Europeans and Southerners, the colonel thinks: "Southerners! They were *Englishmen,* by George." Shaara hardly needed to tell us that Fremantle "was at home" (165), considering the man's enthusiastic comparison of Confederates to the

English: "He felt a part, almost a member, of this marvelous group of outnumbered men. Englishmen. They called themselves Americans, but they were transplanted Englishmen. Look at the names: Lee, Hill, Longstreet, Jackson, Stuart. And Lee was Church of England. Most of them were. All gentlemen. No finer gentlemen in England than Lee" (167).

After deciding that one or two Englishmen compare favorably to Lee after all, Fremantle's thinking unearths some of the deeper issues of Shaara's book: "The great experiment. In democracy. The equality of rabble. In not much more than a generation they have come back to *class*.... The experiment doesn't work. Give them fifty years, and all that equality rot is gone. Here they have that same love of the land and of tradition, of the right form, of breeding, in their horses, their women. Of course slavery is a bit embarrassing, but that, of course, will go. But the point is they do it all exactly as we do in Europe. And the North does not. *That's* what the war is really about." In summation, Fremantle turns to the Northern way of thinking: "The Northerner doesn't give a damn for tradition, or breeding, or the Old Country. He hates the Old Country. Odd. You very rarely hear a Southerner refer to 'the Old Country.'... Well, of course, the South *is* the Old Country. They haven't left Europe. They've merely transplanted it. And *that's* what the war is about" (173–74).

Shaara's canny use of Fremantle depended on his familiarity with the real-life Englishman's 1863 memoir, *Three Months in the Southern States: April–June 1863*. Fremantle entered Texas through Mexico and, as an amiable lieutenant colonel in the British army, soon found himself the welcome guest of Confederates both patrician and common, political and military, western and eastern. Although many foreigners visited and reported on the South during the war years, none "grasped more fully the South's immense size and diversity, [and] none possessed a keener eye or greater facility in committing to paper what he had seen."[45] As one would expect, the published diary of the Englishman influences strongly Shaara's representation of the man and his personality. The novelist captured the tenor of Fremantle's enthused and optimistic prose when relating that the Englishman "was enjoying himself hugely" at Gettysburg, looking "delightfully disreputable" in clothes dirtied by his travels (135). The attention awarded Fremantle's filthy clothes reveals how closely Shaara studied his sources. He not only related the events featured in Fremantle's memoir, "a casual hanging, raw floods, great fires" (135), but also draws on the fact that the foreigner reported having once refused an invitation to an evening party because of what he termed "the extreme badness of my clothes."⁴⁶ Other colorful moments and details from Fremantle's account also make their way into *The Killer Angels*, such as his desire to see Confederate troops form the Hollow Square (156 in Fremantle; 135 in Shaara).

Some early reviews of the novel noted that Shaara included Fremantle as a "stock" character designed to provide "comic relief." Yet Shaara devoted a chapter to Fremantle's point of view not to provide humor but precisely because of the foreigner's observations about Southern ties to England. In *Three Months in the Southern States*, Fremantle routinely looked for (and found) ways to blur the distinction between England and the South. He observed that "all the well-bred Southerners" speak English "exactly like an English gentleman" and claimed that those Southern men with education and money "are proud of their descent from Englishmen. They glory in speaking English as we do . . . their manners and feelings resemble those of the upper classes in the old country." Southern men, he reported Gen. Joseph E. Johnston as saying, are "fond of titles, though they are republicans; and as they can't get any other sort, they all take military ones." Fremantle's comparisons extended beyond speech and manners. The city of Richmond, he argued, "is very pretty, and rather English-looking." The visitor even linked the two nations' flags, noting that the new Confederate flag "bears a strong resemblance to the British white ensign." By contrast, Fremantle drew sharp distinctions between the English and those Americans living in the North. Whereas his narrative praises the virtue of the Southern people and their soldiers, it disparages Northern troops as "bad imitations of soldiers" and generally paints the Northern public as spoiled, hypocritical, and lazy. Probably the highest compliment Fremantle paid the North concerned its locomotive sleeping cars, "a most admirable and ingenious Yankee notion."⁴⁷

Reading *Three Months in the Southern States* alongside *The Killer Angels*, one sees how Shaara came to imagine Fremantle as hoping that the South "will rejoin the Queen" and that its lands might "once again be English soil" (167). Shaara's Fremantle glories in the fact that all the Confederate officers "had insisted that the South would be happier under the Queen than under the Union" (167). Of course, the real-life Fremantle never seemed as naïve on this count as Shaara's version of the man. Looking at the passage in *Three Months* that inspired these lines in the novel, one sees a much wiser Fremantle: one who understood that Southerners would rather serve the Queen than "Uncle Abe" *only* insofar as they would also rather serve the Emperor of France, the

Emperor of Japan, or Satan himself.[48] Yet if the novel removes something of Fremantle's wit, by doing so Shaara could better represent the South as a patrician world ever looking backward toward Europe and the past.

While *The Killer Angels* shows there to be much truth in Fremantle's thinking that the war is about democracy and aristocracy, the Englishman does not speak for Shaara. In fact, contrary to Fremantle's belief that the social outlook in the South has shifted from democratic equality back to the Old World emphases on breeding and class, the novel demonstrates that the reverse is true. For all its outward vitality, Shaara's South represents but the lingering, fading remnant of Old World ideology in America. When Fremantle concludes happily that the Confederates "are *Englishmen*," Shaara meant for the sentiment to carry ironic weight (173). For if these doomed Confederate patricians represent the fortunes of the Old Country in a modern age, then their fall must also portend a decline in English strength and tradition. Writing with the benefit of hindsight, Shaara knew the analogy succeeded. By the 1890s, twenty-five years after Appomattox, the British imperialists "knew by some unadmitted instinct that . . . time was running short." England's "democratic foundation" had won power over "autocratic resolution," and the empire stood on the brink of a world war that would further upend elite rule, efface Napoleonic warfare, and usher in the modern world.[49]

The figure of Lee stands at the center of Shaara's picture of a Southern world collapsing inward upon itself. As Southern aristocracy personified, Lee is a dying old man. Although some historical evidence suggests that the commander suffered from heart disease during the war, Shaara developed this idea far beyond the available facts.[50] We learn in the novel's foreword that Lee "has been down that spring with the first assault of the heart disease which will eventually kill him" (x). And once into the novel proper, the reader cannot escape reminders of Lee's ill health. Before we see the general for the first time, Longstreet notes that "Lee had not been well" (13), and references to his failing heart litter the chapters told from Lee's perspective. An early passage captures the tenor of these moments: "Lee took a deep breath, testing his chest: a windblown vacancy, a breathless pain. He had a sense of enormous unnatural fragility, like hollow glass. . . . Not much pain this morning. Praise God. . . . But it was not the pain that troubled him; it was a sick gray emptiness he knew too well, that sense of a hole clear through him like the blasted vacancy in the air behind a shell burst, an enormous emptiness." Although determined to hide his failing health, to "show no pain, no weakness here" (83), Lee knows that his death looms near: "The great cold message had come in the spring, and Lee carried it inside him every moment of every day and all through the nights—that endless, breathless, inconsolable alarm: *there is not much time, beware, prepare*" (78).

More than any other feature of Shaara's novel, his portrait of Lee rakes against the traditions of the Lost Cause. Many readers have noted that, in meting out blame for Confederate failures at Gettysburg, Shaara targeted Lee more than anyone else. Of course, Shaara never went so far as to repeat Longstreet's infamous assessment of Lee in *From Manassas to Appomattox*. "That he was excited and off his balance was evident on the afternoon of the 1st," Lee's lieutenant declared, "and he labored under that oppression until enough blood was shed to appease him." To this day, these words evoke shock and anger among the custodians of Lee's honor and military reputation; when published in 1896, they secured Longstreet's alienation from the South—perhaps forever.[51] Not wishing to similarly alienate himself and his novel from his readers, Shaara exercised good judgment in paying ample respect to Lee's honor, courage, integrity, duty, and loyalty to his men, state, and nation. And he somewhat excused Lee's shortcomings at Gettysburg by deflecting blame to the general's physical ailments: ailments that drove Lee to gamble everything on a decisive battle for fear of his not surviving a prolonged war. While Early and other Lost Cause advocates would have surely griped over Shaara's picture of Lee, the author risked the presentation with good reason. In order to show that the South and its aristocratic ways could no longer thrive in a modern world, he found it necessary to contrast an elderly and infirm Lee with a robust and modern Longstreet.

To be sure, while one might read Lee's declining health simply as a premonition of the Confederacy's demise, or as a sign that the North had weakened the South during three years of hard fighting, the novel denies these possibilities in the character of Longstreet. Throughout the novel, Longstreet stands at odds with his comrades' Old World, aristocratic principles. We learn that he considers duels "silly" and once refused to fight one against A. P. Hill (254, 140), that he regards as "nonsense" the idea that Southern boys fight harder than Yankees (68), and that he would rather his men fight in trenches than risk failure and death in a glorious charge (142). Were he an outsider or marginal character, we might dismiss him as an anomaly. Yet as "Lee's right hand" (xi), a devoted soldier and Southerner, and a major voice in the book, Longstreet portends that the South, like Lee, is dying from internal conflicts. Tellingly, Shaara portrays Longstreet as more attuned to Lee's decline than anyone else in the army, even the commander's aides. And to Longstreet alone Lee confides that "I've not been well lately" and that "under this beard I'm not a young man" (203, 204). Standing at opposite ends of the Southern spectrum, Lee and Longstreet—more than their fellows or their enemies—can foresee the passing of the Old South.

One of Shaara's most ingenious strategies was to pit the ideas of Longstreet against not only those of his brother Confederates but also those of Fremantle. Discussing the sad case of Gen. Richard B. Garnett, who believes he must die in battle to save his honor, Longstreet shocks Fremantle by saying, "Honor without intelligence is a disaster. Honor could lose the war." Even after Longstreet explains that he appreciates "honor and bravery and courage," but not if it means foolish sacrifice, Fremantle appears exasperated. "But, sir, there is the example of Solferino," the Englishman insists. "And of course the Charge of the Light Brigade." Longstreet listens, sadly realizing that "like all Englishmen, and most Southerners, Fremantle would rather lose the war than his dignity. Dick Garnett would die and die smiling" (141–42). Because Fremantle stands as the novel's purveyor of Old World ideals, and because Longstreet is the South's most progressive and forward-looking soldier, the gulf between them means more than two men's failure to see eye to eye. Rather, that distance illustrates Fremantle's error in thinking that the South will return to the European fold in the wake of a failed democratic experiment. As Longstreet's distrust of honor—the very foundation of gentility—suggests, Southern aristocracy is on the wane.[52]

Like others, however, Fremantle dismisses Longstreet's ideas by pointing out that "Old Pete" does not hail from Virginia. Listening to Longstreet question the value of honor, Fremantle almost instinctively asks, "You are not, ah, Virginia born, sir?" (140). The fact that the general hails from South Carolina means nothing to the logic of the narrative; all that matters is that he is *not* of Virginia. Indeed, having established Virginia as a stand-in for the entire South, Shaara made Longstreet's non-Virginian origins one of the novel's more persistent, if subtle, themes. In the foreword we learn that Longstreet "is one of the few high officers in that army not from Virginia" (xi). Still early in the book, Pickett praises Virginia troops above all others until a thought troubles him: "It occurred to him that Longstreet not being a Virginian, he might have given another insult" (64). And later, when Fremantle develops a theory that Southerners all descend from England, he at first despairs to learn that Longstreet's ancestors were Dutch. But an important fact saves his logic: "Fremantle's theory had taken a jolt. Well. But Longstreet was an exception. He was not a Virginian . . . Fremantle again relaxed" (174).

Why did Shaara reduce the South to Virginia, only to make a non-Virginian one of his two major Southern characters? As I have suggested, one reason involved showing that the South's outward unity and shared customs belied the fact that new ideas and values had eroded that unity from the inside. In addition, Shaara's Longstreet shows us that which only a non-Virginian would have the perspective to see, namely, that what he terms the "Age of Virginia" has no place in the modern world. Shaara illustrated this idea by using military events and strategy as a metaphor for social change. As a dour realist and a soldier whose theories on defensive warfare are "generations ahead of his time," Longstreet believes that Lee's penchant for offensive warfare is not reasoned strategy but just "old Napoleon and a hell of a lot of chivalry" (370, 267). The fact that Lee depends on aristocratic honor to fight a modern war concerns Longstreet, who thinks "there was danger in it; there was even something dangerous in Lee" (69). Why, Longstreet asks, should the outnumbered Confederate army go on the offensive when it might instead maneuver between the Federals and Washington to force a defensive battle? Because Shaara's Lee equates honor with commanding the action and putting his men on the open field rather than in trenches, he orders assaults on July 2 and 3 over the objections of his senior lieutenant. Confederate losses on the second, and terrible defeat on the third, convince us that Longstreet is correct in thinking that chivalrous tactics no longer have a place in modern battle. From there it seems a short leap to the realization that the aristocracy behind those tactics is likewise an anachronism doomed to fade away.

Like Fremantle and Longstreet, Shaara's Northern characters identify the war as a struggle between New and Old World ideology. Early in the novel, Chamberlain expresses his love for America's principles of individuality and equality: "He had grown up believing in America and the individual and it was a stronger faith than his faith in God. This was the land where no man had to bow. In this place at last a man could stand up free of the past, free of tradition and blood ties and the curse of royalty and become what he wished to become. This was the first place on earth where the man mattered more than the state. True freedom had begun here and it would spread eventually over all the earth. But it had begun *here*" (29). Although acknowledging the role slavery plays in the war, Chamberlain seems less interested in freeing slaves than in fighting the germlike spread of aristocracy. "The fact of slavery upon this incredibly beautiful new clean earth was appalling," he thinks, "but more even than that was the horror of old Europe, the curse of nobility, which the South was transplanting to new soil. They were forming a new aristocracy, a new breed of glittering men, and Chamberlain had come to crush it" (29–30).

These passages show that Chamberlain and Fremantle, although at opposite ends of the ideological spectrum, agree that the South's aristocracy is something new, growing, even vibrant. Yet while Fremantle believes Southern slavery to be a passing thing in this New World, Chamberlain views it as the first step toward an Old World aristocracy that will make slaves of *all* Americans. Hoping to inspire the disgruntled men of the 2d Maine to fight, Chamberlain points out that the Union army "is a different kind of army" from those of the past, "an army going out to set other men free" (32). He quickly deflects his audience's attention away from black slavery, however, by emphasizing that all men, black and white, stand to be slaves if the South's way of life survives. "Here we judge you by what *you* do," he argues, "not by what your father was. Here you can be *something*. . . . What we're all fighting for, in the end, is each other" (32).

In general, Shaara's presentation of Chamberlain's words and ideas spring from the officer's postwar writing, specifically from his account of Gettysburg and from his memoir *The Passing of the Armies*. In the latter, Chamberlain observed, "On the Confederate side they were fighting for existing institutions, having historic warrant." By contrast, the North fought for the nation's "guiding and germinant ideals: the expressed intent and purpose of our fathers in establishing the government of one great people, and the inborn right of every human being to make the best of himself, and the duty of all to help him to this." In passages such as these, where Chamberlain emphasized "the duty of all" to help fellow humans obtain freedom, we see the germ for the fictional colonel's claim that Northern soldiers fight for "each other." But more important, we here see how Shaara developed from Chamberlain's writing the idea that slavery did not itself sum up the war so much as represent *one* example of how the South's "existing institutions" meant to corrupt American ideals.[53]

Over the course of the novel, Shaara put Chamberlain's abstract ideas to the test, confronting him with flesh-and-blood members of the Southern aristocracy and one of its black victims. Before arriving at Gettysburg, Chamberlain's men find a wounded, escaped slave in a nearby field. Although undoubtedly the novel's worst scene, the encounter tests Chamberlain's belief that the war is about more than black slavery.[54] Indeed, looking at the prostrate, bleeding, non-English-speaking slave, he thinks: "What could this man know of borders and states' rights and the Constitution and Dred Scott? What did he know of the war? And yet he was truly what it was all about. It simplified to that. Seen in the flesh, the cause of war was brutally clear" (181). Chamberlain seems momentarily happy to have broken through his abstractions to arrive at the truth, but Shaara complicates matters in the voice of Kilrain, Chamberlain's tough old Irish adjutant. When Chamberlain suggests that black men and women have suffered terribly in America, Kilrain says: "True. From any point of view. But your freed black will turn out no better than many the white that's fighting to free him. The point is that we have a country here where the past cannot keep a good man in chains, and that's the nature of the war" (189). "I'm Kilrain, and I God damn all gentlemen," he says, summing up his position in crude but certain terms. "It's the aristocracy I'm after. . . . The people who look at you like a piece of filth, a cockroach" (188–89).

Although it may seem that Kilrain merely brings Chamberlain back to his original way of thinking, the Irishman adds a new dimension to the colonel's view of the war by questioning the truth behind the notion of equality. "There's many a man alive no more value than a dead dog," he says. "What I'm fighting for is the right to prove I'm a better man than many. . . . No two things on earth are equal or have an equal chance, not a leaf nor a tree" (188). The novel shows that Kilrain, while devoted to wiping out America's "lovely, plumed, stinking chivalry" (189), nonetheless supports a *kind* of aristocracy, the aristocracy of mind and merit: "'There's only one aristocracy, and that's right here—' he tapped his white skull with a thick finger—'and *you*, Colonel laddie, are a member of it and don't even know it'" (188). Of all the novel's voices, Kilrain's comes closest to capturing the spirit of *The Killer Angels*. While Chamberlain earlier argues that the war is about freeing other men, or "each other," Kilrain helps him to understand that democracy, and the war itself, finds its roots in the individual.

Coming almost exactly halfway through the novel, Kilrain's words stay with Chamberlain (and the reader) throughout the description of Gettysburg's second and third day. Yet Chamberlain steers the Irishman's ideas in a direction Kilrain himself never intended. While earlier in the novel Chamberlain speaks of his hatred for the enemy, and the grim necessity of killing the "gentlemen" (188), his view of Southerners changes amid the bullets and shells of Little Round Top. Although still willing and able to kill the enemy, the hatred fades. Chamberlain shows this striking transformation in the aftermath of Pickett's charge, on the novel's penultimate page. Recalling the massive Confederate assault that took place just hours before, "the most beautiful thing he had ever seen" (362), Chamberlain thinks about the Confederates who marched against him: "He saw again the bitter face of Kilrain, but Chamberlain did not hate the gentlemen, could not think of them as gentlemen. He felt instead an extraordinary admiration. It was as if they were his own men who had come up the hill and he had been with them as they came, and he had made it across the stone wall to victory, but they had died" (364).

That Chamberlain can now admire the Southerners, forget their aristocratic origins, and imagine *leading* them up the slope shows that he has applied Kilrain's ideas to men in gray as well as blue. Whereas Kilrain believes that Confederate soldiers all fight for aristocracy, Chamberlain is no longer certain. When his brother Tom expresses wonder that the "Johnnies" can fight so hard for slavery, the absurdity of the notion strikes Chamberlain hard: "He had forgotten the Cause. When the guns began firing he had forgotten it completely. It seemed very strange now to think of morality ... or the poor runaway black" (364). Having witnessed the Confederates' determined, mile-long advance into a veritable storm of deadly missiles, Chamberlain cannot believe that what kept those men coming was the wish to preserve slavery, or protect state rights, or even to serve their social betters. In this moment, Shaara opened Chamberlain's eyes to what Longstreet knows and what Lee tries to hide—the fact that Southern aristocracy is not on the rise, but on the decline. Soldiers like these, he realizes, would not die for a "glimmering" aristocrat simply because he has money, land, and a coat of arms. Rather, like Chamberlain and Kilrain and the men of the 20th Maine, the Rebel fights for himself, to prove he is a better man than most. Lee anticipates Chamberlain's epiphany in the preceding chapter. Consoling Longstreet over the army's severe losses, Lee suggests that Southern troops practice the same kind of individualism Kilrain endorses: "They do not die for us. Not for us. That at least is a blessing.... Each man has his own reason to die" (360).

Reunion lies beneath the individualism of the novel's final pages. The last words of *The Killer Angels* make clear that the democratic spirit present at

Gettysburg will unite North and South once the war ends: "It rained all that night. The next day was Saturday, the Fourth of July" (365). Some might read this reference to America's birthday and separation from the Old World as a pronouncement of Northern victory. Such a reading is no doubt valid, but the ending also celebrates America in its entirety. As Chamberlain's musings over Pickett's charge show, reconciliation is already underway. We see this reconciliation earlier in the novel as well, when Longstreet remarks to Lee that the "boys in blue" in front of them seem "never quite the enemy" (201). Yankees and Confederates share common ground figuratively and literally, and in time each side can, like Chamberlain, replace hatred with admiration. If *The Killer Angels* grants the Lost Cause a wide berth, then it also provides more than ample room for another postwar veterans' movement: Reconciliation.

IV.

As with the Myth of the Lost Cause out of which it arose, Reconciliation developed under former Confederates and left a lasting impression on American literature, history, and culture. Like Virginians such as Early and Jones, proponents of Reconciliation offered a "disclaimer against slavery as the cause of the war," defended the South's right to secede, and aimed to create a positive memory of the Confederacy and its people. Unlike the cult of Virginians, however, the proponents of Reconciliation embraced their former enemies, a move that raised the ire of Lost Cause purists. As Foster has described, some unreconstructed Confederates frowned on reunion-minded organizations such as the UCV, viewing fraternization with the North as unacceptable. Yet followers of the "second phase of the veterans' movement," which dominated Confederate memory during the 1890s, believed reunion essential for the South to prosper. Not only would such efforts help restore the South's political and cultural influence on a national scale, but also it would allow Southerners to interpret their wartime sacrifices as honorable and necessary contributions to America's rebirth as a global power. Named for the commander of the UCV from 1889 until his death in 1904, the "John B. Gordon School" attracted far more supporters, North and South, than had the original Lost Cause. Written in "conciliatory tone[s]," Gordon's *Reminiscences of the Civil War* used the war's "Northern name" and famously ends with a statement of triumphant reconciliation: "So the

Republic, rising from its baptism of blood with a national life more robust, a national union more complete, and a national influence ever widening, shall go forever forward in its benign mission to humanity."[55]

Thousands of Northerners welcomed the goodwill message of Gordon and his UCV allies. Determined to heal the wounds of the war, still rankling three decades afterward, the people of the North seemed willing to accept "a segregated memory of [the] Civil War on Southern terms."[56] That meant embracing and celebrating a "Blue-Gray fraternalism" that eclipsed memory of a war fought for emancipation.[57] And the celebration produced a good deal of hyperbole. One Northern veteran, for example, proclaimed that in the world's entire history "there is no record of such fraternal greeting and brotherhood between old-time foes. . . . It will never be repeated again. It could not be except between Americans, the most gallant and dauntless soldiers of the world."[58] Such conciliatory sentiments, completely devoid of references to slavery, echo those found in Gordon's speeches and publications. As a quintessential narrative of Reconciliation, his *Reminiscences* argues that while "it is fair to say that had there been no slavery there would have been no war," neither "its destruction on the one hand, nor its defence on the other, was the energizing force that held the contending armies to four years of bloody conflict."[59] Having dispensed with the issue of slavery, the remainder of Gordon's narrative exists largely as an exaggerated account of the martial brilliance and manhood of all white Civil War soldiers. While today's readers may understandably find it "disarming" that the memoir "lavishes praise on everyone, friend and foe alike," many American readers of the late nineteenth and early twentieth centuries thought that its author struck the right tone.[60]

In particular, Gordon shrewdly mined his personal wartime experiences for examples of North-South fraternity, dwelling most memorably on his role at Appomattox. None other than Gordon himself led the Army of Northern Virginia during the surrender ceremony, where Chamberlain supposedly ordered the Federal troops to offer a formal salute to their defeated countrymen. Although "Gordon made no mention of [the episode] until he saw Chamberlain's published account" in the *New York Times*, four decades after the surrender, the UCV president used the story to his advantage.[61] In his *Reminiscences*, Gordon quoted four paragraphs of Chamberlain's newspaper account and lauded the Maine officer for saluting the conquered South: "One of the knightliest soldiers of the Federal army, General Joshua L. Chamberlain of Maine . . . called his troops into line, and as my men marched in front of them, the veterans in blue gave a soldierly salute to those vanquished heroes—a token of respect from Americans to Americans."[62]

By claiming that veterans themselves had planted the seeds to sectional reconciliation during the final hours of the war, Gordon and Chamberlain fired the American imagination. At the reunion marking the fiftieth anniversary of Gettysburg, ten years after Gordon had ratified Chamberlain's version of the Appomattox surrender, Reconciliation was king. During the anniversary's celebration for New York veterans, a former colonel argued that one "might long search the records of chivalrous deeds in warfare to find a match for Chamberlain's and Gordon's at Appomattox" but would almost certainly return empty-handed.[63]

The Reconciliation movement may explain why Shaara selected Chamberlain as his foremost protagonist. Although the Maine soldier may today seem a logical choice for a novel about Gettysburg, this view depends by and large on the fact that *The Killer Angels* rescued the man from obscurity. Prior to 1974, few Americans knew Chamberlain's name or of the impressive performance of his 20th Maine on July 2, 1863. On that day, the regiment defended a crucial portion of Little Round Top and helped save the Union flank—a feat for which Chamberlain received the Congressional Medal of Honor.[64] In the August 1975 issue of *Civil War Times Illustrated*, the reviewer puzzled over Shaara's decision to include Chamberlain in his cast of characters. Offering rationales for the chapters told from the perspective of Lee, Longstreet, Harrison, Buford, Armistead, and Fremantle, he asked: "But what of Chamberlain, who comes close to being the central character of the novel? Despite his key role at Little Round Top, he was not at that time a prominent officer. The answer must be simply that Shaara was fascinated by this citizen soldier, the only non-professional among the novel's military men."[65] On one level, this explanation makes good sense: Shaara read Chamberlain's postwar writings and clearly admired the spirit and sacrifices of the scholar-turned-soldier. Yet if we consider the choice in light of Shaara's aristocracy-democracy interpretation of the war, then the presence of Chamberlain becomes all the more clear.

Not only did Chamberlain's version of Appomattox place him squarely within the Reconciliation movement, but also—as we have seen—his postwar writings reveal him to be a Northern hero who understood the war beyond the emancipationist vision. Shaara's novel almost always maneuvers indirectly rather than in direct assaults, and in Chamberlain it finds an oblique way to challenge the centrality of slavery to the war. The real-life Chamberlain made the challenge more overt. One of his biographers, Alice Rains Trulock, characterized Chamberlain's view of pre- and postwar America in stark terms: "The white man's country it was, and the white man's country it remained." As evidence, she quoted excerpts from his 1878 *Boston Journal* article, "The Old Flag—What Was Surrendered? And What Was Won?" There Chamberlain agreed that freedmen in the South were "abused," but suggested that "so are the Chinese in California, so are 40,000 poor girls in London, and so are the Indians." He rejected the notion that "the best blood in all the land" had been spilled during the war simply so "that negroes might have no one to stop them in going to the polls." Trulock further noted that Chamberlain voiced "what others would not" when he wrote in the white supremacist vein: "Yes, I say it. The men who have made a country what it is, given it character and built their very lives into its history are to have the foremost hand if we would keep the country true to its mission, true to its ideal." In short, the nation stood "first [for] the men who made it so, then those who are cast upon it."[66]

If Shaara discovered in Chamberlain a historical figure whose sentiments were in step with what he wanted his novel to convey, he was wise in choosing not to simply insert the hero's words into his narrative. Rather, just as he admitted to updating the "naïve" and "quaint" language of the nineteenth century to better fit "the modern ear," so too did Shaara adjust Chamberlain's statements to fit the expectations of his modern audience. Treating with care Chamberlain's postwar rhetoric concerning the division between whites and blacks, he protected the soldier's reputation from readers who would not agree to name America "the white man's country." In fact, at one point in the novel Shaara's Chamberlain says of the two races, "To me there was never any difference," a bold statement that even staunch abolitionists might not have uttered in 1863 (186). Yet in other ways, Shaara remained true to what he read in Chamberlain's postwar writing, especially in the scene involving the black "John Henry." The novel dramatizes Chamberlain's "revulsion" when he sees the escaped slave up close, a feeling "he had not expected" (179). Moreover, the scene portrays the fugitive as incapable of speaking English, wounded, and lying prone on the ground—details that correspond neatly to Chamberlain's vision of Africans "cast upon" the nation's shores. Black people stand as bystanders in America, without a voice, while white men are those who truly "have made [the] country what it is, given it character and built their very lives into its history." Indeed, as the white troops gather and march toward blood and glory at Gettysburg, the abandoned black man wanders "generally east," away from the making of this new, western nation (182).

Whether or not we err in assuming that "Shaara's favorite is obviously Chamberlain," there can be little doubt that Shaara found the soldier a perfect fit for his novel.[67] First, Chamberlain stood as a genuine Gettysburg hero; second, his postwar writings put him at the forefront of the Reconciliation movement; and third, he fought for the victorious North. This last point seems crucial. Although Longstreet's six chapters draw close to Chamberlain's seven, Shaara made sure to place a Northern character at the helm of his narrative. The power of the novel—and its portrait of democratic victory over residual American aristocracy—depends on its championing a figure who fought for national unity. While Gordon also fought at Gettysburg, and played a more important role in postwar Reconciliation than Chamberlain, his allegiance to the South would have virtually excluded him from Shaara's consideration. The author needed Gordon's equivalent in blue. As a Northerner who after the war remarked on the "manly qualities and earnest motives" of Southern soldiers, and who played down in print the relevance of slavery to the war's memory, Chamberlain made an attractive choice.[68]

V.

Some readers, having identified the different principles and ideologies represented by Shaara's major characters, may wish to describe the novel as a literary allegory. In some ways, *The Killer Angels'* use of character, Lee in particular, belongs to this trend in historical fiction. Naomi Jacobs has noted that "certain figures from pop culture and national history can still provide this sort of ready-made allegorical character . . . a convenient code reference to an elaborate set of associations in the reader's and/or writer's mind."[69] Civil War figures seem especially ripe for this kind of coding, particularly because the Lost Cause, Reconciliation, and emancipationist traditions often attempt to assign a given meaning or significance to particular heroes. This phenomenon has long been the case in literary and historical treatments of Lee, Stonewall Jackson, Jefferson Davis, and Abraham Lincoln. Yet not all of the characters in *The Killer Angels* function allegorically, and I believe our understanding of the novel may benefit from looking at it within a broader context of historical fiction. In his study of the fictions of Sir Walter Scott,

Harry E. Shaw observed: "Historical novelists whose works center on history are usually not content to give a panoramic view of an age. They wish to understand, evaluate, and sometimes to rebel against or accommodate themselves to what they have presented. They are faced, in other words, with the problem of giving not only shape but meaning to history." Such writers, Shaw continued, "wish to use their plotted actions and characters to dramatize directly the meaning they have discovered in historical process."[70] These words well describe Shaara as a historical novelist, one interested not only in "living" the events he re-created (as he suggested in his "To The Reader" page) but also in helping his countrymen understand what the Civil War and Northern victory mean for them personally.

Considering the laurels garnered by *The Killer Angels*, it seems important to ask whether the novel has done as much as other famed works of Civil War literature to bring Americans face to face with the war and its issues. In 1978, W. L. Rose pointed out that "four of the most popular reading-viewing events in all American history" have involved the Civil War era and its primary concerns: race and region.[71] Discussing Harriet Beecher Stowe's *Uncle Tom's Cabin* (1852), Thomas Dixon's *The Clansman* (1905), Margaret Mitchell's *Gone with the Wind* (1936), and Alex Haley's *Roots* (1976), Rose argued that each work "appeared at just the moment when a new synthesis was forming concerning the American Civil War and race in America." Surely *The Killer Angels* has not rivaled these works in terms of immediate and explosive popular success. And no one would argue that the film *Gettysburg* has made, in either the short or the long term, the cultural waves of *Birth of a Nation* (1915), *Gone with the Wind* (1939), or even the 1977 television miniseries *Roots*. Yet it seems significant that Shaara's novel did inspire a fifth major reading-viewing event in American history: Ken Burns's nine-part, eleven-hour 1990 PBS documentary *The Civil War*.[72] Burns has explained that he never had the courage to make the film until he read *The Killer Angels* in the final days of 1984: "I had never visited Gettysburg, knew almost nothing about the battle before I read that book, but here it all came alive. . . . I remember sitting straight up after finishing the book and resolving right then and there to make the film, a project that would ultimately take more than five and a half years. . . . I wept. No book, novel or nonfiction, had ever done that to me before."[73] Burns's love for the novel shined through his documentary, a fact not lost on historians who have written about the film and its success among the forty million Americans who tuned in to watch. Gallagher has guessed that "Burns's deep admiration for Michael Shaara's novel *The Killer Angels* contributed to [the filmmaker's] unbalanced treatment of Gettysburg." The film "lavishes nearly 45 minutes on the campaign in Pennsylvania versus fewer than eleven [on the factors] that settled Vicksburg's fate."[74] Similarly, Gabor S. Boritt has noted that *The Killer Angels* made Chamberlain "into a folk hero," a fact borne out in Burns's documentary, where the other soldiers and regiments defending Little Round Top disappear "almost entirely." Shaara's novel and Burns's documentary—read, viewed, and internalized by millions of Americans—hence illustrate what Boritt called "the evolving mythology of the battle."[75]

Above all, the observations of Burns and his critics illustrate that *The Killer Angels* has connected, directly and indirectly, with Americans from varied backgrounds and walks of life. Many would join McPherson in naming it their favorite historical novel. D. Scott Hartwig has noted the book's peculiar ability to fascinate even readers uninterested in American history. He realized "how powerful and moving Michael Shaara's work was" upon learning that his cousin, a foreign exchange student with little interest in the American Civil War, had once listed *The Killer Angels* as a favorite work of fiction: "If it could reach out to a well read, highly intelligent high school student in Japan, Shaara had connected."[76]

I have argued that a great deal of the novel's success rests on the decision by Shaara to represent the war as democratic America's victory over Old World aristocracy.[77] This is not to say that readers lack other good reasons for praising Shaara's novel or that they do not think about it in different ways. To the contrary, *The Killer Angels* connects with the public on many levels, and often for reasons having little to do with the fall of aristocracy. Some like that it comes to grips with "the brutality of Gettysburg," breaking through "the constraints of the folklore and romanticism that have entrapped so many writers in the past." Others seem less interested in the novel's gritty realism than in what they perceive to be a fair, bipartisan representation of the war. Still others find that Shaara's novel bucks the trend—long deplored by Civil War scholars and enthusiasts—of badly written, sentimental, or historically uninformed fictions about the conflict. Yet none of these reasons, taken alone or together, can explain the success of the novel. Without a central concept and message, *The Killer Angels* would have felt hollow—no matter how impressive its historical accuracy, subtle prose, and objectivity.[78]

In representing the war as the nation's triumph over a European world that threatened to enslave all future Americans, Shaara showed that contemporary readers owed their freedom to the events of July 1–3, 1863. His novel can therefore persuade white readers that Northern victory affected them directly, amounting to more than a reconciled America and freedom for blacks. Indeed, by collapsing the evils of slavery within the larger evils of the Old World, Shaara attended to emancipation without alienating those readers who either passionately refute or support its centrality to the war. *The Killer Angels* therefore makes itself attractive to readers weary of seemingly removed or distant explanations for the war's cause and meaning. Even those who come to the novel with a decidedly Southern bias can find much to praise in Shaara's representation of the war. Although he depicted Southern aristocracy as an evil that must be stamped out, he treated Confederate personalities in an evenhanded and usually positive fashion. While some readers may dislike his portrait of Lee as old and feeble, Shaara allowed Lee all of the dignity we would expect of the commander. Moreover, the emphasis on Lee's ill health ties directly to Shaara's picture of an aristocracy already on the decline. By giving us a dying Lee, a Longstreet whose ideas differ from those of the Old World, and Southern soldiers who fight for themselves rather than their "betters," Shaara complicated his portrait of an aristocratic South enough for readers to differentiate between it and Fremantle's England. Certainly by the end of the novel—if not before—we would agree with Tom Chamberlain that the Confederates are "Americans anyway, even if they are Rebs" (364). Because *The Killer Angels* appeals to a shared American, democratic heritage without devaluing Southern valor, even readers sympathetic to the Confederate cause would find it hard to dismiss the novel as partisan.

Singer-songwriter Steve Earle provided one example of how Shaara's readers have acknowledged and taken to heart the message of *The Killer Angels*. On his 1999 album *The Mountain*, Earle performs "Dixieland"—a song narrated from the point of view of Shaara's colorful Kilrain. First recounting something of his life in County Clare, Ireland, and his voyage to America, Kilrain then turns to his role in the Civil War:

> I am Kilrain of the 20th Maine and we fight for Chamberlain
> 'Cause he stood right with us when the Johnnies came like a banshee on the wind
> When the smoke cleared out of Gettysburg many a mother wept
> For many a good boy died there, sure, and the air smelted just like death

In the second half of the song, Earle showed himself to be a careful reader of Shaara's novel:

> I am Kilrain of the 20th Maine and I damn all gentlemen
> Whose only worth is their father's name and the sweat of a workin' man
> Well we come from the farms and the city streets and a hundred foreign lands
> And we spilled our blood in the battle's heat
> Now we're all Americans

Now set to music, Kilrain once again declares his contempt for gentlemen; but here—more so than in *The Killer Angels*—the Irishman leaves the door open to embrace Southerners. In the reunion-laden declaration, "Now we're all Americans," he comes around to Chamberlain's way of thinking. Like Shaara before him, Earle presented the blood and heat of battle as a forge in which true Americans, from Maine to "Dixieland," can split apart the shackles of the Old World.[79]

To what extent has *The Killer Angels* left its mark on Civil War fictions published after 1974? Clearly Shaara's son, the best-selling author Jeff Shaara, owed the novel an enormous debt of gratitude. "Something I will never take for granted," he told an interviewer, "is that it was my father who opened the door for me to be doing this in the first place. Michael Shaara left us a true classic in *The Killer Angels*, and the success of the film *Gettysburg* should have been his success. He died too soon, and never understood the enormous impact his work had on so many people. That is the responsibility I now carry. I'm continuing the story he began, a story that if he were alive would be his to tell. That's an extraordinary privilege." Jeff Shaara's first book, *Gods and Generals* (1996), functioned as a prequel to his father's novel; another, *The Last Full Measure* (1998), was its sequel and the final work of what Random House styles a Civil War "trilogy." The son's comments suggest that he and his publishers either did not realize, or chose to ignore, the fact that his father's novel was meant to stand alone as a representation of the entire war. This point aside, in his books Jeff Shaara followed closely his father's approach to dialogue and characterization. Most notably, he made use of Michael Shaara's method of shifting the point of view among men from both the Northern and Southern armies.[80]

In particular, *The Killer Angels* may have influenced how later writers of fiction depicted famous Civil War personalities, especially Longstreet and Lee. In the acknowledgments section of his Civil War novel *Cold Mountain* (1997), a work that won the National Book Award, Charles Frazier mentioned no works of celebrated Civil War fiction. Yet in an early chapter of his book, Frazier drew brief sketches of Lee and Longstreet that seem congruent with Shaara's portrait of these commanders. The narrator observes that, in the eyes of Frazier's Confederate protagonist, Inman, Longstreet appears quite different from the "noble-looking" Lee and the "befeathered" Stuart: "Longstreet had a grey shawl of wool draped about his shoulders. Compared to the other two men, Longstreet looked like a stout hog drover." But the Virginians' grand appearance means little to the soldier's assessment of his commanders: "From what Inman had seen of Lee's way of thinking, he'd any day rather have Longstreet backing him in a fight. Dull as Longstreet looked, he had a mind that constantly sought ground configured so a man could hunker down and do a world of killing from a position of relative safety." The narrator then shares with the reader Inman's unorthodox thinking about Lee, thoughts "unspeakable" among the ranks: "Even . . . early in the war, his opinion differed considerably from Lee's, for it appeared to him that we like fighting plenty, and the more terrible it is the better. And he suspected that Lee liked it most of all and would, if given his preference, general them right through the gates of death itself." One wonders whether Frazier's confident pictures of a wise, defensive-minded Longstreet, and a dangerous and bloodthirsty Lee, would have existed had not *The Killer Angels* first licensed and popularized these characterizations.[81]

The same question applies to the portrait of Lee found in the 2001 novel *Gettysburg*, authored by James Reasoner. Like Shaara, Reasoner portrayed Lee as aging and possibly ill, "a tired old man with his coat off." Agitated when Longstreet suggests withdrawing from Gettysburg to a defensive position, Lee, we discover, "had come to Pennsylvania to fight . . . running away from a fight rubbed him the wrong way." Reasoner also made use of the Longstreet–Fremantle, New World–Old World opposition drawn by Shaara in *The Killer Angels*. Following Pickett's charge, Reasoner's Fremantle says, "I saw unimaginable gallantry in that field today." In response, Longstreet snaps: "It didn't get us anything. . . . Except for a lot of good men dead." Admittedly, it makes little sense to scour every Civil War novel or story published since 1974 for passages that hearken back to *The Killer Angels*. What matters is that Shaara's interpretation of history, and his literary strategies, appear to have struck a chord among others interested in exploring the war through fiction.[82]

The influence of *The Killer Angels* may extend beyond lay readers, filmmakers, and novelists, and into the very historiography of the war. Shaara wrote the novel during the 1960s and early 1970s, amid a burgeoning period of revisionist Civil War history. While his decision to clothe Longstreet in brighter tones than Lee clashed with a century of myth and tradition, Shaara was not the first to absolve Longstreet of sins at Gettysburg. Glenn Tucker helped revise how twentieth-century Americans thought about Longstreet and the Pennsylvania campaign with his 1958 history, *High Tide at Gettysburg*. The work represented "the first major separate study of the battle since 1873 which did not treat Longstreet as a scapegoat." A number of other works from that period, such as George R. Stewart's *Pickett's Charge: A Microhistory of the Final Attack at Gettysburg, July 3, 1863* (1959), also portrayed Longstreet in positive terms. Stewart concluded that the South turned on Old Pete in part to deny that "Lee had ordered an impossibility" at Gettysburg, and he found indictments of Longstreet's behavior "unfounded, and in fact utterly fantastic." Published as an academic contribution to the war's Centennial, the volume *Why the North Won the Civil War* (1960) contained a now-famous revisionist essay by T. Harry Williams, "The Military Leadership of North and South." While acknowledging Lee's many worthy qualities, Williams took the Confederate commander to task for following the outmoded ideas of Antoine Henri Jomini, a Swiss officer who served with Napoleon and whose published theories on war dominated the thinking of early nineteenth-century strategists. "In many respects," Williams concluded, "Lee was not a modern-minded general." This statement squares neatly with Shaara's backward-looking Lee, a figure wholly unlike Longstreet, "one of the first of the new soldiers, the cold-eyed men who have sensed the birth of the new war of machines" (xi).[83]

In the years leading up to the appearance of *The Killer Angels*, the historian Thomas L. Connelly also published noted revisionist essays. These articles anticipated his controversial books of the 1970s and 1980s, *The Marble Man: Robert E. Lee and His Image in American Society* (1977) and *God and General Longstreet: The Lost Cause and the Southern Mind* (1982). These essays and books cast doubt on Lee's talents as a military strategist and explained the general's modern reputation in terms of postwar mythmaking, not bona fide accomplishments. Connelly and Barbara L. Bellows, his coauthor on the second book, argued that the Lee Cult had often explained the general's failures by relegating blame to his subordinates—particularly Longstreet. Among other issues, they concerned themselves with "the historiographical puzzle" that transformed Longstreet into "the scapegoat of the Lost

Cause." Connelly may have appreciated one particular passage appearing three-fourths of the way into *The Killer Angels*. There Shaara depicted a conversation between Thomas J. Goree and Longstreet, in which Goree reports that Confederates blamed Longstreet rather than Lee for the failed assaults on the Union left: "Thing is, if anything bad happens now, they all blame it on you. I seen it comin'. They can't blame General Lee. Not no more. So they take it out on you. You got to watch yourself, General" (254).[84]

Did the writing of Tucker, Stewart, Williams, and Connelly influence Shaara's thinking? From one perspective, the novelist seemed less interested in revitalizing Longstreet's reputation, and diminishing that of Lee, than in representing a struggle between the Old World and the New. Yet from another perspective, the novel undoubtedly reflected Shaara's own estimation of the historical commander and his lieutenant, and the preference for Longstreet shows. Even if we cannot be sure whether these scholars shaped Shaara's thinking, we must acknowledge that *The Killer Angels*—one of the first "pro-Longstreet" novels ever written—appeared in an era of Civil War revision. To be sure, some serious students of the conflict considered *The Killer Angels* a deliberate contribution to the brewing reassessment of the war and its participants. A reviewer for the *New York Times* thought Shaara might have done better to write a standard historical treatment of Gettysburg: "[It] is not quite clear from this book why a straightforward narrative would not have served Mr. Shaara as well as the fictional form he chose." As if forgetting Shaara was a novelist, the reviewer suggested that his "fictional touches" risked obscuring the book's contribution to historical studies. Clearly, for some readers, Shaara's project amounted to more than the writing of fiction.[85]

The aforementioned *Civil War Times Illustrated* review of the novel, in August 1975, occupied the entire book reviews section of the issue: a space usually divided among reviews of four or more works of scholarly history. The reviewer, Robert Ashley, saw the novel as unique: "Shaara's novel is quite different from Crane's and from any other Civil War novel I have ever read. Its uniqueness lies in the fact that, with one or two minor exceptions, its characters are all historical." For Ashley, Shaara's novel differed from most Civil War fiction in that it participated in the historical debates of the moment. He saw Shaara taking up the revisionist flag: "In the Lee-Longstreet controversy Shaara comes down squarely on the side of Longstreet. Lee is portrayed as grand and noble, but also as old, ill, dangerously over-confident, and too loosely-reigned in command." Ashley argued that the "historical flavor" of the novel "is further enhanced by eighteen superb maps far more readable than those which usually appear in factual accounts of the battle," as well as by Shaara's inclusion of a factual foreword and afterword. At one point comparing the *The Killer Angels* to Freeman's *Lee's Lieutenants,* he ended the review by considering the novel alongside more nonfictional, historical works: "From researchers like Coddington, Dowdey, or Tucker, Civil War buffs can get a more comprehensive and more accurate, but not more stirring, picture of Gettysburg. *The Killer Angels* is both fascinating history and exciting fiction."[86]

If *Civil War Times Illustrated* could designate Shaara's novel "fascinating history," it seems reasonable that *The Killer Angels* might have influenced some of the popular and scholarly accounts of Gettysburg and the war that appeared after 1974. Mapping the novel's influence, however, would be difficult; historians draw on a multitude of sources, and few would acknowledge that their view of the past owes a great deal to a work of fiction. Yet it seems worthwhile to observe that several dimensions of Shaara's presentation reappeared in the pages of academic histories.

A professor at the University of South Carolina, Connelly alerted his graduate students to *The Killer Angels* in the late 1970s. (The scholar may have held a particular interest in Shaara's fiction because, at one point during his life, Connelly had worked on his own novel about Gettysburg.) William Garrett Piston first read Shaara's book while studying under Connelly, then again in 1980 as he developed his dissertation on Longstreet. In 1987, he published the revised work as *Lee's Tarnished Lieutenant: James Longstreet and His Place in Southern History,* a book that explores in detail how Longstreet took on "the image not of a hero but of a villain, even a Judas." Piston credited *The Marble Man* and Glenn Tucker's *Lee and Longstreet at Gettysburg* (1968) as the greatest inspirations for his project, but acknowledged that *The Killer Angels* helped solidify his interest in Longstreet and the Gettysburg controversy. It also helped convince him to examine how works of fiction, from 1865 to the Centennial, contributed to the Southern view of the First Corps commander.[87]

Since the 1990s, academic and independent scholars have continued to show both the direct and indirect influence of *The Killer Angels*. McPherson was correct to say that the modern prominence of Chamberlain grew out of Shaara's presentation. In the wake of the novel and the films it inspired—the Ken Burns documentary and the feature *Gettysburg*—authors produced a deluge of works on Chamberlain and his regiment. A partial list of these studies might include Michael Golay's *To Gettysburg and Beyond: The Parallel Lives of Joshua Lawrence Chamberlain and Edward Porter Alexander*

(1994), Mark Perry's *Conceived in Liberty: Joshua Lawrence Chamberlain, William Oates, and the American Civil War* (1997), Alice Rains Trulock's *In the Hands of Providence: Joshua L. Chamberlain and the American Civil War* (1992), the 1995 reprinting of Willard Mosher Wallace's *Soul of the Lion: A Biography of General Joshua Lawrence Chamberlain* (1960), and Thomas A. Desjardin's *Stand Firm Ye Boys From Maine: The 20th Maine and the Gettysburg Campaign* (2001). Most works have done little to alter Shaara's heroic presentation of Chamberlain. For example, in *Hallowed Ground: A Walk at Gettysburg* (2003), McPherson referred several times to *The Killer Angels* and to its positive effect on tourism at the battlefield park. He concluded that the "hero-worship of Chamberlain" was not unwarranted, as it seemed clear that the soldier "deserved the Congressional Medal of Honor he won." McPherson also agreed with Shaara that it "*is* about time for Longstreet to get his due," and on the issue of Lee's health and temperament observed that "perhaps, as the novelist Michael Shaara suggested in *The Killer Angels*, a flare-up of Lee's heart condition left him by turns belligerent and indecisive, gnawed by the conviction that he had little time left." On the revisionist front, Alan T. Nolan published *Lee Considered* in 1991, a book that produced a storm of controversy. While certainly following in the footsteps of Connelly, Nolan set out less to chart the postwar "apotheosis of Lee" than to "question the historicity" of the Lee tradition. In doing so, he discussed the Lee-Longstreet controversy raised by many writers before him, Shaara included.[88]

    The aforementioned authors and books do not comprise all of the historical work written after 1974 that shares some of the interests and viewpoints of Shaara. Nor do they represent historical efforts that even agree with the ideas put forward by *The Killer Angels*. Rather, they demonstrate that the novel has touched not only the imaginations of lay readers but also the serious debates and trends within the formal study of Civil War history. Admittedly, some scholars have worked hard to dispel the mythologies advanced by veterans' narratives, many of which Shaara reinforced in his novel. Yet nearly all share with Shaara a fascination with the power of soldiers' memoirs to shape and define how Americans view the war.

    We must therefore discount Shaara's claim that in order to portray the authentic battle and war he avoided historical opinion and confined his own interpretation to the realm of character (vii). In truth, by crafting his interpretation of the war from the often competing pieces of veterans' narratives and mythologies, Shaara revealed himself to be in deep conversation with historical opinion—specifically that of veterans. And as an arbiter of their traditions, he demonstrated his control and mastery over his sources. Hayden White has said that every historical narrative "consists, not of one single code monolithically utilized, but of a complex set of codes the interweaving of which by the author ... attests to his talents as an artist, as master rather than servant of the codes available for use."[89] The narratives of Civil War veterans certainly qualify as "a complex set of codes." Yet if not a servant of veterans' codes, Shaara nonetheless strove *not to appear* their master. In fact, in order to create an aura of authenticity, he wanted the reader to believe that he had *not* made choices, that he had *not* manipulated facts, that there was virtually no manipulation at all behind the text.

It should not surprise us, therefore, that Ken Burns so admired *The Killer Angels*. Indeed, Burns's respect for the novel reflected his documentary filmmaker's sense of what an artist should do—make choices and manipulate facts to deliver a message but always *appear* neutral. Robert Brent Toplin explained this approach: "A fine documentary program such as *The Civil War* does not, on its face, appear to have a point of view. Rather, it leaves the impression of having provided a balanced, objective account of the wartime experience."[90] Burns may have learned much from *The Killer Angels*. By playing the role of an unobtrusive writer intending merely to bring alive the story of Gettysburg, Shaara won the confidence of millions of readers and did much to shape popular understanding of the Civil War. Moreover, he made an important contribution to the study of veterans' literature, demonstrating the enduring power of those narratives, when properly managed, to attract and engage modern Americans.

Shaara drew near to revealing his true face at only one point in the novel, when narrating the first chapter from the point of view of Harrison, a Shakespearean actor turned Confederate spy. To avoid suspicion from Yankee patrols and Pennsylvania farmers, Harrison puts his acting to good use, pretending to be "a poor half-witted farmer" scouring the countryside for his runaway wife. Once back in the Confederate camp, Harrison confides to Longstreet: "Strange thing about it all, thing that bothers me is that when you do this job right nobody knows you're doing it, nobody ever watches you work, do you see? And sometimes I can't help but wish I had an audience. I've played some scenes, ah, General, but I've been lovely" (13). Shaara may not have been a spy, but he was certainly an actor. And as the success of *The Killer Angels* shows, he too played some lovely scenes.

Conclusion

GRIEF CROWDED THE SECRET ROOMS OF THEIR HEARTS
Haunted Veterans in *The Judas Field*

> And while my imagination is like the weaver's shuttle, playing backward and forward through these two decades of time, I ask myself, Are these things real? did they happen? ... Did I see those brave and noble countrymen of mine laid low in death and weltering in their blood? Did I see our country laid waste and in ruins? Did I see soldiers marching, the earth trembling and jarring beneath their measured tread?
> —Sam R. Watkins, *"Co. Aytch," Maury Grays, First Tennessee Regiment: or, A Side Show of the Big Show* (1882)

> It is believed that what is herein written will appeal largely to a common experience among soldiers. In full faith that such is the case, [these sketches] are now presented to veterans, their children, and the public as an important contribution of warp to the more majestic woof which comprises the history of the Great Civil War already written. That history, to date, is a history of battles, of campaigns and of generals.
> —John D. Billings, *Hardtack and Coffee; or, The Unwritten Story of Army Life* (1888)

Sam Watkins and John Billings fought on opposite sides during the Civil War, and their published narratives differ widely in content, style, and delivery. In *Co. Aytch*, Watkins told of his own experiences in camp and battle, remembering old friends and reflecting on episodes that were sometimes humorous and often horrific. By contrast, Billings avoided the arena of battles. He created instead a documentary-like account of common soldiers as they ate, slept, foraged, and drilled in the Army of the Potomac.

Today *Co. Aytch* and *Hardtack and Coffee* remain two of the most popular soldiers' accounts of the conflict. Each fills its own niche within the written history of the struggle, and each offers the same underlying vision: that of ordinary Americans caught in the storm of a vast and impersonal war.

As captured in the previous passages, the metaphor of the weaver appealed to both men. Watkins relied on the "shuttle" of his imagination to weave a steady pattern out of memories that were traumatic, jarring, and occasionally surreal. In turn, Billings conceived of his collected sketches as "warp," the supporting threads necessary to make sense of the "more majestic woof" of Civil War history. Readers today may be forgiven if they miss Billings's arcane reference to threads crisscrossing over a weaver's loom. After all, the term "majestic woof" would strike many as an apt way to describe the enormous size and decibel of soldiers' writings about the conflict.

But as the memoirs and fictions discussed in this book prove, not all narratives of the war amount to grand but incoherent barking. Watkins and Billings were joined by thousands of soldiers, of every rank and branch of service, who wrote articulately about the war's human experience. In their massive contribution to American letters, Union and Confederate veterans argued that to understand the Civil War one must explore the thoughts, motivations, and relationships of its participants. Crane and Shaara responded to that vision with narratives about soldiers grappling with a war that threatened not only their nation but also their own families, friendships, and lives. If writers such as Faulkner, Gordon, and Mitchell have attended to men and women *not* in uniform, they have nonetheless done so in the spirit of military memoirists who understood the complexities of their society in terms of personal experience. Each of the Civil War fictions examined here—whether told from the vantage point of uniformed troops or of Southern women and children—grants readers the opportunity to transcend the role of spectator and live the past vicariously through the sensations and voices of those who experienced it firsthand.

But what of Civil War fiction first published during the last few decades? How has the genre evolved since the publication of *The Killer Angels* in 1974 and the close of the Vietnam War, one year later? I would argue that recent Civil War fiction reflects especially the lessons learned from America's twentieth-century wars about the psychological burdens borne by soldiers. The Vietnam War, in particular, fostered a national discussion about the effects of prolonged trauma on combat troops. New war memoirs have contributed to that conversation by providing compelling first-person accounts of suffering and loss. Since the late 1970s several Vietnam memoirs have attracted a wide readership, including *Born on the Fourth of July* by Ron Kovic (1976), *A Rumor of War* by Philip Caputo (1977), and *We Were Soldiers Once . . . and Young* by Harold G. Moore and Joseph L. Galloway (1992). World War II memoirs such as William Manchester's *Goodbye, Darkness* (1980) and E. B. Sledge's *With the Old Breed* (1981) have similarly awakened readers to the emotional and physical aftershocks of battle—including nightmares, flashbacks, panic attacks, and repressed memories of trauma.[1]

These late twentieth-century war memoirs differ dramatically from those penned by most veterans of 1861–65. Restrained by Victorian literary conventions and by their own codes of propriety and manhood, Civil War veterans did not typically record the unspeakable horrors, anger, fear, grief, and vulgarities that they experienced while in uniform. But the soldiers' memoirs of later wars have provided a new lens through which to view the remembrances of Yankees and Confederates. Filling in the narrative "gaps," novelists have often drawn on America's more recent war memoirs when portraying the experiences of Civil War soldiers.

In 2006, Howard Bahr published *The Judas Field*, one of the best Civil War novels of the last thirty years. As I will show in the short analysis to follow, Bahr's novel provides an excellent example of how recent Civil War fiction has responded to the human legacy of America's twentieth-century military conflicts. Set in 1885, the frame narrative portrays the return of three Confederate veterans to the battlefield at Franklin, Tennessee. The men have been asked by a dying friend to recover the bodies of her long-buried father and brother, both of whom died in the Confederate assaults at Franklin. As the action swings back and forth through time, between the battlefields of 1861–65 and the return to Franklin, the novel explores the material and psychic damage left in the wake of a vicious war. Haunted by memories and suffering from alcoholism and addiction, the novel's veterans struggle against physical and mental collapse.

In its use of period detail and antiquated dialogue, *The Judas Field* almost always feels true to its nineteenth-century settings. But Bahr at times borrowed from the memories of twentieth-century veterans in order to add texture and authenticity to his picture of Confederate soldiers. For example, one of the most unforgettable episodes in *With the Old Breed*, Sledge's classic memoir of the Pacific war, occurs during its account of the long battle for Okinawa. The Alabama native remembered that, as a young marine mortarman, he was ordered to entrench along a muddy ridge previously held by the Japanese. Setting about the task, his spade soon unearthed not only a "mass of wriggling maggots," but something altogether more horrific:

> In disgust, I drove the spade into the soil, scooped out the insects, and threw them down the front of the ridge. The next stroke of the spade unearthed buttons and scraps of cloth from a Japanese army jacket buried in the mud—and another mass of maggots. I kept on doggedly. With the next thrust, metal hit the breastbone of a rotting Japanese corpse. I gazed down in horror and disbelief as the metal scraped a clean track through the mud along the dirty whitish bone and cartilage with ribs attached. The shovel skidded into the rotting abdomen with a squishing sound. The odor nearly overwhelmed me as I rocked back on my heels. . . . I began choking and gagging.

The accidental exhumation of an enemy's corpse stood out among the many "vile" sights and experiences that would traumatize Sledge for years. "Having to wallow in war's putrefaction was almost more than the toughest of us could bear," he explained. Digging into the dead Japanese soldier became part of the "the ghastly war nightmares" that haunted him "for many, many years."[2]

In *The Judas Field*, Bahr appeared to incorporate Sledge's experiences into the life of his protagonist, the Confederate soldier Cass Wakefield. During the first battle scene in the novel, the narrator describes in detail the actions of Cass and his comrades in the 21st Mississippi infantry: "[Now] the regiment was going to ground. The boys dug frantically with bayonets and tin plates and frying pans and with unsoldered canteen halves kept just for that purpose." Hysterically burrowing into the loose dirt, Cass makes the same horrible discovery as did Sledge:

> He dug with frantic joy, as if some great treasure lay just below. The ground was soft here, yielding, happy to embrace him. . . . He plunged his hand into a sudden cavity in the loose earth, drew it out—
> And stopped, blinking, trying to understand what he was seeing. He seemed to be holding a glove in his hand: a pale, translucent, oily glove that had come from no place he could imagine. He stared at the thing, trying to make sense of it, until all at once everything came into focus: a spray of white grubs squirming blindly in the sunlight,

an eruption of ants and beetles, the blue sleeve, the delicate bones of the hand he had grasped and stripped—a man buried here after the fighting a week ago, who had lain all this time cooking in the hot earth. And now the man himself burst from the grave, not in body but as an exhalation of gas, violated, crying outrage and humiliation against the still-living man who had shamed him. The smell hit Cass Wakefield full in the face. He screamed.

The two passages are similar enough that almost any reader familiar with Sledge's account will pause to wonder whether Bahr had in mind *With the Old Breed*. But beyond matters of literary homage, the effect of this passage is to build a corridor between worlds: the Civil War and the Pacific war; the nineteenth century and the twentieth; the world of fiction and the world of memoir. In witnessing their shared reactions to the same horrific and pitiful experience, we cannot help but conflate the Mississippi infantryman with the Alabama marine. As a result, the figure of the Civil War soldier becomes less distant in the eyes of the reader. No mythic figure of yore, admired but unknowable, Cass Wakefield here emerges as the same sort of frightened and traumatized figure found in memoirs about World War II, Vietnam, and more recent conflicts.[3]

To be sure, when viewed through the screen of twentieth-century war memoirs, the Civil War becomes a more recognizable phenomenon. Likewise, its participants become less difficult to identify with, because—to use the words of Stephen Crane—we better understand "how they *felt* in those scraps." Not only have later war memoirs helped readers to better imagine the traumas experienced by Civil War soldiers, but these narratives have also complicated our understanding of the Civil War *veteran:* the middle-aged or elderly man so prominent during late nineteenth- and early twentieth-century America. For generations, veterans were understood in largely symbolic terms. At best, they represented the golden age of American manhood, the epitome of self-sacrifice, patriotism, and unalloyed courage. At worst, they stood for historical and masculine exclusivity—a fraternity of holier-than-thou fogies who dismissed the accomplishments of later generations, especially those men who did not serve the nation in uniform and under arms. Complicating both stereotypes, recent war memoirs have led some novelists to contemplate the corrosive and debilitating power that *memory* may have held over those who survived the crucible of Civil War combat. As a result, Civil War fiction has increasingly portrayed veterans of 1861–65 as men akin to the troubled memoirists of later wars, proud of their service but deeply haunted by the past.

Certainly Bahr's novel depicts veteranhood in unhappy, even cynical terms. Just as Sledge noted that nightmares plagued him during the decades following World War II, so is Bahr's middle-aged protagonist terrorized by dreams twenty years after his battles with the Army of Tennessee: "Cass Wakefield woke shivering with anger and dread, the usual residue of his dreams. He did not believe his dreams meant anything—their only purpose seemed to be to scare the shit out of him—and he cursed them in the same way he cursed the deep midnight" (175). Although Cass faces his demons alone, his former comrades also lead damaged lives after the war. Early in the novel, his adopted son, Lucian—who had joined the regiment as an orphanage conscript—reflects on the mental fragility of the unit's survivors: "Rain and dark. Lucian was tired of them both, but he kept his sentiments well hidden, at the very edge of thought, lest Fate mistake him. This rain, this dark, whatever cold might come—these were nothing beside what the soldiers had known once, and now they lived with the fear that, if they pressed too hard, the terrors they remembered would come again" (51–52). The fear that the old hardships will return leads the veterans to adopt superstitious, self-denying behaviors: "Thus Tom Jenkins whistled in the night, Steven Peck always drank his coffee from a tin cup, Bloodworth often went without a coat in the coldest weather, the Craddocks stayed every month of November in hunting camp, living in dog tents, and Carl Nobles kept a bull's-eye canteen wound around his saddle horn. They did these things not from joy or sentiment or habit, but because they knew something was watching, waiting to snatch them up again if they let themselves get too comfortable" (52).

The novel shows that the precarious lifestyle of veterans extends directly from the depleted, shattered world they occupied during the war itself. Like his fellow Mississippi writer William Faulkner, Bahr presents Civil War troops as capable, even dangerous men. But while Faulkner's soldiers often appear stoic, Bahr's cry out under the weight of stress, loss, and survivor's guilt: "Grief crowded the secret rooms of their hearts. Now and then, it passed a shadow over their own faces, trembled in their own voices. Now and then, a man, sitting by a fire perhaps, or strolling through the camp, would suddenly begin to cry. He would weep without shame until he was done, while the boys looked away and were silent. No one ever laughed or ever brought it back again in jest. . . . So they grieved, and more: they were harried by guilt" (113). Whether suffering in public or alone, soldiers in *The Judas Field* appear as victims of post-traumatic stress disorder (PTSD), the anxiety disorder commonly associated with the veterans of modern wars. (The affliction was referred to obscurely as "soldier's heart" during the Civil War, or as "shell shock" or "battle fatigue" during the first half of the twentieth century.) The first prolonged clinical analysis of PTSD occurred during the 1970s and 1980s, when mental health specialists asserted that up to 60 percent of Vietnam veterans suffered from "Post-Vietnam syndrome."[4] Discussed openly in works of journalism and in Vietnam memoirs especially, the anxiety disorder has become yet another way in which novelists have sought to better understand the men who endured and survived the Civil War.

As a Vietnam veteran himself, Bahr may have drawn on his own experiences when peopling his novel with veterans whose outwardly "ordinary" lives conceal "a dark current of memory and violence" (197).[5] Discarding with the stereotype of the wizened veteran who cheerfully relates his war stories to all who will listen, the men of *The Judas Field* take a darker attitude toward the past: "That is how the war did for some people, Lucian thought. It used up everything, stole everything, and what remained—memory, mostly—was just enough to keep the shape of a man, just enough to propel the flesh from one day to the next, only without feeling or interest or desire" (196). The bleak lives led by Bahr's veterans derive, in part, from these men's inability to connect meaningfully with those who had not known combat. The veterans occupy a shadow world apart from civilian life, a prison house of the mind: "So the war did this, too: it put those who suffered by it all together in a glass jar like so many strange, dangerous insects, and they could crawl up and down the glass all they wanted, but they could never reach the other side" (202). Too ruined by past traumas to live happily, the veterans "created their own world out of memory and grief. Here they kept alive their anger and fed on it" (201–2).

The Judas Field also stands at odds with the traditional picture of grand old men happily fraternizing with former comrades and enemies alike. Rather, Bahr's portrait of despondent veterans seems in step with the now-familiar film footage of Vietnam veterans meeting dolefully in support groups, or congregating to commemorate, embrace, and sometimes weep before the Vietnam Veterans' Memorial in Washington, D.C. Some will therefore argue that *The Judas Field* has far more to teach us about the late twentieth century than the nineteenth. But I would caution readers not to dismiss the insights that Bahr's novel offers into the nature of Civil War veteranhood. At the very least, the book raises a series of worthwhile questions. To what extent were Civil War veterans' groups such as the GAR and the UCV popular for their therapeutic, rather than social and financial, qualities? Were such organizations attractive, in part, because they offered members a band of brothers who could understand them as no others could? Were battlefield reunions and tours—such as the famous Gettysburg reunion of 1913—only occasions for nostalgia and reconciliation? Or did many veterans feel deeply conflicted, and even terrified, when walking over the old battlefields to which they were inexplicably drawn?

In Bahr's hands, the return to the battlefield at Franklin inspires flashbacks, mental disassociations, and drug abuse. As Cass and Lucian approach the old gin house, where their unit saw its heaviest fighting twenty years earlier, their minds overflow with memories of deeply traumatic experiences. For example, when Cass notes numerous bullet holes punched through some of the buildings on the field, the sight triggers the memory of "all that lead and iron, rammed and charged, sent on its way toward living men who had to stand it somehow, who trembled behind their works while it hummed overhead, or walked upright into it . . . knowing it had come at last, that thing which happened only to others—bowels spilling out, curls of fat and ligament, dark blood spurting, brains leaking" (207). The old soldier's mind turns especially to the awful moment when the living soldier must comfort the dying one with lies: "*Is it bad?* they would ask, always. *How bad is it?* And a comrade, bending for a moment, would always say, *No, not bad—it's nothing, nothing a-tall*" (207–8). Cass drinks whiskey from a flask to fortify himself during the return to Franklin; for his part, Lucian cannot help but quaff a full bottle of laudanum in order to numb the pain he feels. Far stronger than the marijuana he smokes to dull his war-related headaches, the laudanum leaves him fumbling on his hands and knees in the mud. Yet even this "Black Draught" cannot put his mind at ease. When Lucian at last collapses entirely, drifting in and out of consciousness, he experiences visions of the dead.

Lucian's self-destructive behavior mirrors the accounts of some twentieth-century memoirists who recorded similar postwar addictions and breakdowns. In a postscript to the 1996 edition of *A Rumor of War*, Caputo recounted how survivor's guilt, combined with public interest in his best-selling Vietnam memoir, led to panic attacks and intense drinking: "One night, when I was particularly wound up and knocking back straight scotches, someone offered me a joint—a potent bomber of pure Columbian gold—and I smoked it down to the roach. The combination of exhaustion, anxiety, alcohol, and drugs had the inevitable effect: I had a nervous collapse and spent the next several days in the psychiatric ward of an East Coast hospital, drugged on Thorazine yet happy that no one could get to me." Caputo cast his hospitalization as evidence that he did not revisit his past traumas as a form of therapy: "Writing [the memoir] was a trial; living with its publication an ordeal." Similarly, the visit to the Franklin battlefield grants Cass and Lucian no relief from their horrific memories of combat. The task of exhuming long-dead soldiers, of literally digging up the past, instead inspires only grief, anger, and new acts of violence. As Cass kneels on the battlefield to drink whiskey, he reflects on the lives of veterans, paralyzed by grief: "They had come a long way to this place the first time, and even longer now, but no matter. For all time's turning, nothing important had changed; they still could not move forward, and they could not run away" (212).[6]

As we have seen, Bahr's portrait of Civil War veterans is a far cry from the familiar turn-of-the-century images of jaunty, bearded men cheerfully marching in parades on Decoration Day. The novel helps us to imagine what it meant to live with memory of the war on a daily basis. When we see Ike Gatlin hobbling through the streets of Cumberland, Mississippi, on feet long ago ruined by frostbite, we better appreciate the physical scars of war (51). And when we see Lucian living in a fog of drugs, or Cass avoiding holiday revelers because "easy joy was oddly repulsive to him, the thought of idle conversation unbearable" (21), we better appreciate the psychological burdens of those who escaped the "Death Angel" to become civilians again. By redefining what it meant to wear the label of "veteran" in the decades after 1865, Bahr has sought to improve our understanding of the long-term personal sacrifices made by those men who returned from the Civil War no less than by the survivors of America's twentieth-century conflicts.

Historians are fond of saying that each generation remakes the Civil War in its own image. Without a doubt, fiction has reinforced this axiom time and again. *The Judas Field* and other novels have indeed cast the Civil War soldier in the mold of the World War II, Vietnam, and Gulf War combatant. It may well be fair, at times, to complain of such works being anachronistic. But as I have suggested, it would be wrongheaded to conclude that these novels have lost sight of the participants of the Civil War. In the recent fiction of Allen Ballard, Thomas Dyja, Marie Jakober, Donald McCaig, Marly Youmans, and other writers, we witness the same honest and sustained effort to understand the Civil War veteran as found in the earlier works of Crane, Mitchell, Gordon, Faulkner, and Shaara. If some have drawn on the graphic memoirs of twentieth-century soldiers, or have portrayed Civil War veterans struggling with the same afflictions that have haunted troops returning from Southeast Asia or the Middle East, then these authors have in fact deepened our sympathy for those who endured the traumas of 1861–65. As Bahr and other writers of the last thirty years have demonstrated, the tone and perspectives of Civil War fiction may change over time, but the primary interest of the genre—the war's participants—will ensure its survival well into the twenty-first century.

I believe the continuing popularity of Civil War fiction demonstrates that these works help answer a communal need to participate in our past. In the same vein as reenacting organizations and battlefield tours, they provide an opportunity for readers to experience history firsthand. Yet memoirs and fictions are living things and do more than bring readers into contact with historical figures and events. They also investigate, challenge, revise, and reevaluate the sanctioned memories of the nation. Americans read and write Civil War literature not merely to inhabit the four-year span from 1861 to 1865, but also to negotiate the issues and traumas that inspired the conflict and that stand as its legacy. Veterans' memoirs and Civil War fictions deserve attention from anyone interested in American culture and literary history. Studied together, these narratives remark on the enduring power of the written word to shape American identity.

Notes

Introduction

1. Robert A. Lively, *Fiction Fights the Civil War: An Unfinished Chapter in the Literary History of the American People* (Chapel Hill: Univ. of North Carolina Press, 1957), 14.

2. Walt Whitman, *Memoranda during the War* (1875–76; repr., ed. Peter Coviello, New York: Oxford Univ. Press, 2004), 6.

3. Edmund Wilson, *Patriotic Gore: Studies in the Literature of the American Civil War* (New York: Oxford Univ. Press, 1962); Stephen Crane, *The Red Badge of Courage: An Episode of the American Civil War* (New York: D. Appleton and Company, 1895); Mary Johnston, *The Long Roll* (Boston: Houghton Mifflin, 1911); Margaret Mitchell, *Gone with the Wind* (New York: Macmillan, 1936). Wilson explained the subject of *Patriotic Gore* in straightforward terms: "This book describes some thirty men and women who lived through the Civil War, either playing some special role in connection with it or experiencing its impact in some interesting way, and who have left their personal records of some angle of it" (x).

4. Daniel Aaron, *The Unwritten War: American Writers and the Civil War* (New York: Alfred A. Knopf, 1973), 207–9, 211.

5. Caroline Gordon, *None Shall Look Back* (New York: Scribner's, 1937).

6. William Faulkner, *Absalom, Absalom!* (New York: Random House, 1936); William Faulkner, *The Unvanquished* (New York: Random House, 1938).

7. Michael Shaara, *The Killer Angels: A Novel* (New York: Random House, 1974).

8. Howard Bahr, *The Judas Field: A Novel of the Civil War* (New York: Picador, 2006).

9. Stephen Cushman, *Bloody Promenade: Reflections on a Civil War Battle* (Charlottesville: Univ. Press of Virginia, 1999), 224.

1. Various Veterans Had Told Him Tales

1. Cushman, *Bloody Promenade*, 209.
2. Phyllis Frus and Stanley Corkin, "The Civil War Remembered," in *Stephen Crane: The Red Badge of Courage, Maggie: A Girl of the Streets, and Other Selected Writings*, ed. Phyllis Frus and Stanley Corkin (New York: Houghton Mifflin, 2000), 290.
3. Quoted in Aaron, *Unwritten War*, 210.
4. For example, Stanley Wertheim has demonstrated that the plot, imagery, and themes of *The Red Badge of Courage* may reflect the contents of several postwar memoirs by veterans. Similarly, Philip D. Beidler has argued that veterans' reminiscences and semiautobiographical works are "indisputably" the "main 'objective' source" for the novel. See, respectively, Stanley Wertheim, "*The Red Badge of Courage* and Personal Narratives of the Civil War," *American Literary Realism: 1870–1910* 6 (Winter 1973): 61–65, and Philip D. Beidler, "Stephen Crane's *The Red Badge of Courage*: Henry Fleming's Courage in Its Contexts," *CLIO* 20 (Spring 1991): 240. For a discussion of the similarities between *The Red Badge of Courage* and Wilbur F. Hinman's *Corporal Si Klegg and His "Pard,"* see H. T. Webster, "Wilbur F. Hinman's *Corporal Si Klegg* and Stephen Crane's *The Red Badge of Courage*," *American Literature* 11 (Nov. 1939): 285–93.
5. Wilbur F. Hinman, *Corporal Si Klegg and His "Pard": How They Lived and Talked, and What They Did and Suffered, While Fighting for the Flag* (Cleveland, Ohio: Williams, 1887); Alonzo F. Hill, *Our Boys: The Personal Experiences of a Soldier in the Army of the Potomac* (Philadelphia: J. E. Potter, 1864); John D. Billings, *Hardtack and Coffee; or, The Unwritten Story of Army Life* (Philadelphia: Thompson, 1888); Frank Wilkeson, *Recollections of a Private Soldier in the Army of the Potomac* (New York: G. P. Putnam's Sons, 1887); Warren Lee Goss, *Recollections of a Private* (New York: T. Y. Crowell and Co., 1890).
6. Mrs. Roger A. Pryor, "The Genesis of Decoration Day," *New York Times*, May 29, 1898, 7; David W. Blight, *Race and Reunion: The Civil War in American Memory* (Cambridge, Mass.: Harvard Univ. Press, 2001), 71.
7. Gerald Linderman, *Embattled Courage: The Experience of Combat in the American Civil War* (New York: Free Press, 1987), 287.
8. Blight, *Race and Reunion*, 172; Kirk Savage, *Standing Soldiers, Kneeling Slaves: Race, War, and Monument in Nineteenth-Century America* (Princeton, N.J.: Princeton Univ. Press, 1997), 162, 164, 162.
9. Earl J. Hess, *The Union Soldier in Battle: Enduring the Ordeal of Combat* (Lawrence: Univ. Press of Kansas, 1997), 160, 161.
10. Cushman, *Bloody Promenade*, 167. Earl J. Hess has examined carefully the postwar memoirs of Northern veterans. Contrary to the generalizations of many literary critics, he viewed the narratives as belonging to a sophisticated body of literature marked by multiple subgenres. See Hess, *Union Soldier in Battle*, esp. chap. 9, 158–90.

11. Blight, *Race and Reunion*, 182; Alice Fahs, *The Imagined Civil War: Popular Literature of the North and South, 1861–1865* (Chapel Hill: Univ. of North Carolina Press, 2001), 314; John D. Billings, *Hardtack and Coffee; or, The Unwritten Story of Army Life* (1888; repr., Lincoln: Univ. of Nebraska Press, 1993), 12.

12. Dr. W. W. Parker, "How the Southern Soldier Kept House during the War," *Southern Historical Society Papers* 23 (1895): 328. Parker's article first appeared in the Richmond *Dispatch* on Feb. 9, 1886; George Wilson Booth, *A Maryland Boy in Lee's Army: Personal Reminiscences of a Maryland Soldier in the War between the States, 1861–1865* (Baltimore: Self-published, 1898), 177.

13. Quoted in Linderman, *Embattled Courage*, 286.

14. George H. Allen, *Forty-six Months with the Fourth R.I. Volunteers in the War of 1861 to 1865: Comprising a History of the Marches, Battles, and Camp Life, Compiled from Journals Kept while on Duty in the Field and Camp* (Providence, R.I.: J. A. and R. A. Reid, 1887), 368; Carlton McCarthy, *Detailed Minutiae of Soldier Life in the Army of Northern Virginia, 1861–1865* (Richmond, Va.: Carleton, McCarthy and Co., 1882), 41; Henry Harrison Eby, *Observations of an Illinois Boy in Battle, Camp and Prisons, 1861 to 1865* (Mendota, Ill.: Eby, 1910), 259, 265.

15. Linderman, *Embattled Courage*, 277.

16. Bruce Catton, *Waiting for the Morning Train: An American Boyhood* (New York: Doubleday and Co., 1972), 189–90, 190.

17. On Civil War memory and the reconciliation movement, see Paul H. Buck, *The Road to Reunion: 1865–1900* (Boston: Little, Brown, 1937); Nina Silber, *The Romance of Reunion: Northerners and the South, 1865–1900* (Chapel Hill: Univ. of North Carolina Press, 1993); and Blight, *Race and Reunion*. Blight noted that for those veterans penning remembrances for national publication, "consideration of slavery, emancipation, and Reconstruction became bad taste at best, and bad politics at worst" (189).

18. Stuart McConnell, *Glorious Contentment: The Grand Army of the Republic, 1865–1900* (Chapel Hill: Univ. of North Carolina Press, 1992), 167.

19. Ibid., 179, 202, 204. On Southern veterans' organizations and Confederate hereditary societies, see Gaines M. Foster, *Ghosts of the Confederacy: Defeat, the Lost Cause, and the Emergence of the New South, 1865–1913* (New York: Oxford Univ. Press, 1987), esp. chaps. 8, 9, and 10.

20. "A Short History of the War," review of *A Short History of the War of Secession, 1861–1865*, by Rossiter Johnson, *The Critic: A Weekly Review of Literature and the Arts*, Dec. 1, 1888, 257; Advertisement, *The Dial: A Semi-monthly Journal of Literary Criticism, Discussion, and Information* 9 (Jan. 1889): 105.

21. Elizabeth Young, *Disarming the Nation: Women's Writing and the American Civil War* (Chicago: Univ. of Chicago Press, 1999), 2, 3; David Madden and Peggy Bach, eds., *Classics of Civil War Fiction* (Jackson: Univ. Press of Mississippi, 1991), 2, 10.

22. Aaron, *Unwritten War*, 91, 92, 112.

23. Mark Twain, "The Private History of a Campaign That Failed" (1885; repr. in *Stephen Crane:* The Red Badge of Courage, Maggie: A Girl of the Streets, *and Other Selected Writings*, ed. Phyllis Frus and Stanley Corkin (New York: Houghton Mifflin, 2000), 324, 331.

24. Aaron, *Unwritten War*, 137; Twain, "Private History," 323.

25. Twain, "Private History," 328, 332–33. On the device of humor in Twain's article, see Aaron, *Unwritten War*, 136: "Why did he present himself and his companions as if they were Tom Sawyer and his carefree gang (he was close to twenty-six at the time) . . . ? He may have remained a boy at heart, but the so-called story of the Marion Rangers is utterly unconvincing unless read as the apologia of one who is trying to explain what he thinks might be taken as a discreditable episode."

26. Mark Twain, *Mark Twain's Autobiography*, 2 vols. (1924; repr. as *The Autobiography of Mark Twain*, ed. Charles Neider, New York: Harper and Row, 1959), 139. In the story itself, the greatest general in heaven is described slightly differently. A resident explains: "The greatest military genius our world ever produced was a brick-layer from somewhere back of Boston—died during the Revolution—by the name of Absalom Jones. Wherever he goes, crowds flock to see him. You see, everybody knows that if he had had a chance he would have shown the world some generalship that would have made all generalship before look like child's play and 'prentice work." See Mark Twain, *Extract from Captain Stormfield's Visit to Heaven* (New York: Harper and Brothers, 1909).

27. Aaron, *Unwritten War*, 139. Ulysses S. Grant, *Personal Memoirs of U. S. Grant*, 2 vols. (New York: Charles L. Webster and Co., 1885–86); Wilson, *Patriotic Gore*, 133.

28. Eric Solomon, *Stephen Crane: From Parody to Realism* (Cambridge, Mass.: Harvard Univ. Press, 1966), 74; Amy Kaplan, "The Spectacle of War in Crane's Revision of History," in *New Essays on* The Red Badge of Courage, ed. Lee Clark Mitchell (New York: Cambridge Univ. Press, 1986), 86; Christopher Benfey, *The Double Life of Stephen Crane* (New York: Knopf, 1992), 104.

29. Corwin K. Linson, *My Stephen Crane*, ed. Edwin H. Cady (Syracuse, N.Y.: Syracuse Univ. Press, 1958), 37; Linda H. Davis, *Badge of Courage: The Life of Stephen Crane* (New York: Houghton Mifflin, 1998), 63; Michael W. Schaefer, *Just What War Is: The Civil War Writings of De Forest and Bierce* (Knoxville: Univ. of Tennessee Press, 1997), ix, 17.

30. William L. Alden, "London Literary Letter," *New York Times*, July 7, 1900, BR7.

31. Cushman, *Bloody Promenade*, 170–71; Theodore Gerrish, *Army Life: A Private's Reminiscences of the War* (Portland, Maine: Hoyt, Fogg, and Donham, 1882), 107–8. For more on Gerrish and his account of Gettysburg, see Thomas A. Desjardin, *Stand Firm Ye Boys from Maine: The 20th Maine and the Gettysburg Campaign* (Gettysburg, Pa.: Thomas, 1995), esp. 127–34.

32. Stephen Crane, *The Red Badge of Courage: An Episode of the American Civil War* (1895, repr. in *Stephen Crane: Prose and Poetry*, ed. J. C. Levenson, New York: Library of America, 1996), 83, 86, 87. All quotations are hereafter taken from the Library of America edition and cited parenthetically within the text.

33. Sam R. Watkins, *Co. Aytch: A Confederate Memoir of the Civil War* (1882; repr., New York: Touchstone, 1997), 245, 19.

34. Harold R. Hungerford, "'That Was at Chancellorsville': The Factual Framework of *The Red Badge of Courage*," *American Literature* 34 (Jan. 1963): 526; Andrew B. Wells, "The Charge of the Eighth Pennsylvania Cavalry: III," in *Battles and Leaders*

of the Civil War, vol. 3 (New York: De Vinne, 1887–88), 188. The editors of *Century* magazine drew Wells's account from the *Philadelphia Weekly Press,* where it appeared on Oct. 13, 1866.

35. St. Clair A. Mulholland, *The Story of the 116th Regiment, Pennsylvania Volunteers in the War of the Rebellion: The Record of a Gallant Command* (1903; repr., ed. Lawrence Frederick Kohl, New York: Fordham Univ. Press, 1996), 46.

36. Aaron, *Unwritten War,* xvii.

37. Quoted in Stanley Wertheim and Paul Sorrentino, *The Crane Log: A Documentary Life of Stephen Crane, 1871–1900* (New York: G. K. Hall, 1994), 197. Critical consensus holds that four fiction writers preceded Crane in offering a realistic portrait of Civil War combat: Ambrose Bierce, John W. De Forest, Joseph Kirkland, and Albion Tourgée. All had served in the Union army.

38. *The Red Badge of Courage* achieved critical and popular fame soon after its publication by D. Appleton and Company in 1895 (a shorter version had appeared in late 1894 in numerous American newspapers). Celebrated both in America and abroad, the bestseller "went through ten editions in its first year alone, through as many more in the next dozen, and was accorded a critical reception unusual for the work of a living writer." See Lee Clark Mitchell, introduction to *New Essays on The Red Badge of Courage,* ed. Lee Clark Mitchell (New York: Cambridge Univ. Press, 1986), 5.

39. Quoted in Richard M. Weatherford, *Stephen Crane: The Critical Heritage* (London: Routledge and Kegan Paul, 1973), 86.

40. "Comment on New Books," review of *The Red Badge of Courage: An Episode of the American Civil War,* by Stephen Crane, *Atlantic Monthly* 77 (Mar. 1896): 422.

41. Gaston Pelletier, "*Red Badge* Revisited," *English Journal* 57 (Jan. 1968): 24.

42. Thomas C. Leonard, *Above the Battle: War-Making in America, from Appomattox to Versailles* (New York: Oxford Univ. Press, 1978), 3.

43. Stephen Crane, letter to John Northern Hilliard, 1897, *The Correspondence of Stephen Crane,* ed. Stanley Wertheim and Paul Sorrentino, vol. 1 (New York: Columbia Univ. Press, 1988), 322; quoted in Benfey, *Double Life of Stephen Crane,* 109.

44. R. W. Stallman, *Stephen Crane: A Biography* (New York: Braziller, 1968), 181; Shelby Foote, introduction to The Red Badge of Courage *and "The Veteran,"* (New York: Modern Library, 2000), xxxvi; Alexander C. McClurg, "The Red Badge of Hysteria," letter to *The Dial: A Semi-monthly Journal of Literary Criticism, Discussion, and Information* 20 (Apr. 16, 1896): 227–28. By turns, McClurg might have been both comforted and frustrated by the sequel to *The Red Badge of Courage,* Crane's brief short story, "The Veteran." In the story, a now-elderly Henry explained that his flight at Chancellorsville was *not* due to the cowardly nature of the American soldier; rather, he acknowledged that "lots of men" never ran and that he did simply because it was his first battle. After Chancellorsville, Henry told his townsfolk, "I got kind of use to it. A man does." Moreover, the story's climax demonstrated that Henry had retained the courage and reasoned action he honed during the war, two of the qualities McClurg so prized in the Civil War soldier. But nowhere in the story did Henry discuss the causes for which the Union fought; nor did he express any

overtly patriotic sentiments. The absence of cause and country in "The Veteran" would surely have raised objections from McClurg and like-minded veterans. See Stephen Crane, "The Veteran," *The University of Virginia Edition of the Works of Stephen Crane*, vol. 6, *Tales of War*, ed. Fredson Bowers (Charlottesville: Univ. Press of Virginia, 1970), 82–86.

45. For example, those veterans who were also part of the literary establishment tended to approve of the novel. Both John W. De Forest and Thomas Wentworth Higginson praised *The Red Badge of Courage* and openly admired Crane's imaginative powers. De Forest believed the novel contained "a good deal of really first-class work" and thought the battle scenes were "excellent," even if Crane had exaggerated a detail or two. Higginson believed it remarkable that such a young writer, inexperienced in war, had penned an account of the life of soldiers "not only more vivid than they themselves have ever given, but more accurate." He rejected McClurg's complaint that the novel ignored cause and country, arguing that the book "is not a patriotic tract, but a delineation; a cross section of the daily existence of the raw enlisted-man. In other respects it is reticent, because it is truthful." Of course, De Forest's and Higginson's views were not shared by all veterans who later built their careers upon the written word. One reviewer disagreed with Higginson's account of the novel, explaining: "[Our] recollections of battle are quite devoid of the greens, and golds, and purples, and oranges so lavishly present in Mr. Crane's style of description. We recollect some passages in Colonel Higginson's own *Army Life in a Black Regiment*, much more truly realistic than anything *The Red Badge of Courage* can offer." See Edwin Oviatt, "Authors at Home," *New York Times*, Dec. 17, 1898, BR856; Thomas Wentworth Higginson, "A Bit of War Photography," review of *The Red Badge of Courage*, by Stephen Crane, *Philistine: A Periodical of Protest* (July 1896): 3, 2; "American Essays," review of *Book and Heart: Essays on Literature and Life*, by Thomas Wentworth Higginson, *Chap-Book: Semi-Monthly. A Miscellany & Review of Belles Lettres*, Apr. 15, 1897, 6.

46. "Stephen Crane and Gen. Otis," letter to the editor, *New York Times*, Aug. 7, 1899, 6.

47. McClurg, "Red Badge of Hysteria," 227–28; Hess, *Union Soldier in Battle*, 165, 165–66. For an examination of those factors inspiring soldiers North and South to fight, see James M. McPherson, *For Cause and Comrades* (New York: Oxford Univ. Press, 1997). Contrary to the findings of other historians, McPherson argued that what motivated most Civil War soldiers to fight was "the complex mixture of patriotism, ideology, concepts of duty, honor, manhood, and community or peer pressure that prompted them to enlist in the first place" (13).

48. Blight, *Race and Reunion*, 175; Charles H. Weygant, *History of the One Hundred and Twenty-Fourth Regiment, N.Y.S.V.* (Newburgh, N.Y.: Journal Printing House, 1877), 101.

49. Aaron, *Unwritten War*, 211; Stephen Crane, *The Monster and Other Stories* (New York: Harper, 1899); Andrew Delbanco, "The American Stephen Crane: The Context of *The Red Badge of Courage*," in *New Essays on* The Red Badge of Courage, ed. Lee Clark Mitchell (New York: Cambridge Univ. Press, 1986), 49–76.

50. Delbanco, "American Stephen Crane," 63.

51. McPherson, *For Cause and Comrades*, 5.

52. Sarah E. Gardner, *Blood and Irony: Southern White Women's Narratives of the Civil War, 1861–1937* (Chapel Hill: Univ. of North Carolina Press, 2004), 148–49; Hamilton Wright Mabie, "Books and Writers," review of *The Battle-Ground*, by Ellen Glasgow, *Outlook*, May 24, 1902, 71; Henry James Forman, "James Boyd Writes a Tale of the Civil War," review of *Marching On*, by James Boyd, *New York Times*, May 1, 1927, BR4.

53. Shaara, *Killer Angels*, vii; Foote, introduction, xxxii. As I discuss in a later chapter, Shaara's novel differed from *The Red Badge of Courage* in a number of ways. But because both writers rejected historical abstractions in favor of individual, human experiences, Shaara could identify Crane as his literary antecedent. See chapter 4 in this volume.

54. Stephen Crane, letter to John Phillips, Jan. 9, 1896, *The Correspondence of Stephen Crane*, ed. Wertheim and Sorrentino, vol. 1, 177.

2. FOR WAS I NOT A SOLDIER, ENLISTED FOR THE WAR?

1. Malcolm Cowley, "Going with the Wind," review of *Gone with the Wind*, by Margaret Mitchell, *New Republic*, Sept. 16, 1936, 161–62.

2. Margaret Mitchell, *Gone with the Wind* (New York: Macmillan, 1936), 1003. All citations hereafter appear parenthetically within the text. Margaret Mitchell, letter to Mrs. L. H. Clark, *Margaret Mitchell's* Gone with the Wind *Letters: 1936–1949*, ed. Richard Harwell (New York: Macmillan, 1976), 102.

3. Margaret Mitchell, letter to Mrs. E. L. Sullivan, Aug. 18, 1936, *Margaret Mitchell's* Gone with the Wind *Letters:* "I wish I could tell you what happened to them both [Scarlett and Rhett] after the end of the book but I cannot, for I know no more about them than you do. I wrote my book from back to front. That is, the last chapter first and the first chapter last" (54).

4. Fahs, *Imagined Civil War*, 148–49, 2.

5. Ibid., 137. The anonymous story "Wounded" appeared in *Harper's Weekly*, July 12, 1862, 442–43.

6. Fahs, *Imagined Civil War*, 138; Drew Gilpin Faust, *Mothers of Invention: Women of the Slaveholding South in the American Civil War* (Chapel Hill: Univ. of North Carolina Press, 1996), 5, 233. Faust suggested that during the war, when most men were "preoccupied with military matters," women writers published as a way to maintain and support a distinctive Southern culture. "Culture became to a considerable degree the domain of women in the Confederate South," she noted, "and women were a major source of the articles that filled Confederate periodicals" (167). Faust went on to explain why women could perform this cultural service without breaking gender expectations. "Public discourse expressed fewer reservations about women writers than it did about nurses or teachers. The profession of letters seemed consistent with many of the ideals of domesticity." After all, writing "did not require ladies to leave the house or to undertake demeaning

physical labor that would threaten their class status; although it did expose their words and sometimes their names to public scrutiny, it left their actual persons sheltered within the domestic sphere" (167).

7. Gardner, *Blood and Irony*, 16, 30. Southern propagandist Augusta Jane Evans, for instance, used her 1864 novel *Macaria; or, Altars of Sacrifice* (Richmond, Va.: West and Johnston) to "glorify the pure and noble southern soldier" rather than to argue that the sacrifices of women were indistinguishable from those of men. The heroine of the novel may be willing to lose her life for the South, but she realizes that her gender bars her from a soldier's death in battle. See Gardner, *Blood and Irony*, 23.

8. Fahs, *Imagined Civil War*, 317. See Kaplan, "Spectacle of War," esp. 81–84.

9. Rev. Edward O. Guerrant, "Marshall and Garfield in Eastern Kentucky," *Battles and Leaders of the Civil War*, vol. 1, ed. Robert Underwood Johnson and Clarence C. Buel (New York: De Vinne Press, 1887–88), 397; Fahs, *Imagined Civil War*, 122.

10. Constance Cary Harrison, "Virginia Scenes in '61," *Battles and Leaders*, vol. 1, ed. Johnson and Buel, 163.

11. Quoted in Gardner, *Blood and Irony*, 117, 120; Blight, *Race and Reunion*, 278. For a valuable discussion of Southern commemorative organizations and their role in American culture, see Foster, *Ghosts of the Confederacy*, esp. chaps. 8–10, pp. 104–44. For treatments of these organizations North and South (and their interaction), see Buck, *Road to Reunion*, esp. 236–62. For a discussion of Decoration Day and Memorial Day events, see Blight, *Race and Reunion*, chap. 3, pp. 64–97.

12. Gardner, *Blood and Irony*, 126; quoted in Gardner, *Blood and Irony*, 124.

13. Elisabeth Muhlenfeld, "Mary Chesnut," in *The History of Southern Women's Literature*, ed. Carolyn Perry and Mary Louise Weaks (Baton Rouge: Louisiana State Univ. Press, 2002), 122.

14. Margaret Mitchell, letter to Hunt Clement, July 8, 1936, *Margaret Mitchell's* Gone with the Wind *Letters*, 24; Mitchell, letter to Herschel Brickell, Nov. 13, 1936, *Margaret Mitchell's* Gone with the Wind *Letters*, 88; Mitchell, letter to Clement, July 8, 1936, *Margaret Mitchell's* Gone with the Wind *Letters*, 24; Darden Asbury Pyron, "A Bibliographical Essay," in *Recasting:* Gone with the Wind *in American Culture*, ed. Darden Asbury Pyron (Miami: Univ. Presses of Florida, 1983), 223; Anne Goodwyn Jones, *Tomorrow Is Another Day: The Woman Writer in the South, 1859–1936* (Baton Rouge: Louisiana State Univ. Press, 1981), 339, 349.

15. Anne Goodwyn Jones, "Women Writers and the Myths of Southern Womanhood," in *The History of Southern Women's Literature*, ed. Carolyn Perry and Mary Louise Weaks (Baton Rouge: Louisiana State Univ. Press, 2002), 279.

16. Margaret Mitchell, letter to Miss Ruth Tallman, July 30, 1937, *Margaret Mitchell's* Gone with the Wind *Letters*, 162.

17. Young, *Disarming the Nation*, 252.

18. Margaret Mitchell, letter to Julia Collier Harris, Apr. 28, 1936, *Margaret Mitchell's* Gone with the Wind *Letters*, 3–4; Margaret Mitchell, letter to Col. Telamon Cuyler, Jan. 9, 1940, *Margaret Mitchell's* Gone with the Wind *Letters*, 294; Mitchell, letter to Harris, Apr. 28, 1936, *Margaret Mitchell's* Gone with the Wind *Letters*, 4; and ibid.

19. Margaret Mitchell, letter to Robert C. Taylor, Aug.15, 1936, *Margaret Mitchell's* Gone with the Wind *Letters,* 53; Margaret Mitchell, letter to George Ward, Sept. 1, 1936, *Margaret Mitchell's* Gone with the Wind *Letters,* 58; Margaret Mitchell, letter to Donald Adams, July 9, 1936, *Margaret Mitchell's* Gone with the Wind *Letters,* 31; and ibid.; Margaret Mitchell, letter to Paul Jordan-Smith, May 27, 1936, *Margaret Mitchell's* Gone with the Wind *Letters,* 8.

20. Margaret Mitchell, letter to Mr. and Mrs. Clifford Dowdey, May 13, 1943, *Margaret Mitchell's* Gone with the Wind *Letters,* 368; Margaret Mitchell, letter to Douglas Southall Freeman, Nov. 27, 1939, *Margaret Mitchell's* Gone with the Wind *Letters,* 290.

21. Margaret Mitchell, letter to Sidney Howard, Nov. 21, 1936, *Margaret Mitchell's* Gone with the Wind *Letters,* 95; Margaret Mitchell, letter to Mr. and Mrs. Clifford Dowdey, May 13, 1943, *Margaret Mitchell's* Gone with the Wind *Letters,* 369; Margaret Mitchell, letter to Douglas Southall Freeman, July 21, 1943, *Margaret Mitchell's* Gone with the Wind *Letters,* 373.

22. Mitchell, letter to Jordan-Smith, *Margaret Mitchell's* Gone with the Wind *Letters,* 8.

23. Gardner, *Blood and Irony,* 198; George Garrett, "On Mary Johnston's *The Long Roll,*" in *Classics of Civil War Fiction,* ed. David Madden and Peggy Bach (Jackson: Univ. Press of Mississippi, 1991), 85. See Ellen Glasgow, *The Battle-Ground* (New York: Doubleday, Page, 1902); Johnston, *Long Roll*; and Mary Johnston, *Cease Firing* (Boston: Houghton Mifflin, 1912).

24. Johnston, *Cease Firing,* 439.

25. Gardner, *Blood and Irony,* 231; Evelyn Scott, *The Wave* (New York: Jonathan Cape and Harrison Smith, 1929).

26. Blight, *Race and Reunion,* 177–78; Mary Elizabeth Massey, *Bonnet Brigades* (New York: Knopf, 1966), 175; Faust, *Mothers of Invention,* 162.

27. Muhlenfeld, "Mary Chesnut," 120; Massey, *Bonnet Brigades,* 175–76, 187; Louisa May Alcott, *Hospital Sketches* (Boston: James Redpath, 1863). For two helpful discussions of women's memoirs and published diaries of the Civil War, see Massey, *Bonnet Brigades,* 175–96; and Walter Sullivan, "Civil War Diaries and Memoirs," in *The History of Southern Women's Literature,* ed. Carolyn Perry and Mary Louise Weaks (Baton Rouge: Louisiana State Univ. Press, 2002), 109–18.

28. Gardner, *Blood and Irony,* 64, 4.

29. Margaret Mitchell, letter to Harry Stillwell Edwards, June 18, 1936, *Margaret Mitchell's* Gone with the Wind *Letters,* 14; Margaret Mitchell, letter to Stephen Vincent Benét, July 7, 1936, *Margaret Mitchell's* Gone with the Wind *Letters,* 36; Margaret Mitchell, letter to George Ward, Sept. 1, 1936, *Margaret Mitchell's* Gone with the Wind *Letters,* 58; Mitchell, letter to Freeman, July 21, 1943, *Margaret Mitchell's* Gone with the Wind *Letters,* 372.

30. Eliza Frances Andrews, *The War-Time Journal of a Georgia Girl, 1864–1865* (New York: D. Appleton and Company, 1908), 13, 232.

31. Ibid., 349, 365.

32. J. H. Segars, foreword to Mary A. H. Gay, *Life in Dixie during the War:*

1861–1862–1863–1864–1865, ed. J. H. Segars (Macon, Ga.: Mercer Univ. Press, 2001), vii–iii; Sullivan, "Civil War Diaries and Memoirs," 117.

33. Mary A. H. Gay, *Life in Dixie during the War: 1861–1862–1863–1864–1865*, ed. J. H. Segars (Macon, Ga.: Mercer Univ. Press, 2001), 216, 214, 218.

34. Ibid., 225, 67, 139–40.

35. Cowley, "Going with the Wind," 161–62.

36. Alan T. Nolan, "The Anatomy of the Myth," in *The Myth of the Lost Cause and Civil War History*, ed. Gary W. Gallagher and Alan T. Nolan (Bloomington: Indiana Univ. Press, 2000), 31.

37. Jones, *Tomorrow Is Another Day*, 317; Drew Gilpin Faust, "Clutching the Chains That Bind: Margaret Mitchell and *Gone with the Wind*," *Southern Cultures* 5, no. 1 (1999): 6, 19.

38. Caroline Gordon, letter to Sally Wood, Sept. 10, 1936, *The Southern Mandarins: Letters of Caroline Gordon to Sally Wood, 1924–1937*, ed. Sally Wood (Baton Rouge: Louisiana State Univ. Press, 1984), 202; Caroline Smith, review of *None Shall Look Back*, by Caroline Gordon, *Nation*, Mar. 20, 1937, 332; Edith H. Walton, "Miss Gordon's Civil War Novel," review of *None Shall Look Back*, by Caroline Gordon, *New York Times*, Feb. 21, 1937, 86. John Crowe Ransom congratulated Gordon in a letter for not "sentimentalizing" the war: "It is a terrific experience; real tragedy. It is not half as big as *Gone with the Wind*, I guess, and covers almost precisely the same subject matter, and is many times as powerful"; quoted in Ann Waldron, *Close Connections: Caroline Gordon and the Southern Renaissance* (New York: G. P. Putnam's Sons, 1987), 169.

39. Caroline Gordon, letter to Ward Dorrance, quoted in Veronica Makowsky, "Caroline Gordon on Women Writing: A Contradiction in Terms?" *Southern Quarterly* 28 (Spring 1990): 43. For a recent reiteration of *Gone with the Wind* as a feminized, sensational romance, see Sarah E. Gardner, "Every Man Has Got the Right to Get Killed? The Civil War Narratives of Mary Johnston and Caroline Gordon," *Southern Cultures* 5 (Winter 1999): "Gordon's determination to write in the 'male' mode embodied her visceral reaction against the sentimentalized, romanticized, and idealized Civil War romance usually associated with women audiences. Unfortunately for Gordon, her novel was eclipsed by the publication of the greatest exemplar of that tradition, Margaret Mitchell's *Gone with the Wind*" (27).

40. Caroline Gordon, letter to Ford Madox Ford, Sept. 1936, *A Literary Friendship: Correspondence between Caroline Gordon and Ford Madox Ford*, ed. Brita Lindberg-Seyersted (Knoxville: Univ. of Tennessee Press, 1999), 88; quoted in Nancylee Novell Jonza, *The Underground Stream: The Life and Art of Caroline Gordon* (Athens: Univ. of Georgia Press, 1995), 170, 173, 191; Gordon, letter to Ford, *Literary Friendship*, 89.

41. Quoted in Makowsky, "Caroline Gordon on Women Writing," 43; Katherine Hemple Prown, *Revising Flannery O'Connor: Southern Literary Culture and the Problem of Female Authorship* (Charlottesville: Univ. Press of Virginia, 2001), 90.

42. Prown, *Revising Flannery O'Connor*, 90; Jonza, *Underground Stream*, xii; Helen Taylor, "*Gone with the Wind* and Its Influence," *History of Southern Women's*

Literature, ed. Carolyn Perry and Mary Louise Weaks (Baton Rouge: Louisiana State Univ. Press, 2002), 266. On Gordon's public persona, Jonza explained: "Gordon worked hard to establish a public myth about her life to guide interpretations of her art. According to her public myth she was a conservative southern lady married to an equally conservative southern gentleman, Allen Tate, a critic and poet who taught Gordon everything she knew about writing. Although her fiction was never a popular success, Gordon was known for her technical excellence. A 'writer's writer,' she believed in old-fashioned values: men were meant to be leaders and sometimes heroes; women were always called to be submissive to men." Jonza, *Underground Stream*, ix–x.

43. Quoted in Gardner, "Every Man Has Got the Right to Get Killed?" 27; Jonza, *Underground Stream*, 11–12.

44. Quoted in Makowsky, "Caroline Gordon on Women Writing," 44–45; Caroline Gordon, letter to Sally Wood, Oct. 27, 1935, *Southern Mandarins*, 196.

45. Caroline Gordon, letter to Sally Wood, Nov. 2, 1931, *Southern Mandarins*, 90; quoted in Jonza, *Underground Stream*, 168; Caroline Gordon, letter to Sally Wood, Oct. 27, 1935, *Southern Mandarins*, 197.

46. Walton, "Miss Gordon's Civil War Novel," 86; quoted in Gardner, "Every Man Has Got the Right to Get Killed?" 30; Caroline Gordon, letter to Sally Wood, July 1935, *Southern Mandarins*, 192; Makowsky, "Caroline Gordon on Women Writing," 50. For a brief article touching on Gordon's literary borrowings, see Gregory Marks, "Quotation and Authority: A Note on Caroline Gordon's *Green Centuries*," *Mississippi Quarterly* 52 (Fall 1999): 655–58. Gordon drew numerous passages and images from Wyeth's book, including a memorable scene in which Gen. Nathan B. Forrest climbs a tree to view the Federal troops at Chattanooga. Of Gordon's nonverbatim borrowings from Wyeth, the most striking relates to her use of a scene at Murfreesboro, after the battle of Franklin, in which Forrest shoots a panicked and retreating Confederate color-bearer. In Wyeth's account, Forrest seizes the colors and waves them to rally his broken troops. Gordon borrowed some of Forrest's resolve for her own hero, making it Rives who guns down the fleeing color-bearer. Only after Rives's death does Forrest take up the flag (373–75). See John Allan Wyeth, *Life of Lieutenant-General Nathan Bedford Forrest* (New York: Harper, 1899), 259–60, 552.

47. Gardner, *Blood and Irony*, 100–101. Historians have demonstrated that among George Pickett's letters to his wife, those published by her under the title of *The Heart of a Soldier* (1913) were in fact not written by the general. That his wife had manufactured the letters herself and passed them off as genuine demonstrates the extent to which southern women could depend on the words of men in order to authenticate their own interpretations of the war. For the best discussion of the forged Pickett letters, see Gary W. Gallagher, *Lee and His Generals in War and Memory* (Baton Rouge: Louisiana State Univ. Press, 1998), 227–42.

48. Ashley Brown, "*None Shall Look Back:* The Novel as History," *Southern Review* 7 (Spring 1971): 483.

49. Daniel H. Hill, "Chickamauga: The Great Battle of the West," *Battles and Leaders of the Civil War*, vol. 3, ed. Johnson and Buel, 638; Gordon, *None Shall Look Back*, 225–26, 228. All citations hereafter appear parenthetically within the text.

50. Henry Walke, "The Western Flotilla at Fort Donelson, Island Number Ten, Fort Pillow and Memphis," in *Battles and Leaders of the Civil War*, vol. 1, ed. Johnson and Buel, 434; J. S. Fullerton, "Reënforcing Thomas at Chickamauga," in *Battles and Leaders of the Civil War*, vol. 3, ed. Johnson and Buel, 665–67.

51. Caroline Gordon, letter to Sally Wood, May 1937, *Southern Mandarins*, 208; Caroline Gordon, letter to Sally Wood, Jan. 8, 1937, *Southern Mandarins*, 204.

52. Charles Frazier, *Cold Mountain* (New York: Atlantic Monthly Press, 1997). Frazier upset the typical male (fighting front) versus female (home front) equation by making his male protagonist, Inman, a Confederate deserter. Nonetheless, Inman's violent experiences on the road stand in stark contrast to the mostly domestic and agrarian struggles of his fiancée at home.

53. Jonza, *Underground Stream*, 172.

54. Caroline Gordon, letter to Ford Madox Ford, Sept. 1936, *A Literary Friendship*, 89; and ibid.

55. Nancylee Novell Jonza, "Caroline Gordon," in *The History of Southern Women's Literature*, ed. Carolyn Perry and Mary Louise Weaks (Baton Rouge: Louisiana State Univ. Press, 2002), 369.

56. Quoted in Prown, *Revising Flannery O'Connor*, 96; quoted in Waldron, *Close Connections*, 285; quoted in Richard Dwyer, "Case of the Cool Reception," in *Recasting:* Gone with the Wind *in American Culture*, ed. Darden Asbury Pyron (Miami: Univ. Presses of Florida, 1983), 22; quoted in Darden Asbury Pyron, "The Critical Setting," *Recasting* Gone with the Wind *in American Culture*, ed. Pyron, 5; Dwyer, "Case of the Cool Reception," 29; and ibid., 27.

57. Lively, *Fiction Fights the Civil War*, 12–13; Madden and Bach, "Introduction," *Classics of Civil War Fiction*, 22; Gardner, *Blood and Irony*, 10. With regard to the novels' differing political agendas, Gardner concluded that *Gone with the Wind* and its heroine look "not to Tara for the future but to Atlanta, the symbol of the New South. In the postwar world, Tara inspires nostalgia, but nothing more." By contrast, *None Shall Look Back* reflected the agrarian critique of industrialization and "the crass materialism associated with the postwar South and perhaps even more explicitly with the post-World War I South." See Gardner, *Blood and Irony*, 250, 257.

58. Maurine Weiner Greenwald, *Women, War, and Work: The Impact of World War I on Women Workers in the United States* (Westport, Conn.: Greenwood, 1980). See also Gail Braybon, "Women, War, and Work," in *The Oxford Illustrated History of the First World War*, ed. Hew Strachan (Oxford: Oxford Univ. Press, 1998), 149–62. In a discussion useful for students of American as well as European history, Braybon explained that during World War I, "commentators across Britain, France, and Germany began to talk of [the war's] impact on 'society.' With surprising rapidity, the idea took hold that military and industrial mobilization would have a permanent, possibly radical, effect on class, sex, and familial relations" (149).

With men serving in the European armies, women became laborers in industry and agriculture and adopted public and sometimes outspoken positions in support of the war effort. But Braybon declared it an "enduring myth" that women's wartime activities "led to dramatic social change" (150). After the war, and despite the resistance of some women to return to domestic roles, "there was a general desire that life should return to 'normal'" (161).

59. Helen Taylor, *Scarlett's Women: Gone with the Wind and Its Female Fans* (New Brunswick, N.J.: Rutgers Univ. Press, 1989), 211–12.

60. Flannery O'Connor, "A Late Encounter with the Enemy," *Harper's Bazaar* 87 (Sept. 1953; repr. in *The Oxford Book of American Short Stories*, ed. Joyce Carol Oates, New York: Oxford Univ. Press, 1992), 399, 406, 399, 407.

61. Gardner, *Blood and Irony*, 234.

62. Taylor, *Scarlett's Women*, 211–12; and ibid., 12. For criticism on *None Shall Look Back* that largely excludes gender from its analyses, see Brown, "Novel as History"; Rose Ann C. Fraistat, *Caroline Gordon as Novelist and Woman of Letters* (Baton Rouge: Louisiana State Univ. Press, 1984), 64–73; and—aside from noting Lucy's "heroic qualities"—William J. Stuckey, *Caroline Gordon* (New York: Twayne, 1972), 42–54.

63. Quoted in Susie King Taylor, *Reminiscences of My Life in Camp with the 33d United States Colored Troops, Late 1st S.C., Volunteers* (1902; repr., ed. Patricia W. Romero and Willie Lee Rose, Princeton, N.J.: Markus Wiener, 1995), 142–43. For a discussion of how black feminists and writers have responded negatively to *Gone with the Wind*, see Young, *Disarming the Nation*, 235–36. For Young's larger discussion of race and gender in the novel, see chap. 6, 232–86.

64. Catherine Clinton, "Noble Women as Well," in *Ken Burns's The Civil War: Historians Respond*, ed. Robert Brent Toplin (New York: Oxford Univ. Press, 1996), 64, 69; Elizabeth D. Leonard, *All the Daring of the Soldier: Women of the Civil War Armies* (New York: Penguin, 2001); De Anne Blanton and Lauren M. Cook, *They Fought Like Demons: Women Soldiers in the Civil War* (New York: Vintage, 2003); Bonnie Tsui, *She Went to the Field: Women Soldiers of the Civil War* (Guilford, Conn.: Globe Pequot Press, 2003).

65. Ann Rinaldi, *Girl in Blue* (New York: Scholastic Press, 2001); "Knightley considers cross-dressing for Civil War flick" (Knight Ridder/Tribune News Service, Nov. 7, 2003), http://static.highbeam.com/k/knightriddertribunenewsservice/november072003/ (accessed June 16, 2003).

3. The Eggshell Shibboleth of Caste and Color Too

1. Faulkner made the Civil War a frequent presence in his fiction, both directly and indirectly, from 1927 to 1951. See Michel Gresset, "Faulkner's War with Wars," in *Faulkner and History*, ed. Javier Coy and Michel Gresset (Salamanca, Spain: Univ. of Salamanca Press, 1986), 15.

2. Charles Reagan Wilson, *Judgment and Grace in Dixie: Southern Faiths from Faulkner to Elvis* (Athens: Univ. of Georgia Press, 1995), 65. On the Myth of the Lost Cause, see Thomas L. Connelly, *The Marble Man: Robert E. Lee and His Image in*

American Society (New York: Knopf, 1977); Foster, *Ghosts of the Confederacy*; Gary W. Gallagher and Alan T. Nolan, eds., *The Myth of the Lost Cause and Civil War History* (Bloomington: Indiana Univ. Press, 2000); Alan T. Nolan, *Lee Considered: General Robert E. Lee and Civil War History* (Chapel Hill: Univ. of North Carolina Press, 1991); and William Garrett Piston, *Lee's Tarnished Lieutenant: James Longstreet and His Place in Southern History* (Athens: Univ. of Georgia Press, 1987).

3. Gary W. Gallagher, introduction to *The Myth of the Lost Cause and Civil War History*, ed. Gary W. Gallagher and Alan T. Nolan (Bloomington: Indiana Univ. Press, 2000), 4.

4. Aaron, *Unwritten War*, 317.

5. Several scholars have considered how the Lost Cause fits into Faulkner's vision of the war. Ricky Floyd Dobbs, John T. Matthews, and Glenn Meeter have commented on the Myth as it relates to Faulkner's portrait of race and gender; others, such as Elmo Howell, have likened Faulkner to Sir Walter Scott, finding both writers obsessed with lost causes and the preservation of regional heritage. Few critics have explored the military dimension of the Lost Cause, however, a situation owing less to scholarly oversight than to Faulkner's tendency to focus on *civilian* subject matter when attending to the Civil War and its memory. See Ricky Floyd Dobbs, "Case Study in Social Neurosis: Quentin Compson and the Lost Cause," *Papers on Language and Literature* 33 (Fall 1997); John T. Matthews, *The Sound and the Fury: Faulkner and the Lost Cause* (Boston: Twayne, 1991); Glenn Meeter, "Molly's Vision: Lost Cause Ideology and Genesis in Faulkner's *Go Down, Moses*," in *Faulkner and Ideology: Faulkner and Yoknapatawpha, 1992*, ed. Donald M. Kartiganer and Ann J. Abadie (Jackson: Univ. Press of Mississippi, 1995); Elmo Howell, "Faulkner and Scott and the Legacy of the Lost Cause," *Georgia Review* 26 (Fall 1972).

6. Thomas L. Connelly and Barbara Bellows, *God and General Longstreet: The Lost Cause and the Southern Mind* (Baton Rouge: Louisiana State Univ. Press, 1982), 109.

7. Alan T. Nolan, *"Rally, Once Again!": Selected Civil War Writings of Alan T. Nolan* (Madison, Wis.: Madison House, 2000), 74; Joseph Blotner, *Faulkner: A Biography*, vol. 2 (New York: Random House, 1974), 1413.

8. The Myth of the Lost Cause and its military emphases influenced how generations of Americans, from all regions, understood the war. Alan T. Nolan may not have overstated his point when he concluded, as late as 2000, that in "the popular mind, the Lost Cause represents the national memory of the Civil War; it has been substituted for the *history* of the war." While Faulkner did not prize undiluted, factual history as do Civil War historians like Nolan, he appeared to have reached a similar conclusion years earlier. See Nolan, "Anatomy of the Myth," 12.

9. Louis Rubin Jr., "Scarlett O'Hara and the Two Quentin Compsons," *Recasting* Gone with the Wind *in American Culture*, ed. Darden Asbury Pyron (Miami: Univ. Presses of Florida, 1983), 99, 99–100.

10. Quoted in Blight, *Race and Reunion*, 220 (emphasis in original).

11. Albion Tourgée was not the only exception to this rule. See, for example, Basil W. Duke, *Reminiscences of General Basil W. Duke* (New York: Doubleday, 1911). Duke, a former Confederate general, argued that no "statement now made

could present more forcibly than has been done the chief issue of the fierce debate, or show more plainly how the persistent agitation of the question of slavery, in its varied phases, inflamed sectional passion and resentment, and suggested to the disputants the thought that it could be settled only by civil war" (4). This view stands in contrast to that offered by many memoirs of the Lost Cause tradition, which could ignore slavery altogether or claim, as did Jefferson Davis, that "slavery was in no wise the cause of the conflict." See Jefferson Davis, *The Rise and Fall of the Confederate Government*, vol. 2 (1881; repr., New York: De Capo Press, 1990), iv.

12. John Milton Hubbard, *Notes of a Private* (Memphis, Tenn.: E. H. Clarke and Brother, 1909), 181–83.

13. Henry Kyd Douglas, *I Rode with Stonewall: Being Chiefly the War Experiences of the Youngest Member of Jackson's Staff from the John Brown Raid to the Hanging of Mrs. Surratt* (Chapel Hill: Univ. of North Carolina Press, 1940). At its outset, Douglas's memoir devotes a paragraph to the issue of slavery, but plays down its role in precipitating the war and persuading Southerners to fight. Nonetheless, Douglas could not resist firing a barb at what he perceived to be Northern hypocrisy: "Personally I had no feeling of resentment against the people of the North because of their desire for the emancipation of the slave, for I believed Negro slavery was a curse to the people of the Middle States. As a boy I had determined never to own one. Whether I would have followed the example of shrewd New Englanders in compromising with philanthropy by selling my slaves for a valuable consideration before I became an abolitionist, I will not pretend to say" (3).

14. Faulkner may not have employed military narrators or depicted Civil War combat at length, but he does seem to have drawn on at least one episode from Hubbard's memoir. Hubbard recalled a scene witnessed by his unit on Dec. 2, 1862, in the town of Oxford, Mississippi: "On the verandah of a cottage, somewhere just south of the courthouse, was standing one of the [town's] maidens, who did not seem to be weeping, for her spirit had risen to the occasion. With dark blue eyes and flowing hair, she was animation incarnate. She was most forcibly expressing her opinion about our giving over the town to the merciless Yankees" (42–43). Faulkner made his home in Oxford, and it seems likely that he would have taken special interest in this account of the town's wartime plight. Perhaps the passage stirred his imagination. Indeed, the fiery "maiden" described in the memoir seems akin to Faulkner's Drusilla, also a young woman whose spirit awakens when the war arrives at her doorstep. Hubbard observed: "But who was our little maiden, she of the patriotic impulses? Everybody wanted to know, for we hoped to have her think better of us. Cad Linthicum, our little Kentuckian, who somehow had a penchant for knowing all the girls in divers[e] places, said it was Taylor Cook. And so it was Taylor Cook. Then 'Taylor Cook' went down the line. She had become famous in a twinkling. The Seventh Tennessee Cavalry would have willingly adopted her as 'The Daughter of the Regiment,' if she could have appreciated the honor. She was worthy to become the wife of Nathan Bedford Forrest's only son. And she did" (43–44). The cavalry regiment's wish to adopt the spirited girl seems amplified in *The Unvanquished*, where Drusilla actually does join

the cavalry unit of her uncle John Sartoris. And just as Taylor Cook comes to marry the son of General Forrest, in time Drusilla weds Sartoris himself, her former commander, and kisses his only son.

15. Aaron, *Unwritten War*, 311; Katherine Arn Clark, *Reconsidering Faulkner's Pulp Series: The Unvanquished as Parody, Not Potboiler* (PhD diss., Emory University, 1992), 76–77; Aaron, *Unwritten War*, 311. Those adhering to this view find that an "immense distance separates the pomposities of [the] 'lost-cause' version of the War from Faulkner's" (Aaron, *Unwritten War*, 313). In *Race and Reunion*, for example, Blight lauded the Mississippian (as well as Flannery O'Connor and Robert Penn Warren) for clashing with Lost Cause mythology that had "constricted creative impulses and stultified historical understanding" (293). Noting that the revered mythologies of the South interested Faulkner less than its humanity, white *and* black, Blight concluded that "piety rarely lasts forever as a substitute for knowledge among those determined to probe the depths of human drama" (293).

16. Joseph Blotner, *Faulkner: A Biography* (Jackson: Univ. Press of Mississippi, 2005), 472. For appraisals of Faulkner's service with the RAF, real and imagined, and his supposed rejection by the U.S. Army Signal Corps due to his height and slight build, see Blotner, *Faulkner: A Biography* (2005, Univ. Press of Mississippi ed.), 48, 60–67, 122, 361, 472, 560. See also Donald M. Kartiganer, "'So I, Who Never Had a War . . .': William Faulkner, War, and the Modern Imagination," *Modern Fiction Studies* 44 (1998): 619–45; and Panthea Reid, "William Faulkner's 'War Wound': Reflections on Writing and Doing, Knowing and Remembering," *Virginia Quarterly Review* (Autumn 1998).

17. Joseph Blotner, *Faulkner: A Biography* (New York: Vintage Books, 1991), 211; John Faulkner, *My Brother Bill* (New York: Pocket Books, 1964), 48–49, 231.

18. Blotner, *Faulkner: A Biography* (1991, Vintage Books ed.), 181; Aaron, *Unwritten War*, 181. For an example of Bierce's writing that does consider the role of emancipation in precipitating and justifying the war, see his poem "The Hesitating Veteran" in *The Collected Works of Ambrose Bierce*, vol. 4 (New York: Neale, 1910), 115–18. The narrator concludes that although the "black chap" found his freedom in the war, "many white chaps in the grave / 'Twould puzzle to say what they died for" (lines 29–32).

19. Johnston, *Long Roll*; Caroline Gordon, letter to Sally Wood, summer 1931, *Southern Mandarins*, 80.

20. Frederick L. Gwynn and Joseph L. Blotner, eds., *Faulkner in the University: Class Conferences at the University of Virginia, 1957–1958* (Charlottesville: Univ. Press of Virginia, 1959), 13–14.

21. Clark, *Reconsidering Faulkner's Pulp Series*, 73; Gwynn and Blotner, *Faulkner in the University*, 249.

22. William Faulkner, *Flags in the Dust* (New York: Random House, 1973), 46.

23. William C. Falkner, *The White Rose of Memphis: A Novel* (1881; repr., New York: Coley Taylor, 1953).

24. William Faulkner, *Sartoris* (New York: Harcourt, 1929), 227.

25. Leonard, *Above the Battle*, 192–93. The fact that Sartoris lacks Falkner's literary talent seems all the more striking when we consider that Faulkner made frequent reference to his great-grandfather's writing. For instance, he told audiences that "he may have inherited the ink stain" from W. C. Falkner, and as a child reportedly exclaimed that he would grow up to be a writer like his great-grandfather. See Joseph L. Fant III and Robert Ashley, eds., *Faulkner at West Point* (Jackson: Univ. Press of Mississippi, 2002), 99. In *Faulkner: A Biography* (1991 Vintage Books ed.), Blotner writes: "What image, then, did the growing boy carry in his mind of this ancestor whom he had never seen, yet who loomed so large? . . . What the boy would extract from it was not the dashing figure of the Knight with the Black Plume but that of the writer" (28). It therefore seems a very conscious decision, and perhaps a sacrifice on Faulkner's part, to deny Sartoris the literary powers of Colonel Falkner.

26. William Faulkner, *Requiem for a Nun* (New York: Random House, 1951), 239–40, 240, 240. Faulkner's famous short story, "A Rose for Emily" (1931), also contributes to the author's portrait of veterans as inarticulate men incapable of understanding their own past. After the death of Jefferson's Emily Grierson, "the very old men—some in their brushed Confederate uniforms—[stood] on the porch and the lawn, talking of Miss Emily as if she had been a contemporary of theirs, believing that they had danced with her and courted her, perhaps, confusing time with its mathematical progression" (181). Clearly, Faulkner's old veterans are nothing like the detail-oriented soldiers-turned-historians of the early Lost Cause, led by Jubal A. Early. See William Faulkner, "A Rose for Emily," in *These 13: Stories by William Faulkner* (New York: Jonathan Cape and Harrison Smith, 1931).

27. Faulkner, *Requiem for a Nun*, 246–47, 240; William Faulkner, *Absalom, Absalom!* (1936; repr., New York: Vintage, 1990), 7; quoted in Geoffrey Ward, *The Civil War: An Illustrated History* (New York: Knopf, 1990).

28. Tony Horwitz, *Confederates in the Attic: Dispatches from the Unfinished Civil War* (New York: Vintage, 1998), 277; William Faulkner, *Intruder in the Dust* (New York: Random House, 1948), 194–95; Douglas T. Miller, "Faulkner and the Civil War: Myth and Reality," *American Quarterly* 15 (Summer 1963): 201; Earl J. Hess, *Pickett's Charge, the Last Attack at Gettysburg* (Chapel Hill: Univ. of North Carolina Press, 2001), 397–98; Carol Reardon, *Pickett's Charge in History and Memory* (Chapel Hill: Univ. of North Carolina Press, 1997), 204; Horwitz, *Confederates in the Attic*, 277; Lloyd A. Hunter, "The Immortal Confederacy: Another Look at Lost Cause Religion," in *The Myth of the Lost Cause and Civil War History*, ed. Gary W. Gallagher and Alan T. Nolan (Bloomington: Indiana Univ. Press, 2000), 208–9; quoted in Ward, *Civil War*, 269. We should observe that the famous passage from *Intruder in the Dust* further links Lost Cause commemoration to a juvenile mindset, insofar as it places memory of Pickett's charge in the hands of southern youth. But if Connelly and Bellows were correct that the passage represents a "southern youth's birthright" (*God and General Longstreet*, 31), it was a birthright that southerners did not easily release over time. Several of Faulkner's adult characters—from Gavin Stevens to the Reverend Gail Hightower—continue to embrace the Myth in part

or whole, and by doing so fall prey to a kind of arrested development. As Clark has commented, in Faulkner's fiction "a glorified view of the War and the Old South exists only in a child-like state of consciousness" (16). The Pickett's charge passage therefore works as much as a critique of southern memory as a reflection of its comforting possibilities.

29. Francois Pitavy, "William Faulkner: Fiction as Historiography," in *Faulkner and History*, ed. Javier Coy and Michel Gresset (Salamanca, Spain: Univ. of Salamanca Press, 1986), 46.

30. Gwynn and Blotner, *Faulkner in the University*, 254.

31. For a fine discussion of Lost Cause architect Jubal A. Early and his vision for the future, see Gallagher, *Lee and His Generals in War and Memory*, chap. 10, "Jubal A. Early, the Lost Cause, and Civil War History." Gallagher observes: "Because of Early's passionate interest in how the future would judge the Confederacy . . . it is a mistake to see him as looking only to the past. His opinions about Confederate military history, which he hoped would influence subsequent generations, earned a receptive hearing across the postwar South" (201).

32. Faulkner, *Absalom, Absalom!* 289.

33. Lewis P. Simpson, "On William Faulkner's *Absalom, Absalom!*" in *Classics of Civil War Fiction*, ed. David Madden and Peggy Bach (Jackson: Univ. Press of Mississippi, 199), 171; William Faulkner, *The Unvanquished* (1938; repr., New York: Vintage, 1990), 188; Gwynn and Blotner, *Faulkner in the University*, 254, 249, 254; Charles Reagan Wilson, "Our Land, Our Country: Faulkner, the South, and the American Way of Life," in *Faulkner in America: Faulkner and Yoknapatawpha, 1998*, ed. Joseph R. Urgo and Ann J. Abadie (Jackson: Univ. Press of Mississippi, 2001), 163.

34. Joel Williamson, *William Faulkner and Southern History* (New York: Oxford Univ. Press, 1993), 7; Blotner, *Faulkner: A Biography* (1974, Random House ed.), vol. 2, p. 1252; and ibid., 1686; Faulkner's biographer, Joseph Blotner, concluded that for "a man of his age, time, and place," Faulkner "would be called a gradualist." The writer believed the white South should itself remedy the injustices done to African Americans, not be forced to do so by Federal law or military coercion. Faulkner's ideas about integration appeared to grow more conservative over the years, but in 1955 he first outraged his fellow southerners—including members of his own family—by supporting school integration. Following a letter he wrote to the Memphis *Commercial Appeal* that voiced his opposition to a dual, separate-but-equal school system in Mississippi, Faulkner began to receive threatening phone calls and hate mail. Moreover, numerous southerners repudiated his ideas in print, including his brother John. See Blotner, *Faulkner: A Biography* (1974, Random House ed.), vol. 2, p. 1252, 1531–32, 1687.

35. *The Unvanquished* began as a series of short stories Faulkner published in the mid-1930s in the *Saturday Evening Post* and *Scribner's Magazine*. After the addition of a final story, "An Odor of Verbena," the author set about revising and connecting the earlier stories to create narrative cohesion. The resulting novel was published in 1938, two years after the publication of *Absalom, Absalom!*

36. Clark, *Reconsidering Faulkner's Pulp Series*, 126. As revealed in Faulkner's novel *Sartoris (Flags in the Dust)*, Bayard will in time become the mayor of Jefferson and later serve as president of the Merchants and Farmers Bank until his retirement. See William Faulkner, *Sartoris* and *Flags in the Dust*.

37. John Pilkington, *The Heart of Yoknapatawpha County* (Jackson: Univ. Press of Mississippi, 1981), 358; Robert E. Knoll, "*The Unvanquished* for a Start," *College English* 19 (May 1958): 339; Warren Akin IV, "'Blood and Raising and Background': The Plot of *The Unvanquished*," *Modern Language Studies* 11 (Winter 1980): 8.

38. Similarly, in *The Sound and the Fury* (1929) Faulkner narrated the first three sections from the points of view of the three Compson brothers but did not permit a woman or person of color to narrate any of the story. Dilsey, a black servant of the Compsons, is a major presence in the fourth section of the novel and the character who, in Faulkner's words, "held the whole [family] together." Some readers have lamented that Faulkner allowed his biases regarding gender and race to prevent him from granting Dilsey her own narrative voice. See William Faulkner, *The Sound and the Fury* (New York: J. Cape and H. Smith, 1929); and Gwynn and Blotner, *Faulkner in the University*, 5.

39. Faulkner, *Unvanquished*, 81. All quotations hereafter refer to the Vintage edition and are cited parenthetically within the text.

40. James Hinkle has argued that *The Unvanquished* opens during the first summer of the war, in 1862, rather than with the July 1863 capture of Vicksburg. See James Hinkle, "The Civil War in the Apocrypha according to Faulkner," in *Faulkner and History*, ed. Javier Coy and Michel Gresset (Salamanca, Spain: Univ. of Salamanca Press, 1986), 30–31.

41. My reading of Loosh is informed by Katherine Arn Clark's dissertation, *Reconsidering Faulkner's Pulp Series*. Clark argued convincingly that like "Bayard, Loosh emerges 'unvanquished' during the course of the novel" (195). She also made the fine observation that it "is part of Faulkner's achievement in Loosh that he has drawn a black character who is heroic and at the same time unlikable. Faulkner makes us respect and admire him in spite of the difficulties of his personality" (194).

42. Nolan, "Anatomy of the Myth," 16.

43. Blight, *Race and Reunion*, 192, 196, 196. See Joseph T. Wilson, *The Black Phalanx* (Salem, N.H.: Ayer, 1992); and George Mike Arnold, "Colored Soldiers in the Union Army," *African Methodist Episcopal Church Review* 3 (Jan. 1887): 257–66.

44. Faulkner, *Intruder in the Dust*, 195.

45. Faulkner, *Requiem for a Nun*, 240; Rubin, "Scarlett O'Hara and the Two Quentin Compsons," 100.

46. Speaking to a classroom of West Point cadets in 1962, Faulkner observed: "I wouldn't undertake to guess how many years it will be before the Negro has equality in my country, anything approaching equality. But I am convinced that the Negro is the one that will have to do it, not by getting enough white people on his side to pass laws and bayonets, but to make himself—to improve himself to where the white men in Mississippi say, will say, 'Please join me.' There is too much talk of right and not enough talk of responsibility." See Fant and Ashley, *Faulkner at West Point*, 81.

47. Readers familiar with the events of Civil War history have questioned whether Faulkner did not make a number of chronological errors in *The Unvanquished*. Others, such as James Hinkle, have denied that such mistakes exist. Hinkle argued that Faulkner knew a great deal "about the actual time-table of the war" and concluded that "there is no discrepancy between the chronology of Faulkner's novel and the course of the real war. Faulkner simply knew more about Civil War history than his doubters did." Whether or not *The Unvanquished* contains chronological errors, Faulkner surely helped foster the idea that he lacked interest in historical facts, often claiming to have performed no research for his writing. See Hinkle, "Civil War in the Apocrypha according to Faulkner," 30–31.

48. Faulkner, *Absalom, Absalom!* 53. All quotations hereafter refer to the Vintage edition and are cited parenthetically within the text.

49. Richard Gray, *The Life of William Faulkner: A Critical Biography* (Oxford: Blackwell, 1994), 227.

50. In correspondence, Faulkner referred to *The Unvanquished* as a "pulp series" and went so far as to call it "trash." See Joseph Blotner, *Selected Letters of William Faulkner* (New York: Random House, 1977), 84.

51. Quoted in Blotner, *Faulkner: A Biography* (1991, Vintage Books ed.), 364.

52. Blight, *Race and Reunion*, 258.

53. Michael G. Kammen, *Mystic Chords of Memory: The Transformation of Tradition in American Culture* (New York: Knopf, 1991), 11.

54. For a similar critique of the South's gallant but anachronistic leaders, see section 4 of "The Bear" in Faulkner's *Go Down, Moses* (1942). There Ike McCaslin asks, "Who else could have declared a war against a power with ten times the area and a hundred times the men and a thousand times the resources, except men who could believe that all necessary to conduct a successful war was not acumen nor shrewdness nor politics nor diplomacy nor money nor even integrity and simple arithmetic but just love of land and courage[?]"—to which McCaslin Edmonds adds, "And an unblemished and gallant ancestry and the ability to ride a horse.... Dont leave that out." William Faulkner, *Go Down, Moses, and Other Stories* (1942; repr., New York: Vintage, 1990), 276.

55. Nolan, "Anatomy of the Myth," 18; Donald M. Kartiganer, "Faulkner's *Absalom, Absalom!* The Discovery of Values" *American Literature* 37 (Nov. 1965): 291.

56. One such monument was erected in April 1910 by the Fannie Gordon chapter of the United Daughters of the Confederacy, No. 1143, in Eastman, Georgia. It reads: "No nation rose so pure and white—none ever fell so spotless." Another monument, located on Broad Street in Augusta, Georgia, is inscribed: "No nation rose so white and fair, None fell so pure of crime."

57. Faulkner, *Go Down, Moses*, 266.

58. This passage falls in step with the sentiments voiced in a 1956 essay Faulkner published in *Harper's*, "On Fear: Deep South in Labor; Mississippi." There he argued that the racial apprehensions of southern whites concerned not "the Negro as an individual Negro nor even as a race, but as an economic class or stratum or factor, since what the Negro threatens is not the Southern white man's social system but the Southern white man's economic system." Throughout the South's antebellum

and postwar eras, Faulkner suggested, the "southern white man's shame" grew out of white culture's having secured its own wealth and power by promoting "the artificial inequality of man." See "On Fear: Deep South in Labor; Mississippi," *Essays, Speeches, and Public Letters, by William Faulkner*, ed. James B. Meriwether (London: Chatto and Windus, 1967), 95–96. For a good discussion of this essay as it relates to Faulkner's vision of the South and America, see Wilson, "Our Land, Our Country," 162–65.

59. Patricia Tobin, "The Time of Myth and History in *Absalom, Absalom!*" *American Literature* 45 (May 1973): 258.

60. Kartiganer, "Faulkner's *Absalom, Absalom!*" 297, 304.

61. Ibid., 298.

62. Cleanth Brooks, *William Faulkner: The Yoknapatawpha County* (New Haven, Conn.: Yale Univ. Press, 1963), 310.

63. See Robert Dale Parker, Absalom, Absalom!*: The Questioning of Fictions* (Boston: Twayne, 1991): "It turns out that Rosa did not *see* Judith's marriage forbidden without rhyme, reason, or excuse; she simply heard that people supposed it was forbidden, and she never heard any reason why. . . . In a way, then, Rosa sees little, but is obsessed with her vision" (25).

64. Rubin, "Scarlett O'Hara and the Two Quentin Compsons," 99.

65. Kartiganer, "Faulkner's *Absalom, Absalom!*" 302.

66. Blight, *Race and Reunion*, 177.

67. Brooks, *William Faulkner*, 311.

68. Fant and Ashley, *Faulkner at West Point*, 50–51.

69. Ibid., 80.

70. Clark, *Reconsidering Faulkner's Pulp Series*, 101, 121–22; Lynn Levins, *Faulkner's Heroic Design* (Athens: Univ. of Georgia Press, 1976), 125.

4. Each Man Has His Own Reason to Die

1. James M. McPherson, introduction to *The Passing of the Armies: An Account of the Final Campaign of the Army of the Potomac, Based upon Personal Reminiscences of the Fifth Army Corps*, by Joshua Lawrence Chamberlain (1915; repr., New York: Bantam, 1993), ix.

2. Desjardin, *Stand Firm Ye Boys From Maine*, 163, 159.

3. McPherson, introduction to *The Passing of the Armies*, x.

4. Shaara, *The Killer Angels*, 374. All quotations hereafter refer to this edition and are cited parenthetically within the text.

5. McPherson, introduction to *The Passing of the Armies*, xii. In his recent book *Hallowed Ground*, a walking guide to the Gettysburg battlefield, McPherson again shadowed the language and emphases of *The Killer Angels* when summarizing the career of Chamberlain. And the novel seems to have inspired a number of other lines by McPherson as well. For example, Shaara observed that Confederate lieutenant general Richard Ewell "[is] recently married [and] refers to his new wife absent-mindedly as 'Mrs. Brown'" (xii); in turn, McPherson noted, "Ewell had recently married a widow,

whom he absentmindedly referred to as 'Mrs. Brown.'" Such parallels may seem trivial, but they demonstrate the degree to which Shaara's novel has made an impression on general readers and historians alike. See James M. McPherson, *Hallowed Ground: A Walk at Gettysburg* (New York: Crown, 2003), 83, 32.

6. William Marvel, *A Place Called Appomattox* (Chapel Hill: Univ. of North Carolina Press, 2000), 358–59, n. 38. Marvel's fascinating account of how Chamberlain "convinced himself" of this story, over a forty-year period, demands the attention of anyone interested in Civil War mythology. See 259–60.

7. "My Favorite Historical Novel," *American Heritage* 43 (Oct. 1992): 103; Reardon, *Pickett's Charge in History and Memory*, 205; "My Favorite Historical Novel," 103; Marc Jaffe, ed., *Three Great Novels of the Civil War* (New York: Wing, 1994); MacKinlay Kantor, *Andersonville* (Cleveland, Ohio: World, 1955); Crane, *Red Badge of Courage*.

8. Shelby Foote, *Shiloh: A Novel* (New York: Dial, 1952); Philip Beidler, "Ted Turner *Et Al.* at Gettysburg; or, Re-Enactors in the Attic," *Virginia Quarterly Review* 75 (Summer 1999): 489.

9. The reviewer for the *New York Times* believed Shaara's battle descriptions superior to those found in most Civil War fictions, including works descending from *The Red Badge of Courage*: "Admirably avoided are the panoramic view and the muck and blood view, which tell us too much and too little." See Thomas LeClair, review of *The Killer Angels*, by Michael Shaara, *New York Times*, Oct. 20, 1974, 424.

10. Robert Underwood Johnson and Clarence C. Buel, eds., *Battles and Leaders of the Civil War*, vol. 3 (New York: De Vinne, 1887–88); Cushman, *Bloody Promenade*, 174.

11. Joshua Lawrence Chamberlain, "Through Blood and Fire at Gettysburg," *Hearst's Magazine* 23 (June 1913): 894–909.

12. Blight, *Race and Reunion*, 2.

13. Joseph Moreau, *Schoolbook Nation: Conflicts over American History Textbooks from the Civil War to the Present* (Ann Arbor: Univ. of Michigan Press, 2003), 315. Moreau explained that although American school texts increasingly devoted space (and respect) to African Americans, political and social opposition to such changes meant that "the drive to reform books and teaching fell short of complete victory" (329). See also Frances FitzGerald, *America Revised: History Schoolbooks in the Twentieth Century* (Boston: Little, Brown and Co., 1979).

14. Gallagher, *Lee and His Generals in War and Memory*, 207, 219. Several scholars have examined lines or passages from *The Killer Angels* when discussing matters as varied as Ken Burns's PBS documentary *The Civil War* (1990), the North Carolina versus Virginia "Pickett's Charge" dispute, the shape and meaning of Civil War fictions, the 1993 film adaptation *Gettysburg*, and literary representations of the Civil War during the Vietnam War and at the close of the millennium. See, respectively, Gary W. Gallagher, "How Familiarity Bred Success: Military Campaigns and Leaders in Ken Burns's *The Civil War*," in *Ken Burns's* The Civil War: *Historians Respond*, ed. Toplin, 51; Reardon, *Pickett's Charge in History and Memory*, 205, 211; Cushman, *Bloody Promenade*, 209–11; Beidler, "Ted Turner *Et Al.* at Gettysburg,"

489–90; Kevin Grauke, "Vietnam, Survivalism, and the Civil War: The Use of History in Michael Shaara's *The Killer Angels* and Charles Frazier's *Cold Mountain*," *War, Literature, and the Arts: An International Journal of the Humanities* 14, nos. 1–2 (2002): 45, 46, 50. Grauke's essay is one of the most sophisticated studies of *The Killer Angels* to date, valuable both for its reading of the novel's political moment and for its look at how the 1993 film adaptation responded to the Persian Gulf War. Noting correctly that *The Killer Angels* "forwards the Union's cause at the expense of the Confederacy's," Grauke made the interesting argument that Shaara attempted "to transmit the artistically enhanced gloriousness and patriotism of the Union Army of 1863 to the U.S. armed forces of the 1960s and 1970s that were fighting the red scare in Southeast Asia" (46, 50). The only study I know of that makes *The Killer Angels* its sole focus—comparing Shaara's characters and presentation of Gettysburg to historical personages and fact—is D. Scott Hartwig, *A Killer Angels Companion* (Gettysburg, Pa.: Thomas Publications, 1996). A historian at the Gettysburg National Military Park, Hartwig does not offer an extended interpretation of the work, but he does assess the novel in favorable terms: "It is a classic work of Civil War fiction and justly deserves the laurels it has garnered" (1).

15. Apparently the makers of *Gettysburg* thought viewers would miss Grant. At one point during the film, Longstreet refers to his old friend from the antebellum army, Sam Grant.

16. Connelly, *Marble Man*, 73.

17. See ibid., 74; and Gallagher, *Lee and His Generals*, 211.

18. Gallagher, *Lee and His Generals*, 212. For a valuable collection of essays that explores the Myth, its rise, and the enduring appeal of Lost Cause tenets, see Gallagher and Nolan, eds., *Myth of the Lost Cause*.

19. Gallagher, *Lee and His Generals*, 199.

20. See LeClair, review of *The Killer Angels:* The reviewer noted that new fictional practices, "like new clichés, are scabrous things, neither brittle with experiment nor comfortably worn by use." Despite the potential perils of innovative writing, "[*The Killer Angels*'] method of multiple points of view fasten the reader's attention to the material" (424).

21. Douglas Southall Freeman, *Lee's Lieutenants: A Study in Command*, vol. 2, *Cedar Mountain to Chancellorsville* (New York: Scribner's, 1943), xxiv.

22. On the casualties at Gettysburg, see David J. Eicher, *The Longest Night: A Military History of the Civil War* (New York: Simon and Schuster, 2001), 550. Eicher notes that of "the 93,534 engaged in the Army of the Potomac, the losses were 3,149 killed, 14,503 wounded, and 5,161 missing; Confederate casualties among the 70,274 engaged were reported as 4,637 killed, 12,391 wounded, and 5,846 missing, but probably actually totaled 28,000 or more" (550).

23. Piston, *Lee's Tarnished Lieutenant*, 1.

24. John B. Gordon, *Reminiscences of the Civil War* (New York: Scribner's, 1905), 163–64.

25. Connelly, *Marble Man*, 83.

26. For a fine examination of Longstreet's postwar reputation in the South, see Piston, *Lee's Tarnished Lieutenant*, esp. 95–188. Piston concludes that "James Long-

street's negative image is not likely to change. His role in Southern culture has been that of villain, not hero, and cultural roles cannot be overturned by scholarship.... Longstreet will be remembered primarily as Lee's tarnished lieutenant" (188).

27. Gallagher, *Lee and His Generals*, 219.

28. Foster, *Ghosts of the Confederacy*, 58.

29. Shaara's version of the conversation among Lee, Early, Ewell, and Gen. Robert E. Rodes shadows one of Early's most famous recollections, as printed in the December 1877 issue of the *Southern Historical Society Papers*. Early claimed that during the July 1 meeting with Ewell and his division commanders, Lee himself criticized Longstreet for being "*so slow.*" Shaara sided with Longstreet. Rather than critique his senior lieutenant, Shaara's Lee casts Early in a dim light: "Something too cold here, something disagreeable in the silence of the eyes, the tilt of the head. . . . Nothing happy about the man" (146). For Early's account, see "A Review by General Early," *Southern Historical Society Papers* 4 (Dec. 1877): 274.

30. Shaara seems to have simplified Early's association with the Louisiana lottery as part of his negative characterization of the man. By contrast, Gaines M. Foster noted that Early added "Confederate dignity and legitimacy to the drawings of the corrupt Louisiana Lottery." See Foster, *Ghosts of the Confederacy*, 55.

31. Walter H. Taylor, *Four Years with General Lee: Being a Summary of the More Important Events Touching the Career of General Robert E. Lee, in the War between the States; Together with an Authoritative Statement of the Strength of the Army Which He Commanded in the Field* (New York: D. Appleton and Company, 1878), 100, 101.

32. Charles Marshall, *Lee's Aide-de-Camp: Being the Papers of Colonel Charles Marshall Sometime Aide-de-Camp, Military Secretary, and Assistant Adjutant General on the Staff of Robert E. Lee, 1862–1865*, ed. Frederick Maurice (1927; repr., Lincoln: Univ. of Nebraska Press, 2000), 240, 238. As for the July 2 assaults on the Union left, Marshall noted only that they began later than Lee desired; he directed no critique at Longstreet. See 233–34.

33. For Marshall's critique of Stuart and his command during the Pennsylvania command, see *Lee's Aide-de-Camp*, esp. 221–24. Marshall blamed Stuart for the loss at Gettysburg, concluding bitterly that "the result of General Stuart's action was that two armies invaded Pennsylvania in 1863, instead of one. One of those armies had little cavalry, the other had nothing but cavalry. One was commanded by General Lee, the other by General Stuart" (224).

34. Gary W. Gallagher, introduction to Charles Marshall, *Lee's Aide-de-Camp: Being the Papers of Colonel Charles Marshall Sometime Aide-de-Camp, Military Secretary, and Assistant Adjutant General on the Staff of Robert E. Lee, 1862–1865*, ed. Frederick Maurice (1927; repr., Lincoln: Univ. of Nebraska Press, 2000), xiii.

35. In *Lee's Aide-de-Camp*, Gettysburg is the subject of three chapters: one on the object of the campaign, one on the invasion of Pennsylvania, and one on the battle itself. These chapters together comprise seventy-five pages, slightly more than a fourth of the narrative. See Marshall, *Lee's Aide-de-Camp*, 177–252.

36. Jubal A. Early, "Letter from Gen. J. A. Early," *Southern Historical Society Papers* 4 (Aug. 1877): 56.

37. Edward Porter Alexander, "The Great Charge and Artillery Fighting at Gettysburg," *Battles and Leaders of the Civil War*, vol. 3, ed. Johnson and Buel, 366.

38. Hess, *Pickett's Charge*, 400; Gary W. Gallagher, *Lee and His Army in Confederate History* (Chapel Hill: Univ. of North Carolina Press, 2001), 102. Hess went on to argue that Lee "was fully aware of the persistent lack of victory in each successive campaign fought by his Western colleagues in Tennessee and Mississippi, where the Rebels suffered a series of dismal defeats and consequent loss of territory. No quick strategic victory in Pennsylvania, no matter how spectacular, could offset the loss of Tennessee, Mississippi, and the Mississippi River. . . . [Lee] never looked on the Pennsylvania campaign as the one and only stroke to win Confederate independence" (400–401).

39. Foster concluded that the first Lost Cause movement of the 1870s, spearheaded by "the Virginia coalition," ultimately failed to attract the attention of Southerners uninterested in a return "to the Confederate past." The Virginians' ideas found wider approval in the 1880s, however, when incorporated into more forward-looking veterans' movements. See Foster, *Ghosts of the Confederacy*, 61–62.

40. Connelly and Bellows, *God and General Longstreet*, 42.

41. Connelly, *Marble Man*, 64; James Longstreet, *From Manassas to Appomattox: Memoirs of the Civil War in America* (Philadelphia: J. B. Lippincott, 1903), 377, 382, 401.

42. Longstreet, *From Manassas to Appomattox*, 404, 397. Longstreet marveled at the Virginians for fighting Gettysburg decades afterward, "consum[ing] many of their peaceful hours in publishing their plans for the battle" (377). Many historians have similarly labeled the postwar efforts of Early and other Lost Cause warriors "piquant" and obsessive. Foster characterized this obsession as a "dream of victory, a dream of a return to an undefeated Confederacy." The Virginians, he explained, "seemed to believe that if they wrote their articles and kept southerners from deserting after the war, the Yankees and all that had occurred after Appomattox would simply disappear." See Foster, *Ghosts of the Confederacy*, 60.

43. Connelly, *Marble Man*, 68.

44. During the early years of the war, some Confederates used "heritage" to distance the South from the North—a region they saw as fundamentally different from their own. Newspapers, poets, and politicians insisted that Southerners descended from aristocratic Cavaliers, not the plebian and puritanical ancestors of the North. Yet the portrait of an aristocratic South did not rest well with many Confederates, who by 1863 argued that their nation stood as a democracy, not a patrician republic. For a fine discussion of these matters, see Robert B. Bonner, "Roundheaded Cavaliers? The Context and Limits of a Confederate Racial Project," *Civil War History* 48 (Mar. 2002): esp. 51–53. Shaara's novel, along with other works of fiction and history, suggests that the vision of an aristocratic South survived the war and still finds acceptance today.

45. Gary W. Gallagher, introduction to *Three Months in the Southern States: April–June 1863* by Arthur James Lyon Fremantle (1863; repr., Lincoln: Univ. of Nebraska Press, 1991), ix.

46. Arthur James Lyon Fremantle, *Three Months in the Southern States: April–June 1863* (1863; repr., Lincoln: Univ. of Nebraska Press, 1991), 185.

47. Robert Ashley, review of Michael Shaara, *The Killer Angels: A Novel*, *Civil War Times Illustrated* 14 (Aug. 1975): 49; Fremantle, *Three Months in the Southern States*, 140, 172, 121, 206, 184, 293, 297.

48. Fremantle, *Three Months in the Southern States*, 21. By contrast, Shaara's Fremantle thinks only that it is "hard to say what they meant" when Confederates pledged allegiance to the Queen (167).

49. James Morris, *Heaven's Command: An Imperial Progress* (New York: Harcourt, 1973), 539, 538.

50. See Gallagher, *Lee and His Generals*: "[Lee] suffered considerable discomfort during the campaign in Pennsylvania. In late summer 1863 he had offered to step down from command, citing unhappiness with the Gettysburg campaign and 'the growing failure of my bodily strength'" (80). However, Gallagher cast doubt on claims that Lee was infirm at Gettysburg and suffering from perhaps three different ailments; see 63n25. For a medical doctor's analysis of Lee's health, see Jack D. Welsh, *Medical Histories of Confederate Generals* (Kent, Ohio: Kent State Univ. Press, 1995), 134–36. Of Lee's condition in Pennsylvania, Welsh said little: "During the battle at Gettysburg, Lee had diarrhea and possibly a recurrence of malaria" (135).

51. See Piston, *Lee's Tarnished Lieutenant*, 154–57. Piston noted that by the time of the memoir's publication, Longstreet's earlier writings—along with the work of Lee's defenders—had already turned thousands in the South against him. Many readers of the memoir believed that Longstreet's "unsparing" criticism of Lee's strategy "merely made Lee seem all the more Christ-like and forgiving, and himself petty by contrast.... The book seemed to confirm that Longstreet was the stubborn, jealous subordinate his detractors had claimed" (156).

52. For the historical Fremantle's view of Longstreet at Gettysburg, see Fremantle, *Three Months in the Southern States*, esp. 237–38, 246–47, 256, 261, 265–66, 274–45. Fremantle said nothing of the general's views on honor or the changing face of modern warfare. His judgment of the "taciturn" Longstreet was highly favorable.

53. Joshua Lawrence Chamberlain, *The Passing of the Armies: An Account of the Final Campaign of the Army of the Potomac, Based upon the Personal Reminiscences of the Fifth Army Corps* (1915; repr., New York: Bantam, 1993), 294.

54. The episode stands as the novel's most contrived moment. It is extremely unlikely that a foreign slave brought to America in mid-June would be with the Confederate army in Pennsylvania (particularly in light of the 1808 ban on the importation of slaves). More important, the slave's thematically convenient appearance strains the narrative's credibility. Shaara did make interesting choices with the runaway, however, informing us that a Gettysburg woman wounded him and *not* Confederates determined to thwart his escape. In facts like these, Shaara demonstrated his seemingly neutral position.

55. Blight, *Race and Reunion*, 282; Foster, *Ghosts of the Confederacy*, 108, 104–14; Gallagher, *Lee and His Generals*, 282, and ibid; Cushman, *Bloody Promenade*, 171

(Lost Cause writers such as Jubal Early named it "The War between the States"); Gordon, *Reminiscences of the Civil War,* 465.

56. Blight, *Race and Reunion,* 203, 2. Blight noted that a minority of Northerners in the 1890s found reconciliation distasteful when it meant forgetting what they saw as the true cause of the war and the reason for prosecuting it: slavery. Virtually all African Americans dissented to reunion on such terms. One Union veteran wrote bitterly of the coming 1888 Gettysburg reunion, perhaps with race in mind: "No God-knows-who-was-right bosh must be tolerated at Gettysburg. The men who won the victory there were eternally right, and the men who were defeated were eternally wrong" (203).

57. Ibid., 203.

58. Lewis R. Stegman, quoted in the *Fiftieth Anniversary Celebration, New York Veterans, Gettysburg, 1913: Report of the New York State Monuments Commission for the Battlefields of Gettysburg, Chattanooga, and Antietam* (Albany, N.Y.: J. B. Lyon, 1916), 29.

59. Gordon, *Reminiscences of the Civil War,* 18–19.

60. Cushman, *Bloody Promenade,* 172.

61. Marvel, *A Place Called Appomattox,* 261. Chamberlain's account of this episode, later repeated in his memoir, appeared in the May 4, 1901, issue of the *New York Times.*

62. Gordon, *Reminiscences of the Civil War,* 444.

63. Andrew Cowan, quoted in the *Fiftieth Anniversary Celebration, New York Veterans,* 65.

64. Chamberlain received the Medal of Honor in 1893. The citation lauded his "daring heroism and great tenacity in holding his position on the Little Round Top against repeated assaults, and carrying the advance position on the Great Round Top." Quoted in Desjardin, *Stand Firm Ye Boys from Maine,* 148.

65. Ashley, review of *The Killer Angels,* 49.

66. Alice Rains Trulock, *In the Hands of Providence: Joshua L. Chamberlain and the American Civil War* (Chapel Hill: Univ. of North Carolina Press, 2001), 353; Joshua Lawrence Chamberlain, "The Old Flag—What Was Surrendered? And What Was Won?" *Boston Journal,* Jan. 4, 1878.

67. Ashley, review of *The Killer Angels,* 49.

68. Quoted in Gallagher, *Lee and His Generals,* 269.

69. Naomi Jacobs, *The Character of Truth: Historical Figures in Contemporary Fiction* (Carbondale: Southern Illinois Univ. Press, 1990), 109–10. Hayden White has commented on the larger connections between allegory and historical narrative: "Precisely insofar as the historical narrative endows sets of real events with the kinds of meaning found otherwise only in myth and literature, we are justified in regarding it as a product of *allegoresis.* Therefore, rather than regard every historical narrative as mythic or ideological in nature, we should regard it as allegorical, that is, as saying one thing and meaning another." See Hayden White, *The Content of the Form: Narrative Discourse and Historical Representation* (Baltimore: Johns Hopkins Univ. Press, 1987), 45.

70. Harry E. Shaw, *The Forms of Historical Fiction: Sir Walter Scott and His Successors* (Ithaca, N.Y.: Cornell Univ. Press, 1983), 101.

71. W. L. Rose, *Race and Region in American Historical Fiction: Four Episodes in Popular Culture; An Inaugural Lecture Delivered before the University of Oxford on 4 May 1978* (Oxford: Clarendon, 1979), 2.

72. Rose anticipated, in 1978, that the next major "reading-viewing success" would occur about twenty years into the future: "Celebratory effects, mass participation, an insistence on sharing the experience, these are the universal style of these events.... This combination of circumstances emboldens me to suppose that somewhere around the year 2000 some such thing may occur again." Rose, *Race and Region in American Historical Fiction*, 30. Ken Burns's nine-part documentary drew an audience of forty million Americans in September 1990, transforming Burns into an overnight celebrity just as *Roots* did Alex Haley in 1977. The phenomenon met Rose's definition of a "shared event," as each day Americans discussed the previous night's episode and frequently watched the film with family and friends. When released, the film script of the documentary, published in hardback by Knopf, sold thousands of copies. Similarly, the author Shelby Foote—often featured in the documentary—learned that in the six-month period following the broadcast, his trilogy on the war sold more than one hundred thousand sets. See Robert Brent Toplin, introduction to *Ken Burns's* The Civil War: *Historians Respond*, ed. Robert Brent Toplin (New York: Oxford Univ. Press, 1996), xv–xvi. The Burns/Ward and Foote books, respectively, are *The Civil War: An Illustrated History*, ed. Geoffrey C. Ward, with Ken Burns and Ric Burns (New York: Knopf, 1990), and Shelby Foote, *The Civil War: A Narrative; Fort Sumter to Perryville, Fredericksburg to Meridian, Red River to Appomattox* (New York: Random House, 1958–74).

73. "My Favorite Historical Novel," 103.

74. Gallagher, "How Familiarity Bred Success," 51, 48–49.

75. Gabor S. Boritt, "Lincoln and Gettysburg: The Hero and the Heroic Place," in *Ken Burns's* The Civil War: *Historians Respond*, ed. Toplin, 91.

76. Hartwig, *Killer Angels Companion*, v.

77. Kevin Grauke has made the same point in a related argument: "Had the Confederacy won, the novel implies, the America of the late twentieth century would not have come to pass. Slavery would have continued and spread, as would have the aristocratic mindset that stresses the blood of the father over the achievement of the son." See Grauke, "Vietnam, Survivalism, and the Civil War," 50.

78. Glenn LaFantasie, "Romance vs. Reality at Gettysburg: A Reconnaissance Report on the Books," *New York Times*, June 12, 1994. In the decades before the publication of *The Killer Angels*, many scholars and editors bemoaned the lack of quality fiction about the Civil War. See, for example, David Gerard, "Why Are Most Civil War Novels Mediocre? Here's Why, With Some Tips for Writers," *Civil War Times Illustrated* (June 1962): 34–36; and Lawrence S. Thompson, "The Civil War in Fiction," *Civil War History* 2 (1956): 83–95. Gerard explained that Civil War novels stood to improve if authors followed his instructions: (a) avoid a modern style, (b) be partisan, (c) avoid telling the war from the perspectives of nonofficers,

(d) describe multiple battles, (e) be historically accurate, and (f) keep women out of the story. Thompson remarked that most novelists representing the Civil War "were imitators, at best fourth and fifth raters."

79. Steve Earle, "Dixieland," *The Mountain* [Compact Disc] (E-Squared, 1999).

80. "Interview with Jeff Shaara, Author of *The Last Full Measure*," www.randomhouse.com/BB/promos/lastfullmeasure/interview.html (accessed July 5, 2007). Jeff Shaara is the author of several works of historical fiction. Those referenced here are: *Gods and Generals* (New York: Ballantine, 1996), and *The Last Full Measure* (New York: Ballantine, 1998).

81. Frazier, *Cold Mountain*, 12, 9, 10, 12.

82. James Reasoner, *Gettysburg* (Nashville, Tenn.: Cumberland, 2001), 345, 350, 393.

83. Glenn Tucker, *High Tide at Gettysburg: The Campaign in Pennsylvania* (New York: Bobbs-Merrill, 1958); Piston, *Lee's Tarnished Lieutenant*, 181; George R. Stewart, *Pickett's Charge: A Microhistory of the Final Attack at Gettysburg, July 3, 1863* (Cambridge, Mass.: Houghton, 1959), 285, 286; T. Harry Williams, "The Military Leadership of North and South," *Why the North Won the Civil War*, ed. David Donald (Baton Rouge: Louisiana State Univ. Press, 1960), 40. Williams did not hold Longstreet in the same high regard as Shaara did and said nothing of the soldier's brilliance for defensive warfare. He wrote that Longstreet and Jackson "were outstanding corps leaders, probably the best in the war, but that neither gave much evidence of being able to go higher. Longstreet failed in independent command" (34).

84. Connelly and Bellows, *God and General Longstreet*, 32. See also Thomas L. Connelly, "Robert E. Lee and the Western Confederacy: A Criticism of Lee's Strategic Ability," *Civil War History* 15, no. 2 (1969): 116–32; and Thomas L. Connelly, "The Image and the General: Robert E. Lee in American Historiography," *Civil War History* 19, no. 1 (1973): 50–64.

85. Thomas Lask, "Books of the Times: High Tide of the Confederacy," review of *The Killer Angels*, by Michael Shaara, *New York Times*, May 10, 1975, 27.

86. Robert Ashley, review of *The Killer Angels*, 49–50.

87. Piston, *Lee's Tarnished Lieutenant*, x; Glenn Tucker, *Lee and Longstreet at Gettysburg* (New York: Bobbs-Merrill, 1968); William Garrett Piston, e-mail to Craig A. Warren, Mar. 23, 2002.

88. Michael Golay, *To Gettysburg and Beyond: The Parallel Lives of Joshua Lawrence Chamberlain and Edward Porter Alexander* (New York: Crown, 1994); Mark Perry, *Conceived in Liberty: Joshua Lawrence Chamberlain, William Oates, and the American Civil War* (New York: Viking, 1997); Willard Mosher Wallace, *Soul of the Lion: A Biography of General Joshua Lawrence Chamberlain* (1960; repr., Gettysburg, Pa.: Stan Clark Military Books, 1993); McPherson, *Hallowed Ground*, 82, 83, 68, 93; Nolan, *Lee Considered*, 5, xi.

89. White, *The Content of the Form*, 41–42.

90. Robert Brent Toplin, "Ken Burns's *The Civil War* as an Interpretation of History," in *Ken Burns's* The Civil War: *Historians Respond*, ed. Toplin, 20–21.

CONCLUSION

1. Ron Kovic, *Born on the Fourth of July* (New York: McGraw-Hill, 1976); Philip Caputo, *A Rumor of War* (New York: Holt, Rinehart and Winston, 1977); Harold G. Moore and Joseph L. Galloway, *We Were Soldiers Once . . . and Young: Ia Drang, the Battle That Changed the War in Vietnam* (New York: Random House, 1992); William Manchester, *Goodbye, Darkness: A Memoir of the Pacific* (Boston: Little, Brown, 1980); E. B. Sledge, *With the Old Breed: At Peleliu and Okinawa* (Novato, Calif.: Presidio Press, 1981).

2. E. B. Sledge, *With the Old Breed: At Peleliu and Okinawa* (1981; repr., New York: Oxford Univ. Press, 1990), 277–78, 278, 235.

3. Howard Bahr, *The Judas Field: A Novel of the Civil War* (New York: Picador, 2006), 89, 93–94. All citations hereafter appear parenthetically in the text.

4. See Matthew J. Friedman, "Post-Vietnam Syndrome: Recognition and Management," *Psychosomatics* 22 (1981): 931–42.

5. On Bahr's Vietnam experiences, including combat, see Alden Mudge, "A Poetic Tale and a Writer Whose Time Has Finally Come," interview with Howard Bahr (*BookPage: America's Book Review*, Apr. 1998), www.bookpage.com/9804bp/howard_bahr.html (accessed Jan. 20, 2008).

6. Philip Caputo, *A Rumor of War* (1977; repr., New York: Henry Holt and Company, 1996), 352.

Bibliography

Memoirs and Other Narratives by Veterans

Alexander, Edward Porter. "The Great Charge and Artillery Fighting at Gettysburg." In *Battles and Leaders of the Civil War*, vol. 3, ed. Robert Underwood Johnson and Clarence C. Buel, 357–68. New York: De Vinne, 1887–88.

Allen, George H. *Forty-six Months with the Fourth R.I. Volunteers in the War of 1861 to 1865: Comprising a History of the Marches, Battles, and Camp Life, Compiled from Journals Kept While on Duty in the Field and Camp.* Providence, R.I.: J. A. and R. A. Reid, 1887.

Arnold, George Mike. "Colored Soldiers in the Union Army." *African Methodist Episcopal Church Review* 3 (Jan. 1887): 257–66.

Bierce, Ambrose. *The Collected Works of Ambrose Bierce.* 12 vols. New York: Neale, 1909–12.

Billings, John D. *Hardtack and Coffee; or, The Unwritten Story of Army Life.* Philadelphia: Thompson, 1888. Reprint, Lincoln: Univ. of Nebraska Press, 1993.

Booth, George Wilson. *A Maryland Boy in Lee's Army: Personal Reminiscences of a Maryland Soldier in the War between the States, 1861–1865.* Baltimore: Self-published, 1898.

Caputo, Philip. *A Rumor of War.* New York: Holt, Rinehart and Winston, 1977.

Chamberlain, Joshua Lawrence. "The Old Flag—What Was Surrendered? And What Was Won?" *Boston Journal,* Jan. 4, 1878.

———. *The Passing of the Armies: An Account of the Final Campaign of the Army of the Potomac, Based upon Personal Reminiscences of the Fifth Army Corps.* New York: G. P. Putnam's Sons, 1915. Reprint, New York: Bantam, 1993.

———. "Through Blood and Fire at Gettysburg." *Hearst's Magazine* 23 (June 1913): 894–909.

Douglas, Henry Kyd. *I Rode with Stonewall: Being Chiefly the War Experiences of the Youngest Member of Jackson's Staff from the John Brown Raid to the Hanging of Mrs. Surratt.* Chapel Hill: Univ. of North Carolina Press, 1940.

Duke, Basil W. *Reminiscences of General Basil W. Duke.* New York: Doubleday, 1911.
Early, Jubal A. "Letter from Gen. J. A. Early." *Southern Historical Society Papers* 4 (Aug. 1877): 50–66.
———. "A Review by General Early." *Southern Historical Society Papers* 4 (Dec. 1877): 241–81.
Eby, Henry Harrison. *Observations of an Illinois Boy in Battle, Camp and Prisons, 1861 to 1865.* Mendota, Ill.: Eby, 1910.
Fiftieth Anniversary Celebration, New York Veterans, Gettysburg, 1913: Report of the New York State Monuments Commission for the Battlefields of Gettysburg, Chattanooga, and Antietam. Albany, N.Y.: J. B. Lyon, 1916.
Fullerton, J. S. "Reënforcing Thomas at Chickamauga." In *Battles and Leaders of the Civil War.* vol. 3, ed. Robert Underwood Johnson and Clarence C. Buel, 665–67. New York: De Vinne, 1887–88.
Gerrish, Theodore. *Army Life: A Private's Reminiscences of the War.* Portland, Maine: Hoyt, Fogg, and Donham, 1882.
Gordon, John B. *Reminiscences of the Civil War.* New York: Scribner's, 1905.
Goss, Warren Lee. *Recollections of a Private.* New York: T. Y. Crowell and Co., 1890.
Grant, Ulysses S. *Personal Memoirs of U. S. Grant.* 2 vols. New York: Charles L. Webster and Co., 1885–86.
Guerrant, Rev. Edward O. "Marshall and Garfield in Eastern Kentucky." In *Battles and Leaders of the Civil War,* vol. 1, ed. Robert Underwood Johnson and Clarence C. Buel, 393–97. New York: De Vinne, 1887–88.
Hill, Alonzo F. *Our Boys: The Personal Experiences of a Soldier in the Army of the Potomac.* Philadelphia: J. E. Potter, 1864.
Hill, Daniel H. "Chickamauga: The Great Battle of the West." In *Battles and Leaders of the Civil War,* vol. 3, ed. Robert Underwood Johnson and Clarence C. Buel, 638–62. New York: De Vinne, 1887–88.
Hinman, Wilbur F. *Corporal Si Klegg and His "Pard": How They Lived and Talked, and What They Did and Suffered, While Fighting for the Flag.* Cleveland, Ohio: Williams, 1887.
Hubbard, John Milton. *Notes of a Private.* Memphis, Tenn.: E. H. Clarke and Brother, 1909.
Johnson, Robert Underwood, and Clarence C. Buel, eds. *Battles and Leaders of the Civil War.* 4 vols. New York: De Vinne, 1887–88.
Kovic, Ron. *Born on the Fourth of July.* New York: McGraw-Hill, 1976.
Longstreet, James. *From Manassas to Appomattox: Memoirs of the Civil War in America.* Philadelphia: J. B. Lippincott, 1903.
Manchester, William. *Goodbye, Darkness: A Memoir of the Pacific.* Boston: Little, Brown, 1980.
Marshall, Charles. *Lee's Aide-de-Camp: Being the Papers of Colonel Charles Marshall Sometime Aide-de-Camp, Military Secretary, and Assistant Adjutant General on the Staff of Robert E. Lee, 1862–1865,* ed. Frederick Maurice. Boston: Little, Brown, and Company, 1927. Reprint, Lincoln: Bison Books [Univ. of Nebraska Press], 2000.

McCarthy, Carlton. *Detailed Minutiae of Soldier Life in the Army of Northern Virginia, 1861–1865.* Richmond, Va.: Carleton, McCarthy and Co., 1882.

Moore, Harold G., and Joseph L. Galloway. *We Were Soldiers Once... and Young: Ia Drang, the Battle That Changed the War in Vietnam.* New York: Random House, 1992.

Mulholland, St. Clair A. *The Story of the 116th Regiment, Pennsylvania Volunteers in the War of the Rebellion: The Record of a Gallant Command.* Philadelphia: F. McManus, 1903. Reprint, ed. Lawrence Frederick Kohl, New York: Fordham Univ. Press, 1996.

Parker, Dr. W. W. "How the Southern Soldier Kept House during the War." *Southern Historical Society Papers* 23 (1895): 318–28.

Sledge, E. B. *With the Old Breed: At Peleliu and Okinawa.* Novato, Calif.: Presidio Press, 1981. Reprint, New York: Oxford Univ. Press, 1990.

Taylor, Walter H. *Four Years with General Lee: Being a Summary of the More Important Events Touching the Career of General Robert E. Lee, in the War between the States; Together with an Authoritative Statement of the Strength of the Army Which He Commanded in the Field.* New York: D. Appleton and Company, 1878.

Walke, Henry. "The Western Flotilla at Fort Donelson, Island Number Ten, Fort Pillow and Memphis." In *Battles and Leaders of the Civil War,* vol. 1, ed. Robert Underwood Johnson and Clarence C. Buel, 430–52. New York: De Vinne, 1887–88.

Watkins, Sam R. *"Co. Aytch," Maury Grays, First Tennessee Regiment; or, A Side Show of the Big Show.* Nashville, Tenn.: Cumberland Presbyterian, 1882. Reprint, as *Co. Aytch: A Confederate Memoir of the Civil War.* New York: Touchstone, 1997.

Wells, Andrew B. "The Charge of the Eighth Pennsylvania Cavalry: III." In *Battles and Leaders of the Civil War,* vol. 3, ed. Robert Underwood Johnson and Clarence C. Buel, 187–88. New York: De Vinne, 1887–88.

Weygant, Charles H. *History of the One Hundred and Twenty-Fourth Regiment, N.Y.S.V.* Newburgh, N.Y.: Journal Printing House, 1877.

Wilkeson, Frank. *Recollections of a Private Soldier in the Army of the Potomac.* New York: G. P. Putnam's Sons, 1887.

Wilson, Joseph T. *The Black Phalanx.* Salem, N.H.: Ayer, 1992.

Wyeth, John Allan. *Life of Lieutenant-General Nathan Bedford Forrest.* New York: Harper, 1899.

OTHER MEMOIRS

Alcott, Louisa May. *Hospital Sketches.* Boston: James Redpath, 1863.

Andrews, Eliza Frances. *The War-Time Journal of a Georgia Girl, 1864–1865.* New York: D. Appleton and Company, 1908.

Catton, Bruce. *Waiting for the Morning Train: An American Boyhood.* New York: Doubleday and Company, 1972.

Davis, Jefferson. *The Rise and Fall of the Confederate Government.* 2 vols. New York: D. Appleton and Company, 1881. Reprint, New York: De Capo Press, 1990.
Faulkner, John. *My Brother Bill.* New York: Pocket Books, 1964.
Fremantle, Arthur James Lyon. *Three Months in the Southern States: April–June 1863.* London: W. Blackwood and Sons, 1863. Reprint, Lincoln: Univ. of Nebraska Press, 1991.
Gay, Mary A. H. *Life in Dixie during the War: 1861–1862–1863–1864–1865.* Atlanta, Ga.: C. P. Byrd, 1892. Reprint, ed. J. H. Segars, Macon, Ga.: Mercer Univ. Press, 2001.
Harrison, Constance Cary. "Virginia Scenes in '61." In *Battles and Leaders of the Civil War,* vol. 1, ed. Robert Underwood Johnson and Clarence C. Buel, 160–66. New York: De Vinne, 1887–88.
Taylor, Susie King. *Reminiscences of My Life in Camp with the 33d United States Colored Troops, Late 1st S.C., Volunteers.* Boston: Self-published, 1902. Reprint, ed. Patricia W. Romero and Willie Lee Rose, Princeton, N.J.: Markus Wiener, 1995.
Twain, Mark. *Mark Twain's Autobiography.* 2 vols. New York: Harper and Brothers, 1924. Reprinted as *The Autobiography of Mark Twain,* ed. Charles Neider. New York: Harper and Row, 1959.
———. "The Private History of a Campaign That Failed." *Century Magazine* 31 (Dec. 1885): 193–204. Reprinted in *Stephen Crane: The Red Badge of Courage, Maggie: A Girl of the Streets, and Other Selected Writings,* ed. Phyllis Frus and Stanley Corkin, 323–33. New York: Houghton Mifflin, 2000.
Whitman, Walt. *Memoranda during the War.* Camden, N.J.: Self-published, 1875–76. Reprint, ed. Peter Coviello, New York: Oxford Univ. Press, 2004.

Biographies, Speeches, Interviews, and Collected Letters

Blotner, Joseph. *Faulkner: A Biography.* 2 vols. New York: Random House, 1974.
———. *Faulkner: A Biography.* New York: Vintage Books, 1991.
———. *Faulkner: A Biography.* Jackson: Univ. Press of Mississippi, 2005.
———. *Selected Letters of William Faulkner.* New York: Random House, 1977.
Davis, Linda H. *Badge of Courage: The Life of Stephen Crane.* New York: Houghton Mifflin, 1998.
Fant, Joseph L., III, and Robert Ashley, eds. *Faulkner at West Point.* Jackson: Univ. Press of Mississippi, 2002.
Golay, Michael. *To Gettysburg and Beyond: The Parallel Lives of Joshua Lawrence Chamberlain and Edward Porter Alexander.* New York: Crown, 1994.
Gwynn, Frederick L., and Joseph L. Blotner, eds. *Faulkner in the University: Class Conferences at the University of Virginia, 1957–1958.* Charlottesville: Univ. Press of Virginia, 1959.
Harwell, Richard, ed. *Margaret Mitchell's* Gone with the Wind *Letters: 1936–1949.* New York: Macmillan, 1976.
"Interview with Jeff Shaara, Author of *The Last Full Measure.*" www.randomhouse.com/BB/promos/lastfullmeasure/interview.html (accessed Aug. 30, 2007).

Jonza, Nancylee Novell. *The Underground Stream: The Life and Art of Caroline Gordon.* Athens: Univ. of Georgia Press, 1995.
"Knightley considers cross-dressing for Civil War flick." Knight Ridder/Tribune News Service. Nov. 7, 2003. http://static.highbeam.com/k/knightriddertribune newsservice/november072003/ (accessed June 16, 2003).
Lindberg-Seyersted, Brita, ed. *A Literary Friendship: Correspondence between Caroline Gordon and Ford Madox Ford.* Knoxville: Univ. of Tennessee Press, 1999.
Linson, Corwin K. *My Stephen Crane,* ed. Edwin H. Cady. Syracuse, N.Y.: Syracuse Univ. Press, 1958.
Mudge, Alden. "A Poetic Tale and a Writer Whose Time Has Finally Come." Interview with Howard Bahr. *BookPage: America's Book Review* (Apr. 1998). www.bookpage.com/9804bp/howard_bahr.html (accessed Jan. 20, 2008).
Perry, Mark. *Conceived in Liberty: Joshua Lawrence Chamberlain, William Oates, and the American Civil War.* New York: Viking, 1997.
Pickett, George E. [La Salle Corbell Pickett]. *The Heart of a Soldier: As Revealed in the Intimate Letters of Genl. George Pickett.* New York: S. Moyle, 1913.
Stallman, R. W. *Stephen Crane: A Biography.* New York: Braziller, 1968.
Trulock, Alice Rains. *In the Hands of Providence: Joshua L. Chamberlain and the American Civil War.* Chapel Hill: Univ. of North Carolina Press, 2001.
Wallace, Willard Mosher. *Soul of the Lion: A Biography of General Joshua Lawrence Chamberlain.* New York: T. Nelson, 1960. Reprint, Gettysburg, Pa.: Stan Clark Military Books, 1993.
Wertheim, Stanley, and Paul Sorrentino, eds. *The Correspondence of Stephen Crane.* 2 vols. New York: Columbia Univ. Press, 1988.
——. *The Crane Log: A Documentary Life of Stephen Crane, 1871–1900.* New York: G. K. Hall, 1994.
Wood, Sally, ed. *The Southern Mandarins: Letters of Caroline Gordon to Sally Wood, 1924–1937.* Baton Rouge: Louisiana State Univ. Press, 1984.

BOOK REVIEWS, NEWSPAPER ARTICLES, AND EDITORIALS

Advertisement. *The Dial: A Semi-Monthly Journal of Literary Criticism, Discussion, and Information* 9 (Jan. 1889): 105.
Alden, William L. "London Literary Letter." *New York Times,* July 7, 1900, BR7.
"American Essays." Review of *Book and Heart: Essays on Literature and Life,* by Thomas Wentworth Higginson. *The Chap-Book: Semi-Monthly. A Miscellany & Review of Belles Lettres,* Apr. 15, 1897, 6.
Ashley, Robert. Review of *The Killer Angels: A Novel,* by Michael Shaara. *Civil War Times Illustrated* 14 (Aug. 1975): 49–50.
"Comment on New Books." Review of *The Red Badge of Courage: An Episode of the American Civil War,* by Stephen Crane. *Atlantic Monthly* 77 (Mar. 1896): 422.
Cowley, Malcolm. "Going with the Wind." Review of *Gone with the Wind,* by Margaret Mitchell. *New Republic,* Sept. 16, 1936, 161–62.

Faulkner, William. "On Fear: Deep South in Labor; Mississippi." In *Essays, Speeches, and Public Letters, by William Faulkner*, ed. James B. Meriwether, 92–106. London: Chatto and Windus, 1967.
Forman, Henry James. "James Boyd Writes a Tale of the Civil War." Review of *Marching On*, by James Boyd. *New York Times*, May 1, 1927, BR4.
Higginson, Thomas Wentworth. "A Bit of War Photography." Review of *The Red Badge of Courage*, by Stephen Crane. *The Philistine: A Periodical of Protest*, July 1896, 2–3.
LaFantasie, Glenn. "Romance vs. Reality at Gettysburg: A Reconnaissance Report on the Books." *New York Times*, June 12, 1994, BR18–21.
Lask, Thomas. "Books of the Times: High Tide of the Confederacy." Review of *The Killer Angels*, by Michael Shaara. *New York Times*, May 10, 1975, 27.
LeClair, Thomas. Review of *The Killer Angels*, by Michael Shaara. *New York Times*, Oct. 20, 1974, 424.
Mabie, Hamilton Wright. "Books and Writers." Review of *The Battle-Ground*, by Ellen Glasgow. *Outlook*, May 24, 1902, 71.
McClurg, Alexander C. "The Red Badge of Hysteria." Letter to *The Dial: A Semimonthly Journal of Literary Criticism, Discussion, and Information* 20 (Apr. 16, 1896): 227–28.
Oviatt, Edwin. "Authors at Home." *New York Times*, Dec. 17, 1898, BR856.
Pryor, Mrs. Roger A. "The Genesis of Decoration Day." *New York Times*, May 29, 1898, 7.
"A Short History of the War." Review of *A Short History of the War of Secession, 1861–1865*, by Rossiter Johnson. *The Critic: A Weekly Review of Literature and the Arts*, Dec. 1, 1888, 257.
Smith, Caroline. Review of *None Shall Look Back*, by Caroline Gordon. *Nation*, Mar. 20, 1937, 332.
"Stephen Crane and Gen. Otis." Letter to the editor. *New York Times*, Aug. 7, 1899, 6.
Walton, Edith H. "Miss Gordon's Civil War Novel." Review of *None Shall Look Back*, by Caroline Gordon. *New York Times*, Feb. 21, 1937, 86.

FICTION

Bahr, Howard. *The Judas Field: A Novel of the Civil War*. New York: Picador, 2006.
Boyd, James. *Marching On*. New York: Scriber's, 1927.
Crane, Stephen. *The Monster and Other Stories*. New York: Harper, 1899.
———. *The Red Badge of Courage: An Episode of the American Civil War*. New York: D. Appleton and Company, 1895. Reprinted in *Stephen Crane: Prose and Poetry*, ed. J. C. Levenson. New York: Library of America, 1996.
———. "The Veteran." *The University of Virginia Edition of the Works of Stephen Crane*. Vol. 6, *Tales of War*. Ed. Fredson Bowers, 82–86. Charlottesville: Univ. Press of Virginia, 1970.

Dixon, Thomas. *The Clansman: An Historical Romance of the Ku Klux Klan.* New York: Doubleday, Page and Company, 1905.

Evans, Augusta Jane. *Macaria; or, Altars of Sacrifice.* Richmond, Va.: West and Johnston, 1864.

Falkner, William C. *The White Rose of Memphis: A Novel.* New York: G. W. Carleton and Company, 1881. Reprint, New York: Coley Taylor, 1953.

Faulkner, William. *Absalom, Absalom!* New York: Random House, 1936. Reprint, New York: Vintage, 1990.

———. *Flags in the Dust.* New York: Random House, 1973.

———. *Go Down, Moses, and Other Stories.* New York: Random House, 1942. Reprint, New York: Vintage, 1990.

———. *Intruder in the Dust.* New York: Random House, 1948.

———. *Requiem for a Nun.* New York: Random House, 1951.

———. "A Rose for Emily." In *These 13: Stories by William Faulkner*, 167–82. New York: Jonathan Cape and Harrison Smith, 1931.

———. *Sartoris.* New York: Harcourt, 1929.

———. *The Sound and the Fury.* New York: Jonathan Cape and Harrison Smith, 1929.

———. *The Unvanquished.* New York: Random House, 1938. Reprint, New York: Vintage, 1990.

Foote, Shelby. *Shiloh: A Novel.* New York: Dial, 1952.

Frazier, Charles. *Cold Mountain.* New York: Atlantic Monthly Press, 1997.

Glasgow, Ellen. *The Battle-Ground.* New York: Doubleday, 1902.

Gordon, Caroline. *None Shall Look Back.* New York: Scribner's, 1937.

———. *Penhally.* New York: Scribner's, 1931.

Haley, Alex. *Roots.* Garden City, N.Y.: Doubleday, 1976.

Jaffe, Marc, ed. *Three Great Novels of the Civil War.* New York: Wing, 1994.

Johnston, Mary. *Cease Firing.* Boston: Houghton Mifflin, 1912.

———. *The Long Roll.* Boston: Houghton Mifflin, 1911.

Kantor, MacKinlay. *Andersonville.* Cleveland, Ohio: World, 1955.

Lytle, Andrew. *The Long Night.* Indianapolis, Ind.: Bobbs-Merrill, 1936.

Mitchell, Margaret. *Gone with the Wind.* New York: Macmillan, 1936.

O'Connor, Flannery. "A Late Encounter with the Enemy." *Harper's Bazaar* 87 (Sept. 1953). Reprinted in *The Oxford Book of American Short Stories*, ed. Joyce Carol Oates, 398–407. New York: Oxford Univ. Press, 1992.

———. *Wise Blood.* New York: Harcourt, Brace and Co., 1952.

Reasoner, James. *Gettysburg.* Nashville, Tenn.: Cumberland, 2001.

Rinaldi, Ann. *Girl in Blue.* New York: Scholastic Press, 2001.

Scott, Evelyn. *The Wave.* New York: Jonathan Cape and Harrison Smith, 1929.

Shaara, Jeff. *Gods and Generals.* New York: Ballantine, 1996.

———. *The Last Full Measure.* New York: Ballantine, 1998.

Shaara, Michael. *The Killer Angels: A Novel.* New York: Random House, 1974.

Stowe, Harriet Beecher. *Uncle Tom's Cabin; or, Life among the Lowly.* Boston: J. P. Jewett, 1852.

Tate, Allen. *The Fathers.* New York: Putnam, 1938.
Tourgée, Albion. *A Fool's Errand.* New York: Fords, Howard, and Hulbert, 1879.
Twain, Mark. *Extract from Captain Stormfield's Visit to Heaven.* New York: Harper and Brothers, 1909.
"Wounded." *Harper's Weekly.* July 12, 1862, 442–43.

FILM, TELEVISION, AND MUSIC

Birth of a Nation. DVD. Directed by D. W. Griffith, 1915. Chatsworth, Calif.: Image Entertainment, 1998.
The Civil War: A Film by Ken Burns. DVD. Directed by Ken Burns, 1990. Alexandria, Va.: PBS Paramount, 2004.
Earle, Steve. "Dixieland." *The Mountain* [Compact Disc]. E-Squared, 1999.
Gettysburg. DVD. Directed by Ronald F. Maxwell, 1993. Atlanta, Ga.: Turner Home Entertainment, 2004.
Gone with the Wind. DVD. Directed by Victor Fleming, 1939. Burbank, Calif.: Warner Home Video, 2006.
Roots. DVD. Directed by Marvin J. Chompsky, John Erman, David Greene, and Gilbert Moses, 1977. Burbank, Calif.: Warner Home Video, 2002.

HISTORICAL SCHOLARSHIP AND LITERARY CRITICISM

Aaron, Daniel. *The Unwritten War: American Writers and the Civil War.* New York: Alfred A. Knopf, 1973.
Akin, Warren, IV. "'Blood and Raising and Background': The Plot of *The Unvanquished.*" *Modern Language Studies* 11 (Winter 1980): 3–11.
Beidler, Philip D. "Stephen Crane's *The Red Badge of Courage:* Henry Fleming's Courage in Its Contexts." *CLIO* 20 (Spring 1991): 235–51.
———. "Ted Turner *Et Al.* At Gettysburg; or, Re-Enactors in the Attic." *Virginia Quarterly Review* 75 (Summer 1999): 488–503.
Benfey, Christopher. *The Double Life of Stephen Crane.* New York: Knopf, 1992.
Blanton, De Anne, and Lauren M. Cook. *They Fought Like Demons: Women Soldiers in the Civil War.* New York: Vintage, 2003.
Blight, David W. *Race and Reunion: The Civil War in American Memory.* Cambridge, Mass.: Harvard Univ. Press, 2001.
Bonner, Robert B. "Roundheaded Cavaliers? The Context and Limits of a Confederate Racial Project." *Civil War History* 48 (Mar. 2002): 34–59.
Boritt, Gabor S. "Lincoln and Gettysburg: The Hero and the Heroic Place." In *Ken Burns's* The Civil War: *Historians Respond,* ed. Robert Brent Toplin, 81–100. New York: Oxford Univ. Press, 1996.
Braybon, Gail. "Women, War, and Work." In *The Oxford Illustrated History of the First World War,* ed. Hew Strachan, 149–62. Oxford: Oxford Univ. Press, 1998.
Brooks, Cleanth. *William Faulkner: The Yoknapatawpha County.* New Haven, Conn.: Yale Univ. Press, 1963.

Brown, Ashley. *"None Shall Look Back:* The Novel as History." *Southern Review* 7 (Spring 1971): 483.

Buck, Paul H. *The Road to Reunion: 1865–1900.* Boston: Little, Brown, 1937.

Clark, Katherine Arn. *Reconsidering Faulkner's Pulp Series:* The Unvanquished *as Parody, Not Potboiler.* PhD diss., Emory University, 1992. UMI Dissertation Services, Order No. 9300543.

Clinton, Catherine. "'Noble Women as Well.'" In *Ken Burns's* The Civil War: *Historians Respond,* ed. Robert Brent Toplin, 61–80. New York: Oxford Univ. Press, 1996.

Connelly, Thomas L. "The Image and the General: Robert E. Lee in American Historiography." *Civil War History* 19, no. 1 (1973): 50–64.

———. *The Marble Man: Robert E. Lee and His Image in American Society.* New York: Knopf, 1977.

———. "Robert E. Lee and the Western Confederacy: A Criticism of Lee's Strategic Ability." *Civil War History* 15, no. 2 (1969): 116–32.

Connelly, Thomas L., and Barbara Bellows. *God and General Longstreet: The Lost Cause and the Southern Mind.* Baton Rouge: Louisiana State Univ. Press, 1982.

Cushman, Stephen. *Bloody Promenade: Reflections on a Civil War Battle.* Charlottesville, Va.: Univ. Press of Virginia, 1999.

Delbanco, Andrew. "The American Stephen Crane: The Context of *The Red Badge of Courage.*" In *New Essays on* The Red Badge of Courage, ed. Lee Clark Mitchell, 49–76. New York: Cambridge Univ. Press, 1986.

Desjardin, Thomas A. *Stand Firm Ye Boys from Maine: The 20th Maine and the Gettysburg Campaign.* Gettysburg, Pa.: Thomas Publications, 1995. Reprint, New York: Oxford Univ. Press, 2001.

Dobbs, Ricky Floyd. "Case Study in Social Neurosis: Quentin Compson and the Lost Cause." *Papers on Language and Literature* 33 (Fall 1997): 366–91.

Donald, David, ed. *Why the North Won the Civil War.* Baton Rouge: Louisiana State Univ. Press, 1960.

Dwyer, Richard. "The Case of the Cool Reception." In *Recasting:* Gone with the Wind *in American Culture,* ed. Darden Asbury Pyron, 21–32. Miami: Univ. Presses of Florida, 1983.

Eicher, David J. *The Longest Night: A Military History of the Civil War.* New York: Simon and Schuster, 2001.

Fahs, Alice. *The Imagined Civil War: Popular Literature of the North and South, 1861–1865.* Chapel Hill: Univ. of North Carolina Press, 2001.

Faust, Drew Gilpin. "Clutching the Chains That Bind: Margaret Mitchell and *Gone With the Wind.*" *Southern Cultures* 5, no. 1 (1999): 6–20.

———. *Mothers of Invention: Women of the Slaveholding South in the American Civil War.* Chapel Hill: Univ. of North Carolina Press, 1996.

FitzGerald, Frances. *America Revised: History Schoolbooks in the Twentieth Century.* Boston: Little, Brown and Co., 1979.

Foote, Shelby. *The Civil War: A Narrative: Fort Sumter to Perryville, Fredericksburg to Meridian, Red River to Appomattox.* New York: Random House, 1958–74.

———. Introduction to *The Red Badge of Courage and "The Veteran,"* by Stephen Crane, xi–liv. New York: Modern Library, 2000.

Foster, Gaines M. *Ghosts of the Confederacy: Defeat, the Lost Cause, and the Emergence of the New South, 1865–1913.* New York: Oxford Univ. Press, 1987.
Fraistat, Rose Ann C. *Caroline Gordon as Novelist and Woman of Letters.* Baton Rouge: Louisiana State Univ. Press, 1984.
Freeman, Douglas Southall. *Lee's Lieutenants: A Study in Command.* Vol. 2, *Cedar Mountain to Chancellorsville.* New York: Scribner's, 1943.
Friedman, Matthew J. "Post-Vietnam Syndrome: Recognition and Management." *Psychosomatics* 22 (1981): 931–42.
Frus, Phyllis, and Stanley Corkin. "The Civil War Remembered." In *Stephen Crane: The Red Badge of Courage, Maggie: A Girl of the Streets, and Other Selected Writings,* ed. Phyllis Frus and Stanley Corkin, 287–300. New York: Houghton Mifflin, 2000.
Gallagher, Gary W. "How Familiarity Bred Success: Military Campaigns and Leaders in Ken Burns's *The Civil War.*" In *Ken Burns's* The Civil War: *Historians Respond,* ed. Robert Brent Toplin, 37–60. New York: Oxford Univ. Press, 1996.
———. Introduction to *Lee's Aide-de-Camp: Being the Papers of Colonel Charles Marshall Sometime Aide-de-Camp, Military Secretary, and Assistant Adjutant General on the Staff of Robert E. Lee, 1862–1865,* by Charles Marshall, ed. Frederick Maurice, ix–xx. Lincoln: Bison Books [Univ. of Nebraska Press], 2000.
———. Introduction to *The Myth of the Lost Cause and Civil War History,* ed. Gary W. Gallagher and Alan T. Nolan, 1–10. Bloomington: Indiana Univ. Press, 2000.
———. Introduction to *Three Months in the Southern States: April–June 1863* by Arthur James Lyon Fremantle, vii–xxix. Lincoln: Univ. of Nebraska Press, 1991.
———. *Lee and His Army in Confederate History.* Chapel Hill: Univ. of North Carolina Press, 2001.
———. *Lee and His Generals in War and Memory.* Baton Rouge: Louisiana State Univ. Press, 1998.
Gallagher, Gary W., and Alan T. Nolan, eds. *The Myth of the Lost Cause and Civil War History.* Bloomington: Indiana Univ. Press, 2000.
Gardner, Sarah E. *Blood and Irony: Southern White Women's Narratives of the Civil War, 1861–1937.* Chapel Hill: Univ. of North Carolina Press, 2004.
———. "Every Man Has Got the Right to Get Killed? The Civil War Narratives of Mary Johnston and Caroline Gordon." *Southern Cultures* 5 (Winter 1999): 14–40.
Garrett, George. "On Mary Johnston's *The Long Roll.*" In *Classics of Civil War Fiction,* ed. David Madden and Peggy Bach, 83–95. Jackson: Univ. Press of Mississippi, 1991.
Gerard, David. "Why Are Most Civil War Novels Mediocre? Here's Why, With Some Tips for Writers." *Civil War Times Illustrated* (June 1962): 34–36.
Grauke, Kevin. "Vietnam, Survivalism, and the Civil War: The Use of History in Michael Shaara's *The Killer Angels* and Charles Frazier's *Cold Mountain.*" *War, Literature, and the Arts: An International Journal of the Humanities* 14, nos. 1–2 (2002): 45–58.
Gray, Richard. *The Life of William Faulkner: A Critical Biography.* Oxford: Blackwell, 1994.

Greenwald, Maurine Weiner. *Women, War, and Work: The Impact of World War I on Women Workers in the United States.* Westport, Conn.: Greenwood, 1980.

Gresset, Michel. "Faulkner's War with Wars." In *Faulkner and History*, ed. Javier Coy and Michel Gresset, 13–28. Salamanca, Spain: Univ. of Salamanca Press, 1986.

Hartwig, D. Scott. *A* Killer Angels *Companion.* Gettysburg, Pa.: Thomas Publications, 1996.

Hess, Earl J. *Pickett's Charge, the Last Attack at Gettysburg.* Chapel Hill: Univ. of North Carolina Press, 2001.

———. *The Union Soldier in Battle: Enduring the Ordeal of Combat.* Lawrence: Univ. Press of Kansas, 1997.

Higginson, Thomas Wentworth. *Book and Heart: Essays on Literature and Life.* New York: Harper and Brothers, 1897.

Hinkle, James. "The Civil War in the Apocrypha according to Faulkner." In *Faulkner and History*, ed. Javier Coy and Michel Gresset, 29–38. Salamanca, Spain: Univ. of Salamanca Press, 1986.

Horwitz, Tony. *Confederates in the Attic: Dispatches from the Unfinished Civil War.* New York: Vintage, 1998.

Howell, Elmo. "Faulkner and Scott and the Legacy of the Lost Cause." *Georgia Review* 26 (Fall 1972): 314–25.

Hungerford, Harold R. "'That Was at Chancellorsville': The Factual Framework of *The Red Badge of Courage*." *American Literature* 34 (Jan. 1963): 520–31. Reprinted in *The Red Badge of Courage by Stephen Crane: A Norton Critical Edition*, ed. Donald Pizer, 147–56. New York: W. W. Norton and Company, 1994.

Hunter, Lloyd A. "The Immortal Confederacy: Another Look at Lost Cause Religion." In *The Myth of the Lost Cause and Civil War History*, ed. Gary W. Gallagher and Alan T. Nolan, 185–218. Bloomington: Indiana Univ. Press, 2000.

Jacobs, Naomi. *The Character of Truth: Historical Figures in Contemporary Fiction.* Carbondale: Southern Illinois Univ. Press, 1990.

Johnson, Rossiter. *A Short History of the War of Secession, 1861–1865.* Boston: Ticknor and Company, 1888.

Jones, Anne Goodwyn. *Tomorrow Is Another Day: The Woman Writer in the South, 1859–1936.* Baton Rouge: Louisiana State Univ. Press, 1981.

———. "Women Writers and the Myths of Southern Womanhood." In *The History of Southern Women's Literature*, ed. Carolyn Perry and Mary Louise Weaks, 275–89. Baton Rouge: Louisiana State Univ. Press, 2002.

Jonza, Nancylee Novell. "Caroline Gordon." In *The History of Southern Women's Literature*, ed. Carolyn Perry and Mary Louise Weaks, 369–73. Baton Rouge: Louisiana State Univ. Press, 2002.

Kammen, Michael G. *Mystic Chords of Memory: The Transformation of Tradition in American Culture.* New York: Knopf, 1991.

Kaplan, Amy. "The Spectacle of War in Crane's Revision of History." In *New Essays on* The Red Badge of Courage, ed. Lee Clark Mitchell, 77–108. New York: Cambridge Univ. Press, 1986.

Kartiganer, Donald M. "Faulkner's *Absalom, Absalom!* The Discovery of Values." *American Literature* 37 (Nov. 1965): 291–306.

———. "'So I, Who Never Had a War . . .': William Faulkner, War, and the Modern Imagination." *Modern Fiction Studies* 44 (1998): 619–45.

Knoll, Robert E. "*The Unvanquished* for a Start." *College English* 19 (May 1958): 339.

Leonard, Elizabeth D. *All the Daring of the Soldier: Women of the Civil War Armies.* New York: Penguin, 2001.

Leonard, Thomas C. *Above the Battle: War-Making in America, from Appomattox to Versailles.* New York: Oxford Univ. Press, 1978.

Levins, Lynn. *Faulkner's Heroic Design.* Athens: Univ. of Georgia Press, 1976.

Linderman, Gerald. *Embattled Courage: The Experience of Combat in the American Civil War.* New York: Free Press, 1987.

Lively, Robert A. *Fiction Fights the Civil War: An Unfinished Chapter in the Literary History of the American People.* Chapel Hill: Univ. of North Carolina Press, 1957.

Madden, David, and Peggy Bach, eds. *Classics of Civil War Fiction.* Jackson: Univ. Press of Mississippi, 1991.

Makowsky, Veronica. "Caroline Gordon on Women Writing: A Contradiction in Terms?" *Southern Quarterly* 28 (Spring 1990): 43–52.

Marks, Gregory. "Quotation and Authority: A Note on Caroline Gordon's *Green Centuries.*" *Mississippi Quarterly* 52 (Fall 1999): 655–58.

Marvel, William. *A Place Called Appomattox.* Chapel Hill: Univ. of North Carolina Press, 2000.

Massey, Mary Elizabeth. *Bonnet Brigades.* New York: Knopf, 1966.

Matthews, John T. *The Sound and the Fury: Faulkner and the Lost Cause.* Boston: Twayne, 1991.

McConnell, Stuart. *Glorious Contentment: The Grand Army of the Republic, 1865–1900.* Chapel Hill: Univ. of North Carolina Press, 1992.

McPherson, James M. *For Cause and Comrades.* New York: Oxford Univ. Press, 1997.

———. *Hallowed Ground: A Walk at Gettysburg.* New York: Crown, 2003.

———. Introduction to *The Passing of the Armies: An Account of the Final Campaign of the Army of the Potomac, Based upon Personal Reminiscences of the Fifth Army Corps*, by Joshua Lawrence Chamberlain, ix–xvi. 1915. Reprint, New York: Bantam, 1993.

Meeter, Glenn. "Molly's Vision: Lost Cause Ideology and Genesis in Faulkner's *Go Down, Moses.*" In *Faulkner and Ideology: Faulkner and Yoknapatawpha, 1992*, ed. Donald M. Kartiganer and Ann J. Abadie, 277–96. Jackson: Univ. Press of Mississippi, 1995.

Miller, Douglas T. "Faulkner and the Civil War: Myth and Reality." *American Quarterly* 15 (Summer 1963): 200–209.

Mitchell, Lee Clark. Introduction to *New Essays on* The Red Badge of Courage, ed. Lee Clark Mitchell, 1–23. New York: Cambridge Univ. Press, 1986.

Moreau, Joseph. *Schoolbook Nation: Conflicts over American History Textbooks from the Civil War to the Present.* Ann Arbor: Univ. of Michigan Press, 2003.

Morris, James. *Heaven's Command: An Imperial Progress.* New York: Harcourt, 1973.

Muhlenfeld, Elisabeth. "Mary Chesnut." In *The History of Southern Women's Literature,* ed. Carolyn Perry and Mary Louise Weaks, 119–24. Baton Rouge: Louisiana State Univ. Press, 2002.

"My Favorite Historical Novel." *American Heritage* 43 (Oct. 1992): 103.

Nolan, Alan T. "The Anatomy of the Myth." In *The Myth of the Lost Cause and Civil War History,* ed. Gary W. Gallagher and Alan T. Nolan, 11–34. Bloomington: Indiana Univ. Press, 2000.

———. *Lee Considered: General Robert E. Lee and Civil War History.* Chapel Hill: Univ. of North Carolina Press, 1991.

———. *"Rally, Once Again!": Selected Civil War Writings of Alan T. Nolan.* Madison, Wis.: Madison House, 2000.

Parker, Robert Dale. Absalom, Absalom! *The Questioning of Fictions.* Boston: Twayne, 1991.

Pelletier, Gaston. "*Red Badge* Revisited." *English Journal* 57 (Jan. 1968): 24–25, 99.

Pilkington, John. *The Heart of Yoknapatawpha County.* Jackson: Univ. Press of Mississippi, 1981.

Piston, William Garrett. *Lee's Tarnished Lieutenant: James Longstreet and His Place in Southern History.* Athens: Univ. of Georgia Press, 1987.

Pitavy, Francois. "William Faulkner: Fiction as Historiography." In *Faulkner and History,* ed. Javier Coy and Michel Gresset, 39–50. Salamanca, Spain: Univ. of Salamanca Press, 1986.

Prown, Katherine Hemple. *Revising Flannery O'Connor: Southern Literary Culture and the Problem of Female Authorship.* Charlottesville: Univ. Press of Virginia, 2001.

Pyron, Darden Asbury. "A Bibliographical Essay." In *Recasting:* Gone with the Wind *in American Culture,* ed. Darden Asbury Pyron, 203–24. Miami: Univ. Presses of Florida, 1983.

———. "The Critical Setting." In *Recasting:* Gone with the Wind *in American Culture,* ed. Darden Asbury Pyron, 5–10. Miami: Univ. Presses of Florida, 1983.

Reardon, Carol. *Pickett's Charge in History and Memory.* Chapel Hill: Univ. of North Carolina Press, 1997.

Reid, Panthea. "William Faulkner's 'War Wound': Reflections on Writing and Doing, Knowing and Remembering." *Virginia Quarterly Review* 74 (Autumn 1998): 597–615.

Rose, W. L. *Race and Region in American Historical Fiction: Four Episodes in Popular Culture; An Inaugural Lecture Delivered before the University of Oxford on 4 May 1978.* Oxford: Clarendon, 1979.

Rubin, Louis, Jr. "Scarlett O'Hara and the Two Quentin Compsons." In *Recasting* Gone with the Wind *in American Culture,* ed. Darden Asbury Pyron, 81–104. Miami: Univ. Presses of Florida, 1983.

Savage, Kirk. *Standing Soldiers, Kneeling Slaves: Race, War, and Monument in Nineteenth-Century America.* Princeton, N.J.: Princeton Univ. Press, 1997.

Schaefer, Michael W. *Just What War Is: The Civil War Writings of De Forest and Bierce*. Knoxville: Univ. of Tennessee Press, 1997.

Segars, J. H. Foreword to *Life in Dixie during the War: 1861–1862–1863–1864–1865*, by Mary A. H. Gay, ed. J. H. Segars, iii–viii. Macon, Ga.: Mercer Univ. Press, 2001.

Shaw, Harry E. *The Forms of Historical Fiction: Sir Walter Scott and His Successors*. Ithaca, N.Y.: Cornell Univ. Press, 1983.

Silber, Nina. *The Romance of Reunion: Northerners and the South, 1865–1900*. Chapel Hill: Univ. of North Carolina Press, 1993.

Simpson, Lewis P. "On William Faulkner's *Absalom, Absalom!*" In *Classics of Civil War Fiction*, ed. David Madden and Peggy Bach, 151–73. Jackson: Univ. Press of Mississippi, 1991.

Solomon, Eric. *Stephen Crane: From Parody to Realism*. Cambridge, Mass.: Harvard Univ. Press, 1966.

Stewart, George R. *Pickett's Charge: A Microhistory of the Final Attack at Gettysburg, July 3, 1863*. Cambridge, Mass.: Houghton, 1959.

Stuckey, William J. *Caroline Gordon*. New York: Twayne, 1972.

Sullivan, Walter. "Civil War Diaries and Memoirs." In *The History of Southern Women's Literature*, ed. Carolyn Perry and Mary Louise Weaks, 109–18. Baton Rouge: Louisiana State Univ. Press, 2002.

Taylor, Helen. "*Gone with the Wind* and Its Influence." In *The History of Southern Women's Literature*, ed. Carolyn Perry and Mary Louise Weaks, 258–67. Baton Rouge: Louisiana State Univ. Press, 2002.

———. *Scarlett's Women:* Gone with the Wind *and Its Female Fans*. New Brunswick, N.J.: Rutgers Univ. Press, 1989.

Thompson, Lawrence S. "The Civil War in Fiction." *Civil War History* 2 (1956): 83–95.

Tobin, Patricia. "The Time of Myth and History in *Absalom, Absalom!*" *American Literature* 45 (May 1973): 258.

Toplin, Robert Brent. Introduction to *Ken Burns's* The Civil War: *Historians Respond*, ed. Robert Brent Toplin, xiii–xxvi. New York: Oxford Univ. Press, 1996.

———. "Ken Burns's *The Civil War* as an Interpretation of History." In *Ken Burns's* The Civil War: *Historians Respond*, ed. Robert Brent Toplin, 17–36. New York: Oxford Univ. Press, 1996.

———, ed. *Ken Burns's* The Civil War: *Historians Respond*. New York: Oxford Univ. Press, 1996.

Tsui, Bonnie. *She Went to the Field: Women Soldiers of the Civil War*. Guilford, Conn.: Globe Pequot Press, 2003.

Tucker, Glenn. *High Tide at Gettysburg: The Campaign in Pennsylvania*. New York: Bobbs-Merrill, 1958.

———. *Lee and Longstreet at Gettysburg*. New York: Bobbs-Merrill, 1968.

Waldron, Ann. *Close Connections: Caroline Gordon and the Southern Renaissance*. New York: G. P. Putnam's Sons, 1987.

Ward, Geoffrey. *The Civil War: An Illustrated History*. New York: Knopf, 1990.

Weatherford, Richard M. *Stephen Crane: The Critical Heritage*. London: Routledge and Kegan Paul, 1973.

Webster, H. T. "Wilbur F. Hinman's *Corporal Si Klegg* and Stephen Crane's *The Red Badge of Courage.*" *American Literature* 11 (Nov. 1939): 285–93.

Welsh, Jack D. *Medical Histories of Confederate Generals.* Kent, Ohio: Kent State Univ. Press, 1995.

Wertheim, Stanley. "*The Red Badge of Courage* and Personal Narratives of the Civil War." *American Literary Realism: 1870–1910* 6 (Winter 1973): 61–65.

White, Hayden. *The Content of the Form: Narrative Discourse and Historical Representation.* Baltimore: Johns Hopkins Univ. Press, 1987.

Williams, T. Harry. "The Military Leadership of North and South." In *Why the North Won the Civil War,* ed. David Donald, 23–48. Baton Rouge: Louisiana State Univ. Press, 1960.

Williamson, Joel. *William Faulkner and Southern History.* New York: Oxford Univ. Press, 1993.

Wilson, Charles Reagan. *Judgment and Grace in Dixie: Southern Faiths from Faulkner to Elvis.* Athens: Univ. of Georgia Press, 1995.

———. "Our Land, Our Country: Faulkner, the South, and the American Way of Life." In *Faulkner in America: Faulkner and Yoknapatawpha, 1998,* ed. Joseph R. Urgo and Ann J. Abadie, 153–66. Jackson: Univ. Press of Mississippi, 2001.

Wilson, Edmund. *Patriotic Gore: Studies in the Literature of the American Civil War.* New York: Oxford Univ. Press, 1962.

Young, Elizabeth. *Disarming the Nation: Women's Writing and the American Civil War.* Chicago: Univ. of Chicago Press, 1999.

Index

Fictional characters alphabetized by first name.

Aaron, Daniel, 3–4, 18–19, 21, 29, 87
Absalom, Absalom! (W. Faulkner): audience, 62; ending, 114–17; W. Faulkner on, 106; Lost Cause in, 93, 95–96, 106; narrator of, 97, 105; presentation and marketability, 105; race and race relations in, 84, 97; slavery in, 108–9, 112; soldiers' portrayal in, 117; *The Unvanquished* comparisons, 105–6. *See also names of individual characters*
Adams, Henry, 18–19
Adams, J. Donald, 75
Adventures of Huckleberry Finn (Twain), 18
Alcott, Louisa May, 55
Alden, William L., 23
Alexander, Edward Porter, 123, 132
allegory, 149, 196n69
All the Daring of a Soldier (E. Leonard), 81
Andersonville (Kantor), 120
Andrews, Eliza, 56–57, 60
Annals of the Army of Tennessee, 126
Appomattox, 146–47
aristocracy, 124–25, 135, 151, 194n44
Armistead, Lewis A., 126
Army Life (Gerrish), 23
Army Life in a Black Regiment (Higginson), 175n45
Ashhurst, R. L., 32
Ashley, Robert, 156–57
Atlantic Monthly, 30
Autobiography (Twain), 21

Bach, Peggy, 18
Bahr, Howard, 162–68
Baldwin, James, 123
Ballard, Allen, 168
battlefield descriptions: by Bierce, 174n37; by De Forest, 174n37; in *Gone with the Wind*, 52, 82; C. Gordon on, 64–66; by Kirkland, 174n37; in *None Shall Look Back*, 69–72; in *The Red Badge of Courage*, 28, 29–31, 34; by soldiers and veterans, 28–29; by Tourgée, 174n37; in veterans' memoirs, 28–29
Battle-Ground, The (Glasgow), 36, 53
Battles and Leaders of the Civil War (*Century* articles): Crane on, 23; description, 13; ironies in, 26; *The Killer Angels* and, 123; use in *None Shall Look Back*, 66–67, 68–69; women in, 44–45
Bayard Sartoris (*The Unvanquished*), 91, 97–101, 103–4, 105
"Bear, The" (W. Faulkner), 108, 189n54
Beidler, Philip D., 120, 171n4
Bellows, Barbara, 84, 133, 155
Benét, Stephen Vincent, 56
Bierce, Ambrose, 18, 29, 89, 174n37, 185n17
Billings, John D., 10, 13, 160–61
Birth of a Nation (film), 150
Blanton, De Anne, 81
Blight, David W., 11, 13, 45–46, 115, 185n15, 196n56
Blood and Irony (Gardner), 43–44
Blotner, Joseph, 88, 187n34
Boritt, Gabor S., 151
Born on the Fourth of July (Kovic), 162

215

Boston Journal, 148
Boyd, James, 37
Bragg, Braxton, 68
Braybon, Gail, 181–82n58
Brickell, Herschel, 47
Brooks, Cleanth, 111
Buffalo Express, 17
Buford, John, 126
Burns, Ken, 26, 94, 150–51, 159, 197n72

Captain Linton (*None Shall Look Back*), 73–74
"Captain Stormfield's Visit to Heaven" (Twain), 21
Caputo, Philip, 162, 167–68
Cass Wakefield (*The Judas Field*), 163–65, 167, 168
Catton, Bruce, 15–16
Cease Firing (M. Johnston), 52, 53–54
Century War Series, 13, 19, 20, 22–23, 26, 33. See also *Battles and Leaders of the Civil War* (*Century* articles)
Chamberlain, Joshua Lawrence: at Appomattox, 146–47; in The *Killer Angels*, 118–19, 126, 141–44, 147, 148–49, 151, 158; McPherson on, 118–19; Medal of Honor, 196n64; published narratives of, 118, 119, 123, 142; slavery and, 142–43, 148; works on, 157–58
Chamberlain, Joshua Lawrence: Works: *The Passing of the Armies*, 118, 119, 142; "Through Blood and Fire at Gettysburg," 123
Chancellorsville battle, 27
Charles Bon (*Absalom! Absalom!*), 112–14
Chesnut, Mary Boykin, 55
Chicago-Tribune, 17
Chickamauga battle, 67
Churchill, Winston, 129
Civil War: black women and, 81; emancipation and, 124; fascination, 49–50; W. Faulkner's portrayal of, 83–85, 87–91, 102, 104, 182n1, 183n5; histories with Eastern focus, 126–27; literature (see Civil War literature); monuments, 51–52, 189n56; race and, 84; slavery and, 124, 184n11
Civil War, The (documentary), 94, 150–51, 159, 197n72
Civil War literature: amount of, 1; David Madden Collection of Civil War Fiction, 1; feminized, 42, 44, 45; memoirs vs. novels, 24; recent fiction, 52, 161, 162, 164–65, 169; *The Red Badge of Courage* influence on, 10, 29, 36–38; soldiers and veterans in, 44, 80, 189n5; South and, 39, 43; by women, 39, 43–44, 46, 52, 60, 66–67, 76–77, 176–77n6; women in, 81
Civil War Times Illustrated, 147, 156–57
Clansman, The (Dixon), 150
Clark, Katherine Arn, 87, 116–17, 188n41
Classics of Civil War Fiction (Madden & Bach, eds.), 18
Clinton, Catherine, 81
Co. Aytch (Watkins), 26, 50–51, 160–61
Cold Mountain (Frazier), 154, 181n52
Colonel Sartoris (*Absalom! Absalom!*), 116–17
Columbus Inquirer-Sun, 66
Combat. See battlefield descriptions
Commager, Henry Steele, 50
Conceived in Liberty (Perry), 158
Confederacy, 107, 108. See also Lost Cause; soldiers and veterans
Confederate flag, 90
Confederate soldiers, 89–90, 92, 116–17, 125. See also Rebel yell
Confederate Veteran (journal), 126
Connelly, Thomas L., 84, 126, 129, 133, 155–56, 157
Cook, Lauren M., 81
Corporal Si Klegg and his "Pard" (Hinman), 10
Cowley, Malcolm, 39
Crane, Stephen: on *Battles and Leaders of the Civil War*, 23; Bierce on, 29; *Century* War Series and, 26; as Civil War author, 22–25, 31–33; M. Shaara on, 37, 176n53
Crane, Stephen: Works: *The Monster*, 34; *The Red Badge of Courage* (see *Red Badge of Courage, The* [Crane]); "The Veteran," 174–75n44
Cushman, Stephen, 12, 23, 123

David Madden Collection of Civil War Fiction (Louisiana State University), 1
Davidson, Donald, 89
Davis, Jefferson, 66
Davis, Varina, 66
Decoration Day, 10, 11
De Forest, John W., 18, 174n37, 175n45
Delbanco, Andrew, 35

Desjardin, Thomas A., 158
De Voto, Richard, 75
Dial, 31
Dilsey (*The Sound and the Fury*), 188n38
"Dixieland" (song), 152–53
Dixon, Thomas, 150
Donald, David, 155
Douglas, Henry Kyd, 87, 184n13
Dowdey, Clifford, 50, 52, 89
Drusilla Hawk *(The Unvanquished)*, 91, 184–85n14
Dwyer, Richard, 75
Dyja, Thomas, 168

Earle, Steve, 152–53
Early, Jubal A., 123, 125, 130, 134, 187n31, 193n30
emancipation, 34, 124
Evans, Augusta Jane, 177n7
Ewell, Richard S., 129

Fahs, Alice, 42, 43, 44
Falkner, William Clark, 91–92, 186n25
Fathers, The (Tate), 62
Faulkner, John, 88–89
Faulkner, William: on *Absalom! Absalom!*, 106; Civil War portrayal by, 83–85, 87–91, 102, 104, 182n1, 183n5; on Confederate flag, 90; on integration, 187n34; Lost Cause portrayal, 183n5; race and, 87, 97, 123, 188n46, 189–90n58; RAF service, 88, 185n16; soldiers' and veterans' portrayal, 91–92, 95, 116–17, 164, 186n26; on the Southern past, 85; on veterans, 95
Faulkner, William: Works: *Absalom, Absalom!* (see *Absalom, Absalom!* [W. Faulkner]); "The Bear," 108, 189n54; *Flags in the Dust*, 91, 117; *Go Down Moses, and Other Stories*, 108, 189n54; *Intruder in the Dust*, 93–95, 104, 186n28; *Light in August*, 117; "An Odor of Verbena," 187n35; "On Fear," 189n58; *Requiem for a Nun*, 92–93, 104–5, 117; "A Rose for Emily," 186n26; *Sartoris*, 92, 117, 188n36; *The Sound and the Fury*, 188n38; *The Unvanquished* (see *Unvanquished, The* [W. Faulkner])
Faust, Drew Gilpin, 43, 176–77n6
flag, Confederate, 90
Flags in the Dust (W. Faulkner), 91, 117
Fool's Errand, A (Tourgée), 85

Foote, Shelby, 89–90, 93, 94, 197n72
For Cause and Comrades (McPherson), 175n47
Ford, Ford Madox, 62
Forrest, Nathan Bedford, 67
Foster, Gaines M., 133, 194n39, 194n42
Four Years with General Lee (W. Taylor), 131
Frazier, Charles, 37, 154, 181n52
Fredericksburg battle, 28
Freeman, Douglas Southall, 50, 127–28, 157
Fremantle, Arthur James Lyon: in *Gettysburg*, 154; in *The Killer Angels*, 135–38, 140, 142; J. Longstreet and, 195n52; slavery and, 142; *Three Months in the Southern States*, 136; writings, 123, 136
From Manassas to Appomattox (J. Longstreet), 133, 139
Fullerton, S., 69

Gallagher, Gary W., 83, 125, 130, 150, 195n50
Galloway, Joseph L., 162
Gardner, Sarah E., 36, 42, 43–44, 52–53, 55, 66
GAR (Grand Army of the Republic), 16–17, 167
Garnett, Richard B., 140
Gavin Stevens (*Intruder in the Dust*), 93–94
Gay, Mary Ann Harris, 56–57, 58–59
George Rowan (*None Shall Look Back*), 73
Gerard, David, 197–98n78
Gerrish, Theodore, 23–24
Gettysburg battle, 128–30, 132, 133–34, 192n22
Gettysburg (film), 125, 150, 151, 153
Gettysburg (Reasoner), 154
Ghosts of the Confederacy (Foster), 133
Girl in Blue (Rinaldi), 82
Glasgow, Ellen, 36, 52–53, 90
God and General and Longstreet (Connelly), 155
Go Down Moses, and Other Stories (W. Faulkner), 108, 189n54
Gods and Generals (J. Shaara), 153
Golay, Michael, 157
Gone with the Wind (film), 75, 79, 150
Gone with the Wind (M. Mitchell): battlefield descriptions in, 52, 82; black wartime service in, 80; Civil War novels by women and, 52; criticism, 75; female perspective in, 41, 51, 59–60; gender distinctions in, 48, 61; C. Gordon on,

Gone with the Wind (cont.): 61, 62–63; influences on, 56–57, 58–59; Ku Klux Klan in, 60–61; masculine glory absence in, 51; *None Shall Look Back* comparisons, 62, 76, 181n57; Pulitzer Prize, 6, 75; racial politics in, 57–58, 81, 150; Reconstruction in, 60; *The Red Badge of Courage* and, 37; region in, 79–80, 150; reputation and success, 61, 75–76; research for, 56; social objectives of, 47; veterans' memoirs and, 78; women in, 41–47, 77–78, 80

Goodbye, Darkness (Manchester), 162

Gordon, Caroline: background, 64; on battlefield descriptions, 64–66; Civil War writing and, 64–65; Confederate soldiers and, 90; on gender roles, 63; on *Gone with the Wind*, 61, 62–63; on M. Mitchell, 63; public persona, 180n42; *The Red Badge of Courage* and, 37; veterans' memoirs and narratives and, 65, 67–69; on women veterans, 82; writing in the 'male' mode, 179n39; Wyeth and, 180n46

Gordon, Caroline: Works: *None Shall Look Back* (see *None Shall Look Back* [C. Gordon]); *Penhally*, 65; "The Women on the Battlefield," 71

Gordon, John Brown, 51, 126, 129, 145–46, 149

Goree, Thomas J., 156

Goss, Warren Lee, 10

Grand Army of the Republic (GAR), 16–17, 167

Grant, Ulysses S., 21

Grauke, Kevin, 192n14, 197n77

Gray, Richard, 106

Greenwald, Maurine Weiner, 77

Haley, Alex, 150, 197n72

Hallowed Ground (McPherson), 158, 190n5

Hampton, Wade, 51

Hancock, Winfield S., 126

Hardtack and Coffee (Billings), 10, 13, 160–61

Hardwicke, Catherine, 82

Harper's Weekly, 43, 189n58

Harrison, Constance Cary, 45

Hartwig, D. Scott, 151, 192n14

Harwell, Richard, 47

Heart of a Soldier, The (L. Pickett), 180n47

Henry Fleming *(Red Badge of Courage)*, 25–26, 27–28, 174–75n44

Henry Sutpin *(Absalom! Absalom!)*, 114–16

Hess, Earl J., 32, 94, 171n10, 194n38

Higginson, Thomas Wentworth, 175n45

High Tide at Gettysburg (Tucker), 155

Hill, Alonzo F., 10

Hill, Ambrose Powell, 129

Hill, Daniel H., 67–69, 134

Hinkle, James, 188n40, 189n47

Hinman, Wilbur F., 10

Hood, John Bell, 51, 123, 132

Horwitz, Tony, 94

Hospital Sketches (Alcott), 55

Howard, Sidney, 51

Howells, William Dean, 18–19

Hubbard, John Milton, 85–87, 184n14

Hughes, Langston, 123

Hungerford, Harold R., 27

Hunter, Lloyd A., 94

Ike McCaslin ("The Bear"), 108

Imagined Civil War, The (Fahs), 42

integration, 187n34

In the Hands of Providence (Trulock), 158

Intruder in the Dust (W. Faulkner), 93–95, 104, 186n28

I Rode with Stonewall (Douglas), 87, 184n13

irony, 26–27

Jackson, Mary Anna, 66

Jackson, Thomas J. "Stonewall," 66, 126, 134

Jacobs, Naomi, 149

Jaffe, Marc, 120

Jakober, Marie, 168

James, Henry, 18–19

Jeffrey Forrest (*None Shall Look Back*), 74

John B. Gordon School, 145

John Sartoris (*The Unvanquished*), 91–92

Johnson, Rossiter, 17

Johnston, Joseph E., 51, 90, 137

Johnston, Mary, 37, 52–54, 90

Jomini, Antoine Henri, 155

Jones, Absalom, 173n26

Jones, Anne Goodwyn, 47–48, 61

Jones, J. William, 125

Jonza, Nancylee Novell, 64

Judas Field, The (Bahr), 162–68. See also names of individual characters

Kantor, MacKinlay, 120
Kaplan, Amy, 22, 44
Kartiganer, Donald M., 107, 110
Killer Angels, The (M. Shaara): as allegory, 149; approaches to the past, 121–22; background in, 121; *Battles and Leaders of the Civil War* and, 123; Burns on, 150–51; Chamberlain in, 118–19, 126, 141–44, 147, 148–49, 151, 158; Early in, 130, 193n30; Eastern focus of, 126, 127, 132–35; Fremantle in, 135–38, 140, 142; Gettysburg focus of, 128–29; influence on historiography of the war, 155–59; influence on later writers, 153–54, 190–91n5; Lee Cult and, 130; R. Lee in, 138–39, 141, 152, 158; J. Longstreet in, 128, 130, 140–41, 156; McPherson on, 120, 151, 157; Myth of the Lost Cause and, 125, 130, 131–32; G. Pickett in, 140–41; point of view, 120, 153, 192n20; popularity, 118, 119–20, 150–52; Pulitzer Prize, 6, 118; race in, 150; reconciliation in, 145; *The Red Badge of Courage* comparisons, 120–22; reviews, 156–57; slavery in, 142–43, 195n54; summary, 124; veterans' memoirs and, 120, 123, 124–25, 128, 158–59
Killer Angels Companion, A (Hartwig), 192n14
Kirkland, Joseph, 174n37
Kovic, Ron, 162
Ku Klux Klan, 60–61

Last Full Measure, The (J. Shaara), 153
"Late Encounter with the Enemy, A" (O'Connor), 78–79
Lee, Fitzhugh, 125, 134
Lee, Robert E., 51, 126; in *Cold Mountain*, 154; Early and, 130; in *Gettysburg*, 154; Gettysburg and, 129–30, 132; health, 139–40, 152, 158, 195n50; in *The Killer Angels*, 138–39, 141, 152, 158; J. Longstreet and, 139. See also Lee Cult
Lee and Longstreet at Gettysburg (Tucker), 157
Lee Considered (Nolan), 158
Lee Cult, 129–30, 155
Lee's Aide-de-Camp (Marshall), 193n33, 193n35
Lee's Lieutenants (Freeman), 127–28, 157
Lee's Tarnished Lieutenant (Piston), 157

Leonard, Elizabeth D., 81
Leonard, Thomas C., 92
Levins, Lynn, 117
Life in Dixie during the War (Gay), 56, 58–59
Life of Lieutenant-General Nathan Bedford Forrest (Wyeth), 66, 180n46
Light in August (W. Faulkner), 117
Linderman, Gerald, 15
Linson, Corwin K., 22
Lively, Robert A., 76
Long Night, The (Lytle), 62
Long Roll, The (M. Johnston), 53, 90
Longstreet, Helen Dortch, 66
Longstreet, James: in *Cold Mountain*, 154; Early and, 130, 134; in the Eastern theater, 126; Fremantle and, 195n52; in *Gettysburg*, 154; Gettysburg loss and, 129–30, 133–34; H. Longstreet's writings and, 66; in *High Tide at Gettysburg*, 155; in *The Killer Angels*, 128, 130, 140–41, 156; R. Lee and, 139; in *Lee's Lieutenants*, 128; *From Manassas to Appomattox*, 133, 139; in *Pickett's Charge*, 155; postwar, 192–93n26, 194n42, 195n51; published narratives of, 123; slavery and, 124; Williams on, 198n83
Loosh (*The Unvanquished*), 100–101, 105, 188n41
Lost Cause: in *Absalom! Absalom!*, 93, 95–96, 106; Early and, 187n31; W. Faulkner's portrayal of, 183n5; in *The Unvanquished*, 106, 185n15; Virginians and, 133; writers on Gettysburg, 129. See also Confederacy
Lost Cause, Myth of the, 83, 125, 130, 131–32, 183n8
Louisiana State University, 1
Louivinia (*The Unvanquished*), 100
Lucian Wakefield (*The Judas Field*), 164, 167, 168
Lucy Allard (*None Shall Look Back*), 70–73
Lytle, Andrew, 62, 63, 90

Macaria (Evans), 177n7
Madden, David, 18
Makowsky, Veronica, 66
Manchester, William, 162
Marble Man, The (Connelly), 155, 157
Marching On (Boyd), 37
Marion Rangers, 19, 173n25
Marshall, Charles, 131, 193n33, 193n35

Marvel, William, 119
Massey, Mary Elizabeth, 55
McCaig, Donald, 168
McClellan, George B., 126
McClurg, Alexander C., 31–32, 174–75n44
McConnell, Stuart, 16
McCullers, Carson, 123
McPherson, James: on Chamberlain, 118–19; on *The Killer Angels*, 120, 151, 157; on soldiers' motivation, 36, 175n47
McPherson, James: Works: *For Cause and Comrades*, 175n47; *Hallowed Ground*, 158, 190n5
Meade, George G., 126
Melanie Wilkes (*Gone with the Wind*), 41–42, 48
memoirs *vs.* novels, 24
Memoranda during the War (Whitman), 2
Memorial Day, 10
"Military Leadership of North and South, The" (Williams), 155
Miller, Douglas T., 94
Mitchell, Kirk, 37
Mitchell, Margaret: on Civil War monuments, 51–52; Civil War fascination, 49–50; *Gone with the Wind* (see *Gone with the Wind* [M. Mitchell]); C. Gordon on, 63; on veterans' memoirs, 52; on women veterans, 82
Monster, The (Crane), 34
Moore, Harold G., 162
Mountain, The (album), 152–53
Mrs. Allard (*None Shall Look Back*), 70–71
Mulholland, St. Clair A., 28
My Brother Bill (J. Faulkner), 88
Myth of the Lost Cause, 83, 125, 130, 131–32, 183n8

Nation, 62
national unity, 26
Ned Allard (*None Shall Look Back*), 73
New York Sun, 75
New York Times, 10–11, 32, 62, 65, 146, 156
Nolan, Alan T., 107, 158, 183n8
None Shall Look Back (C. Gordon): audience, 62; battlefield descriptions in, 69–72; *Battles and Leaders of the Civil War* used in, 66–67, 68–69; black wartime service in, 80; Confederate home front in, 72; criticism, 62, 66; *Gone with the Wind* comparisons, 62, 76, 181n57; historical sources and research for, 65–66, 71; lost voices in, 73–75; male-female scenes, 69–71; popularity, 76; publication, 63; racial politics in, 81; region in, 79–80; reputation and success, 61, 76; reviews, 76, 80; veterans' memoirs and, 65, 67–69, 73, 78; as woman writer, 63; women in, 69, 72, 80. *See also names of individual characters*
North-South fraternity, 146
Notes of a Private (Hubbard), 85–87
novels *vs.* memoirs, 24

Oates, Stephen B., 120
O'Connor, Flannery, 75, 78–79, 123
"Odor of Verbena, An" (W. Faulkner), 187n35
116th Pennsylvania, 28
"On Fear" (W. Faulkner), 189n58
Our Boys (A. F. Hill), 10
Outlook, 36

Passing of the Armies, The (Chamberlain), 118, 119, 142
Patriotic Gore (Wilson), 3, 170n3
Pendleton, William N., 133
Penhally (C. Gordon), 65
Perkins, Max, 66
Perry, Mark, 158
Personal Memoirs (Grant), 21
Pettigrew, James Johnston, 132
Philadelphia Weekly Press, 174n34
Pickett, George E., 66, 126, 140–41. *See also* Pickett's charge
Pickett, La Salle Corbell, 66, 180n47
Pickett's charge, 93–94, 103–4
Pickett's Charge (Stewart), 155
Piston, William Garrett, 129, 157, 195n51
Pitavy, Francois, 95
Place Called Appomattox, A (Marvel), 119
post-traumatic stress disorder (PTSD), 165–66
"Private History of a Campaign That Failed, The" (Twain), 19–21, 22
Prown, Katherine Hemple, 63
PTSD (post-traumatic stress disorder), 165–66
Pulitzer Prize, 6, 75, 118

Quentin Compson (*Absalom! Absalom!*), 93, 95–96, 112, 116

race and race relations: in *Absalom! Absalom!*, 84, 97; Civil War and, 84; W. Faulkner and, 87, 97, 123, 188n46,

189–90n58; in *Gone with the Wind*, 57–58, 81, 150; in *The Killer Angels*, 150; narratives drawing attention to, 123–24; in *None Shall Look Back*, 81; in *The Red Badge of Courage*, 34–35; in *The Unvanquished*, 84–85, 97–105. *See also* emancipation; integration; slavery
RAF (Royal Air Force), 88, 185n16
Ransom, John Crowe, 179n38
Reardon, Carol, 94, 120
Reasoner, James, 154
Rebel soldiers, 89–90, 92, 116–17, 125
Rebel yell, 92, 93
Recollections of a Private (Goss), 10
Recollections of a Private Soldier in the Army of the Potomac (Wilkeson), 10
reconciliation, 145–47, 196n56
Reconsidering Faulkner's Pulp Series (Clark), 188n41
Reconstruction, 60
Red Badge of Courage, The (Crane): approaches to the past, 121–22; background excluded from, 121; battlefields descriptions, 28, 29–31, 34; criticism, 22, 175n45; emancipation in, 34; *Gone with the Wind* and, 37; C. Gordon and, 37; influence of Civil War literature on, 10, 29, 36–38; irony in, 26–27; *The Killer Angels* comparisons, 120–22; narrative perspective, 30; political controversies excluded from, 33, 34–35, 120, 175n45; race in, 34–35; reviews, 30, 31; slavery in, 33, 34; success, 174n38; in *Three Great Novels of the Civil War*, 120; veterans' memoirs and, 9–10, 25–26; veterans' reactions to, 31–33. *See also names of individual characters*
"Reënforcing Thomas" (Fullerton), 69
Reminiscences of My Life in Camp with the 33d United States Colored Troops, Late 1st S.C., Volunteers (S. Taylor), 81
Reminiscences of the Civil War (J. Gordon), 145–47
Requiem for a Nun (W. Faulkner), 92–93, 104–5, 117
Rhett Butler (*Gone with the Wind*), 48
Rinaldi, Ann, 82
Ringo (*The Unvanquished*), 98–101
Rives Allard (*None Shall Look Back*), 70–71
Roots (Haley), 150, 197n72
Roots (miniseries), 150
Rosa Coldfield (*Absalom! Absalom!*), 107, 109–13, 114–16, 190n63

Rose, W. L., 150, 194n72
"Rose for Emily, A" (W. Faulkner), 186n26
Royal Air Force (RAF), 88, 185n16
Rubin, Louis, Jr., 85
Rumor of War, A (Caputo), 162, 167–68

Sartoris (W. Faulkner), 92, 117, 188n36
Saturday Evening Post, 187n35
Saturday Review, 31, 75
Savage, Kirk, 11
Scarlett O'Hara (*Gone with the Wind*), 40–41, 48
Scott, Evelyn, 54, 90
Scribner's Magazine, 187n35
Settle, Mary Lee, 90
Shaara, Jeff, 153
Shaara, Michael: on Crane, 37, 176n53; *The Killer Angels* (see *Killer Angels, The* [M. Shaara]); veterans' memoirs and, 123, 158–59
Shaw, Harry E., 150
Sherman, William Tecumseh, 17, 51
She Went to the Field (Tsui), 81
Short History of the War of Secession, A (Johnson), 17
Shreve McCannon (*Absalom! Absalom!*), 95–96
slavery: in *Absalom, Absalom!*, 108–9, 112; Chamberlain and, 142–43, 148; Civil War and, 124, 184n11; Fremantle and, 142; in *The Killer Angels*, 142–43, 195n54; J. Longstreet and, 124; in *The Red Badge of Courage*, 33, 34. *See also* emancipation; race and race relations
Sledge, E. B., 162–63
Smith-Jordan, Paul, 52
Soldier Girl (film), 82
soldiers and veterans: in *Absalom! Absalom!*, 117; battlefield descriptions by, 28–29; black wartime service in fiction, 80; black veterans, 80, 102; in Civil War literature, 44, 80, 189n5; commemoration of, 10–12, 45; Confederate, 89–90, 92, 116–17, 125; W. Faulkner on, 95; W. Faulkner's portrayal of, 91–92, 95, 116–17, 164, 186n26; in *Gone with the Wind*, 80; C. Gordon and, 90; in *The Judas Field*, 165, 166–67, 168; McPherson on, 36, 175n47; memoirs (see veterans' memoirs and narratives); M. Mitchell on women veterans, 123; motivation, 36, 175n47; Myth of the Lost Cause and, 125; in *None Shall*

soldiers and veterans (cont.):
  Look Back, 80; organizations, 16–17;
  reactions to *The Red Badge of Courage*,
  31–33; reputation, 15; stereotypes, 164;
  in *The Unvanquished*, 117; women,
  41–47, 77–78, 81–82, 123; as writers,
  2–3, 12–16, 23
Solomon, Eric, 22
Sons of Confederate Veterans, 17
Sons of Veterans, 17
Soul of the Lion (Wallace), 158
Sound and the Fury, The (W. Faulkner), 188n38
Southern Bivouac (journal), 126
Southern Historical Society Papers, 13, 126, 129, 131–32, 193n26
Southern Review, 71
Spencer Rowe (*None Shall Look Back*), 73
Stand Firm Ye Boys From Maine (Desjardin), 158
Stewart, George R., 155
Stowe, Harriet Beecher, 150
Stryron, William, 123
Stuart, James E. B. "Jeb," 126, 129

Tallman, Ruth, 49
Tate, Allen, 62, 76, 90, 180n42
Taylor, Robert C., 50
Taylor, Susie King, 81
Taylor, Walter H., 131
They Fought Like Demons (Blanton & Cook), 81
Thomas Sutpin (*Absalom! Absalom!*), 105, 107–8
Thompson, Lawrence S., 198n78
Three Great Novels of the Civil War (Jaffe, ed.), 120
Three Months in the Southern States (Fremantle), 136
"Through Blood and Fire at Gettysburg" (Chamberlain), 123
To Gettysburg and Beyond (Golay), 157
Toplin, Robert Brent, 159
Tourgée, Albion, 85, 174n37
Trimble, Isaac R., 132
Trulock, Alice Rains, 147, 158
Tsui, Bonnie, 81
Tucker, Glen, 155, 157
Twain, Mark, 18–21, 22
20th Maine, 24

UCV (United Confederate Veterans), 16, 167
UDC (United Daughters of the Confederacy), 17, 45–46, 77
Uncle Tom's Cabin (Stowe), 150
United Confederate Veterans (UCV), 16, 167
United Daughters of the Confederacy (UDC), 17, 45–46, 77
Unvanquished, The (W. Faulkner): *Absalom! Absalom!* comparisons, 105–6; chronology of, 189n47; Lost Cause in, 106, 185n15; narrator of, 97; opening, 188n40; presentation and marketability, 105; publication, 187n35; race and race relations in, 84–85, 97–105; soldiers' treatment in, 117; surrender in, 96. *See also* names of individual characters
Unwritten War, The (Aaron), 3–4, 18–19

"Veteran, The" (Crane), 174–75n44
Veterans. *See* soldiers and veterans
veterans' memoirs and narratives: battlefield descriptions, 28–29; Beidler on, 171n4; blacks and, 81, 102; distance from civilians and, 14; *Gone with the Wind* and, 78; C. Gordon and, 65, 67–69; Hess on, 171n10; human experience in, 161; *The Killer Angels* and, 120, 123, 124–25, 128, 158–59; male domination of, 44, 45; M. Mitchell on, 52; *None Shall Look Back* and, 65, 67–69, 73, 78; reasons for, 23; *The Red Badge of Courage* and, 9–10, 25–26; M. Shaara and, 123, 158–59; 20th century, 161–62, 164, 167; Victorian literary conventions of, 162; Vietnam memoirs, 162; Wertheim on, 171n4; by women, 54–57, 59
"Vietnam, Survivalism, and the Civil War" (Grauke), 192n14
Vietnam War, 161–62
Virginia and Virginians, 132–35
"Virginia Scenes in '61" (Harrison), 45

Wallace, Willard Mosher, 158
Ward, George, 50, 56
Ward, Mary Ketcham, 56
War-Time Journal of a Georgia Girl, The (Andrews), 56–57, 60

Watkins, Sam, 26–27, 50–51, 160–61
Wave, The (Scott), 54
Wells, Andrew B., 26–27
Welty, Eudora, 123
Wertheim, Stanley, 171n4
We Were Soldiers Once . . . and Young (Moore & Galloway), 162
White, Hayden, 159, 196n69
White Rose of Memphis, The (Falkner), 92
Whitman, Walt, 2
Why the North Won the Civil War (Donald, ed.), 155
Wilkeson, Frank, 10
William Faulkner and Southern History (Williamson), 97
Williams, T. Harry, 155, 198n83
Williamson, Joel, 97
Wilson, Edmund, 3, 21, 170n3
Wise Blood (O'Connor), 75
With the Old Breed (Sledge), 162–63

women: battlefield roles of, 72–73; in *Battles and Leaders of the Civil War*, 44–45; black women and the Civil War, 81; in Civil War literature, 81; Civil War literature by, 39, 43–44, 46, 52, 60, 66–67, 76–77, 176–77n6; in *Gone with the Wind*, 41–47, 77–78, 80; C. Gordon on women veterans, 82; memoirs by, 54–57, 59; M. Mitchell on women veterans, 123; in *None Shall Look Back*, 69, 72, 80; soldiers and veterans, 41–47, 77–78, 81–82, 123; wartime activities of, 182n58
"Women on the Battlefield, The" (C. Gordon), 71
"Wounded" (anonymous), 43
Wright, Richard, 123
Wyeth, John Allan, 66, 180n46

Youmans, Marly, 168
Young, Elizabeth, 18, 49

www.ingramcontent.com/pod-product-compliance
Lightning Source LLC
Chambersburg PA
CBHW020652230426
43665CB00008B/405